Next Generation Performance Management

Next Generation Performance Management

The Triumph of Science Over Myth and Superstition

Alan L. Colquitt

INFORMATION AGE PUBLISHING, INC.
Charlotte, NC • www.infoagepub.com

Library of Congress Cataloging-in-Publication Data

A CIP record for this book is available from the Library of Congress
http://www.loc.gov

ISBN: 978-1-68123-932-3 (Paperback)
      978-1-68123-933-0 (Hardcover)
      978-1-68123-934-7 (ebook)

Contents

SECTION **I**

Context

v

SECTION **II**

What to Stop

SECTION **III**

What to Start

Preface and Introduction

Do We Really Need Another Book About Performance Management?

A few years ago I attended a conference on performance management (PM). Everyone was there to learn about best practices being implemented by top companies. By this time, I was well into my own journey to discover what's wrong with PM and how to fix it, and I was knee deep in my own project to fix PM at my own company. I met a woman from a mid-sized hospital system. Like everyone else she was sent there to learn how the best companies do PM and to bring back what she learned to apply it to her company. Her company had no formal PM process to speak of, nor did they have individual merit pay or bonuses or a pay-for-performance (P4P) philosophy. During a break I asked her why she wanted to introduce these practices into her company. She looked at me, confused as to why I would ask this question. I asked her if they had trouble attracting top talent to her company and she said no. This hospital system has a very strong and deeply ingrained purpose and mission, and people were lined up to work there. I asked her if employees were unhappy there and she replied no, employees were generally happy and engaged. I asked her if their top performers were leaving for better opportunities elsewhere, and she replied no, their overall turnover rate was relatively low. I told her it was my turn to be confused. I told her I couldn't understand why she would want to implement practices everyone hated and that didn't seem to work, in a company that seemed to

Next Generation Performance Management, pages xi–xviii
Copyright © 2017 by Information Age Publishing
All rights of reproduction in any form reserved.

be doing perfectly well without them. After that conversation, I was hooked and I decided the world needed another book about PM.

Companies that don't have PM processes are implementing them, and those that have them are trying to fix them. It is no secret that companies are unhappy with PM. The headlines from the business press say it all. *Businessweek* called PM a "worthless corporate ritual."[1] The Wharton School at the University of Pennsylvania ran an article in their business publication with the title "Should Performance Reviews Be Fired?" (The answer was yes, by the way).[2] Finally, you know your process is in trouble when *The Washington Post* calls it *kabuki*.[3] I have been around PM my entire career, and I think the word kabuki describes it pretty well. This dissatisfaction has led to an explosion in writing on the topic from academics and consultants to HR thinktanks and business pundits.

At the time of this writing, an Amazon search yields nearly 74,000 results for "performance management" and nearly 21,000 results for "pay-for-performance." A Google search nets some 27 million results for the term performance management, and nearly 300 million results for the term pay-for-performance. There have been countless magazine and newspaper articles, blog posts, white papers, and research reports written on this topic in the past 5 years. It has been a very popular topic in the academic press as well.[4] There have been entire issues of academic and practitioner journals devoted to this subject. In my own files I have well over 1,000 different articles and reports from nearly 100 different sources. Nearly every major HR consulting firm and think tank has conducted its own research on this subject surveying their clients or members. Some have even formed special subgroups to study this topic further.

All of these writers have their own ideas about what's wrong and how to fix it. Most of them suggest we blow it up or abandon the practice altogether, replacing it with something else. And companies have begun to follow their advice. Some have gotten rid of PM entirely or have gotten rid of key elements (e.g., performance ratings). While it is still early for many of these experiments, you would be hard pressed to call them successes. Companies abandoning ratings, for example, find they have a hard time filling the void. Companies that still want to differentiate pay (and nearly every one of them does) find it difficult to make these decisions without ratings. Other companies are radically simplifying their PM processes by getting rid of ratings and extensive documentation and focusing more on continuous feedback and coaching. These companies are finding the benefits of these changes don't materialize. Their supervisors and employees like the simple process because it takes less time and is less of a burden.

Who wouldn't? When someone sitting on your chest gets up, it feels better. However, supervisors typically end up spending less time on feedback, coaching, and development, not more. Recent research suggests companies are actually less productive after getting rid of performance ratings.[5]

Everyone in the room at that performance management conference that day was looking for answers. Seven out of 10 companies are making or planning to make changes to their process in the near future.[6] We have been searching for solutions to the PM problem for decades. Douglas McGregor summed up the situation in 1957, and it still rings true today:[7]

> I have sought to show that the conventional approach to performance appraisal stands condemned as a personnel method. It places the manager in the untenable position of judging the personal worth of his subordinates, and of acting on these judgments. No manager possesses, nor could he acquire, the skill necessary to carry out this responsibility effectively.

PM is a miserable failure, and the investment organizations make in it isn't trivial. How much time in aggregate do employees and supervisors spend on this process every year? What value do organizations get for that investment? What impact do evaluations of performance have on other critical decisions like rewards, promotions, leadership succession, development, and terminations? How much money do organizations spend each year on base pay increases and bonuses that are tied to performance evaluations? It is not a stretch to say the impact could be in the hundreds of millions of dollars or more for a large company, and in the hundreds of billions of dollars for business globally.

What return do organizations get for that investment? There is also an important human dimension to the impact of PM. Evaluations of performance can make or break careers. I have witnessed this firsthand. Employees get one bad rating and their career never recovers.

Despite its miserable track record, PM is here to stay. Companies, business leaders, and HR professionals still believe in it. Ed Lawler and his colleagues surveyed 100 companies and every company had a PM system in some form.[8] This was the same result he found 10 years prior. A survey by the Institute for Corporate Productivity (i4cp) found only 6% of companies were considering eliminating appraisals for some or all of their employees.[9] Everyone remains eternally optimistic; however; we believe success is just around the corner. Ultimate Software's report says:

> Traditional once-a-year reviews are hectic, limited and stressful for both managers and employees. In 6 simple steps, you can completely revolution-

ize your company's performance management process—turning it into a powerful collaborative and strategic tool.[10]

PM isn't working. Our efforts to fix it don't seem to help, and we still believe it can be fixed. This is "the PM problem." What I have learned over the past 6 years suggests that "6 simple steps" will not solve it. My own PM journey began in 2010 when I assumed responsibility for PM in my organization. I had been around it my entire career, evaluating it and designing and redesigning it, but I had never owned it. It wasn't long before I was getting the phone calls and hate mail about our process. Employees had strong, visceral reactions to this process, much of which I can't share in writing here. They didn't like it and since I now owned it, it was my responsibility to fix it. So I set about starting to fixing it by doing my homework. I read everything there was to read, I went to every conference and session on PM I could find, and I talked to everyone I knew, both inside and outside of the company. I worked with our organization to redesign and implement a new PM process. This book is a report on what I learned, and no one was more surprised by what I learned than I was. What I learned surprised me, fascinated me, and intrigued me as a student of organizations and as a practitioner responsible for changing in organizations. Here is my summary after 6 years of studying the PM problem:

- We focus on the wrong purpose for PM
- Much of what we do is wrong
- We do what's popular, not what works
- Good solutions exist, but they aren't palatable for most companies
- We look in the wrong places and listen to the wrong people when looking for insight
- We *believe* our principles are right that it's our design and execution that is wrong. We just need to try harder. Trying harder won't help. Our principles are wrong; better design and execution won't solve the problem.
- Solving the PM problem is simple, but it won't be easy
- The previous point is an understatement

I make these statements with all humility, and I come by these views honestly after a lot of study and head scratching about the "eco-system" of the PM problem. Why do we continue to substitute one bad practice for another, over and over again? Why do we believe more tweaking will help when this has been our strategy for decades and we have little improvement to show for it? Why don't we take a more fundamental look at this problem? These questions confounded me and this book describes how I sorted out the PM problem for myself. PM is fundamentally about motivation and control in organizations; how we motivate employees to achieve on behalf of the organization, and how we focus their efforts on the areas that really matter. The root of the PM problem isn't with our practices, it is with the values, beliefs, and assumptions behind our practices. The real problem with PM is in our heads, and solving it requires spending time "on the couch" confronting our assumptions and beliefs about motivation and control, replacing them with new ones grounded in science and sound research.

Approach to This Book

Behind the Practices

This book goes beyond PM practices. We all have our own mental models and lay theories about how to motivate and control the behavior of people in organizations. We cannot (and will not) fundamentally change PM practices until we change our beliefs and mental models. This book will challenge your thinking and beliefs, and will force you to confront your programming.

Evidence-Based

This book is evidence-based. It places a premium on rigorous academic and applied research studies from top sources where results have been peer reviewed. Other books about PM claim to be evidence- based, but they are light on actual evidence and the evidence they rely on isn't always high quality. Other books and articles highlight the practices of top companies or even a single company, with little discussion of whether or not the success of these companies can reasonably be attributed to their PM practices. I am not indicting this work, only saying that it may not provide hard evidence as to the effectiveness of their practices. For example, would you change your PM process because a *Vanity Fair* article said it caused 10 years of famine at Microsoft? Maybe not. This is journalism, not rigorous research. This article reflects one person's perspective after discussions with insiders. Would you change your PM process if I told you that decades of rigorous research studies have found that traditional PM and reward practices negatively affect teamwork, collaboration and innovation? *There is a difference.* Rigorous research tells you our practices don't work. The *Vanity Fair* article puts a face on this research, and it illustrates how these practices can affect real businesses and real people.

This book looks at evidence from multiple disciplines. Much of the research that makes its way into the business press comes from psychology and management. One of the strongest influences on thinking and practice in this area today comes from economics. Very few writers and consultants are paying attention to the influence of economic models, frameworks, and research in this area. There is also much to be learned from other areas struggling with similar issues such as healthcare, education, and public personnel management.

Systemic

This book puts the PM problem in context. It is clear from benchmarking research that organizations, leaders, and HR professionals expect a lot from PM. This is one reason it frequently comes up short in meeting the expectations of stakeholders. I will place PM firmly in the context of organization strategy, design, and culture, and will make concrete recommendations about what PM should and should not do for a company. I will then describe why you don't need to do the things PM did in the past or I will help you find a better way to do them.

What This Book Is Not

This book is not about a specific solution or silver bullet. I do not have a new, integrated program or solution to replace PM. I don't think PM is a bankrupt practice that needs to be replaced. Instead, I think it simply needs to be focused on a core purpose and designed well to achieve that purpose.

This book is also not about benchmarking. While I will discuss what other companies do, I will use science and rigorous research to identify practices you should emulate and practices you should abandon. I will highlight companies engaging in these practices.

This book is not a how-to book. I will not lay out a buffet of all of the choices and options available to you at each stage of a PM design effort. I will not describe every detail of what you should do. In some cases, I won't talk about a particular practice simply because I don't think you should do it in the first place. I won't tell you to "crowdsource feedback" for example. However, I *will* tell you feedback is important, but that supervisors should focus their feedback on the work and not make it personal. If you want to implement work-related feedback using a social media platform, that's fine.

Just make sure it is based on sound principles. While there is no grand solution or program, I will steer you toward principles and general recommendations that have merit based on research. You can implement these ideas in ways that work best for your company.

Finally this book is not an academic research review. While this book is strongly research-based, it does not provide a detailed review of all the research studies. You don't need to be dragged through all the details of the research. You need to know what this research *says*. Much of the research reviewed is listed in the endnotes. Where it is meaningful, I highlight specific, important studies and I provide my own commentary on the state of the research. This book is not full of studies and findings; it is full of research implications for practice.

Who This Book Is For

This book is for anyone who drew the "short straw" and is working on a PM design project or is involved with this process inside organizations. This may be HR professionals, HR generalists, line managers, or other HR experts. This book is also for HR experts who are guiding leaders or other HR professionals in carrying out PM projects or responsibilities. Business and HR leaders who are involved in the architecture of the organization's people and management systems and processes will also find value in this book. Finally, while this book is not designed specifically for academic researchers, they may find it useful for three reasons: First, it may expose them to research areas they are not aware of; Second, it may help stimulate ideas for new research; and last, it can help better frame the debate and discourse.

Academic researchers need to play a prominent role in this debate, and their voices have been too quiet to this point.

Overview of the Book

Section I (Chapters 1–3) is about context. You can't change something without understanding it and understanding why it is the way it is. This is the central flaw in the efforts to fix PM today; they aren't addressing the root cause of the problem. Chapter 1 begins by describing the typical PM system in most organizations today—"Last Generation Performance Management: PM 1.0." This chapter also discusses what we know about how well it works (not very well) and it proposes a new, refined purpose for PM, grounding it in organization design thinking. Chapter 2 puts PM 1.0 on the couch, explaining why it is designed the way it is, and then identifying and discussing the theories and principles behind the practices. You can't change PM practices unless you understand the principles on which they are based. Chapter 3 highlights why nothing has changed despite decades of effort and study. The forces against change are numerous and powerful.

We can't hope to make progress with PM until we understand how these forces act to maintain the status quo.

Section II (Chapters 4–6) discusses what we should stop doing. It makes a case to tear down the primary structure that is PM 1.0, abandoning our old paradigms. Chapter 4 makes a case to abandon formal, quantitative evaluations of performance. Chapter 5 makes a case to stop overrelying on money to motivate. Chapter 6 makes a case to abandon pay-for-performance and differentiation of rewards.

In each of these chapters I make my case using rigorous scientific research, and I provide suggestions on how you can fill the void left by abandoning these practices.

Section III (Chapters 7–9) is about what we should start doing. This section rebuilds PM using new principles and paradigms that are supported by rigorous research. Chapter 7 focuses on goals, direction, meaning, and purpose, the centerpiece of PM 2.0. Chapter 8 focuses on feedback, coaching, and progress, key enablers of individual and organizational performance. Chapter 9 argues we need to change our frame, from seeing PM as a way of optimizing individual performance to one where we focus on the performance of the teams, leveraging the power of collaboration instead of competition. Like Section II, these chapters take a hard scientific look at the research identifying new paradigms and practices for PM 2.0 that are better supported by scientific evidence.

Finally, Chapter 10 integrates the findings from the book and provides a more detailed description of "Next Generation Performance Management"—PM 2.0.

At the end, I hope you will have a better understanding of why you do PM the way you do, why it works so poorly, and what you can do instead. My experience so far indicates this journey will be painful, but it seems nothing worth doing in organizations is ever easy.

Acknowledgments

This book represents the culmination of a 5-year journey for me. I have been wrestling with this topic for the last 5 years and I'm grateful for the opportunity to share what I've learned. While I enjoyed writing this book I'm glad to be done with it. I have always referred to this as my "manifesto," mostly because when I talk about this topic I almost always end up ranting about it. You can imagine my pleasure at reading Sam Culbert's book on PM and talking with him personally about this topic. I realized you could write and rant at the same time. The writing of this book was truly a defensive act for me. I did not want to write a book about PM; I did not have the time to write a book. I had all I could handle with my career and my personal and family life, both of which were plenty demanding and challenging during this period. I did everything I could not to write this book. However this topic would not leave me alone. Every conference I attended, every article, report, and blog post I read outraged me. I felt we were paying attention to the wrong things and as a result our efforts to fix PM would continue to fail. I wrote this book so I could quit thinking about PM.

This book probably would not have happened had I not "drawn the short straw" and assumed responsibility for this process in 2010. At the time I didn't have a lot of preconceived notions about PM, despite being around it for the better part of my career. I was quite surprised when the hate mail started coming in and when my neighbors started interrupting my weekend

Next Generation Performance Management, pages xix–xxi
Copyright © 2017 by Information Age Publishing
All rights of reproduction in any form reserved.

yard work to yell at me about it. And although this book isn't about PM at my company, it certainly benefited from my experiences trying to change PM at my company.

Writing this book has been an eye-opening process. I had a simple goal after a few months of owning PM: Improve this process using science. I didn't know where else to turn. I needed something to anchor my thinking and the science seemed like the most sensible place to start, which it turns out made me an anomaly. Most start with benchmarking. As a result, and I say this often, every position I take in this book I come by honestly (he says so humbly).

Needless to say I was very surprised by what I learned from the science and from sharing the science with others. Despite 30 years of trying to change people and organizations, I was still naïve. What the science says and what people do are frequently two different things, and those two are sometimes in violent opposition. People do not simply kneel down at the altar of science, especially HR-related science. Quite the contrary.

I owe a debt of gratitude to a lot of people in creating this book. In the very early days of this work I assembled a small group of people to think with me about this topic. David Futrell, Bill Cowley, and Kim Melnick, and I had many early conversations about what was wrong with PM. These discussions, along with a lot of research David Futrell and I conducted, led me to realize fairly quickly how badly off course this process had gotten in organizations.

This book also benefited from the experiences of countless others who tried to change PM at their companies. I owe much to the loyal members of the Mayflower Group's PM support group that met diligently over a couple of years. My thinking was greatly sharpened as a result of these monthly calls. I owe big thanks to Hank Jonas, Gail Baity, Michael Harris, Scott Smith, Allen Kamin, and several others for allowing me to learn from their experiences and for helping shape my own thinking. I hope I have given them half as much as they have given me.

This book would not have been possible without research—real research. I owe much to the scientists and practitioners who put PM practices under the microscope. I was surprised to find a robust scientific literature to draw on that far exceeded my expectations. There is very good research being done by first-rate scientists, much of it outside the friendly confines of psychology. I hope this book provides an additional voice to their research and I hope I have done justice to their findings. I am especially thankful for my early association with Paul Levy and Deirdre Schleicher. It was through my early professional discussions with them that I began to gain an appreciation for the science behind PM.

I also owe a lot to the other people who are calling bulls*@t on traditional PM practices. Many of them played a large role in this book. I am especially grateful for a couple of conversations and email exchanges with Dan Pink, who ultimately asked me why I wasn't writing about this. I am also grateful for early conversations with Jean Louis Manzoni and Sam Culbert. Discussions with these two people helped me realize that I wasn't crazy, that the science and the practice in many instances were in direct opposition. They helped reassure me that it was possible that almost everyone else was wrong.

This book benefited greatly from early reviews by Chip Heath, Marty Benson, and three other writers and editors. They all gave me very helpful, candid, if not painful feedback on parts of this manuscript (one generously read the whole thing). Any "life" and "color" you see in these pages is a direct result of their feedback. My brother Jason (the most accomplished Colquitt) was also a big help in the very early stages of this project. One early discussion at a bar during a professional conference (somewhere I can't remember) was particularly helpful. I can only hope that in the future he will have people coming up to him at conferences asking him if he wrote that book on PM. That would be sweet indeed.

This book has also benefited greatly from early partnerships and collaborations with people who allowed me to start road testing many of the ideas in this book. I'm glad people like John Boudreau, Seymour Adler, Steve Ash, and Deb Blackman felt I had something useful to say and were willing to allow me to write about it and talk about it. I have certainly benefited from writing and presenting with (and associating with) such great people, and I believe this book is better because of these experiences.

I also need to thank my parents Ron and Joyce, both of whom passed away before this work was finished. I am sad that I never got the chance to lay the finished product on the shelf in their living room. I think they would have been proud. Lastly, I want to thank my family, my kids Kylie, Jack and Corey, and my wife Dianne. I gave up countless evenings, weekends, and holidays to work on this project. It was a long march indeed. I'm especially fortunate that my wife is a night owl, sleeping in the morning while I wrote in the morning. She also endured years with a massive debris pile that was my office. This project involved working with hundreds of articles and reports and dozens of books that I simply couldn't put away until the work was done. I don't write neatly and she graciously tolerated a big mess for a long time.

And lastly, a disclaimer. The views expressed in this book are my own; they do not necessarily reflect the views of any particular company with whom I am or have been associated. If you have a beef with it, take it up with me.

SECTION I

Context

1

Last Generation Performance Management: PM 1.0

Wrong does not cease to be wrong because the majority share in it.
—Leo Tolstoy

One day everything will be well, that is our hope.
Everything's fine today; that is our illusion.
—Voltaire

In February of 2010, *Businessweek* published an article titled "Ten Management Practices to Axe." This article was a reaction to all the recent best-selling business books advising managers on how to manage and lead their employees.[1] In the name of journalistic excellence, *Businessweek* would sort out all the management BS for us. While I would never advise that you abandon a practice because *Businessweek* tells you to do so, it can be instructive to monitor the musings of the business press to understand where executives feel pain. Even to a persistent critic like me, it was eye-opening that three of the ten practices were related to performance

3

management (PM). The number one practice on their list was forced rank-ing. The other two were 360-degree feedback programs (frequently used as part of PM) and mandatory performance review bell curves. It might be worth taking a second look at a process when 30% of *Businessweek's* hit list has something to do with it.

It's pretty clear people from reading the popular business press PM is in trouble, and its trials and tribulations seem to make good reading. I don't need to read *Businessweek* to know this; I know it from my own experience. I have talked with many people in many companies about PM. People have compared it to the movie *The Hunger Games*. For those of you unfamiliar with this movie (or the book on which it's based), teenagers are selected to fight to the death against one another. This sounds a lot like PM.

Last-Generation Performance Management: PM 1.0

Before I further indict PM, it might be helpful to define what I'm indict-ing. Let me introduce you to Red Lodge Manufacturing. Their PM process starts with a list of corporate priorities and objectives for the upcoming year. Each department translates these into objectives for their department, which are used as input to goals for each employee in the department. In January, supervisors have planning meetings with each of their employees. Each employee lists their goals on their performance plan and submits it to their supervisor. They meet to review the plan and revise it as needed, then both sign off on the plan. Midway through the year, the supervisor and employee meet again to review progress. The employee documents ac-complishments and the supervisor reviews them and provides his/her own input. The supervisor delivers messages to the employee about their per-formance to date and whether they are on track relative to the goals in the plan. Once again the supervisor and the employee both sign off on the doc-ument. The supervisor and employee meet again at the end of the year for a final review. The employee documents his or her accomplishments and they meet to review and discuss them. The employee makes any changes to the document and submits it for approval. The supervisor drafts an overall performance summary and assigns the employee an overall performance rating on a 1 to 5 scale. Both sign the final document. The performance rat-ing is transferred into the compensation system and used to make decisions about base pay increases and bonuses.

We can quibble about the details, but the process Red Lodge Manufac-turing uses (a completely fictitious company) is the process used in most organizations. I call this "Last Generation Performance Management"—or

PM 1.0 for short. For the purposes of this book, I define PM 1.0 broadly to include not just the setting of objectives and evaluation of performance, but also the linkage of performance to rewards and other downstream outcomes. These downstream linkages are pervasive in organizations, and employees and supervisors do not separate in their minds the planning and review of performance from the outcomes and decisions linked to judgments about performance. PM 1.0 consists of a number of common steps similar to those used by Red Lodge Manufacturing:[2]

- **Planning.** Ninety-five percent of companies set individual objectives as a part of their PM process and 80% have formal planning sessions with employees. Employees and supervisors decide on specific goals and objectives for the coming year. This can include developmental objectives as well as traditional work-related objectives.
- **Feedback and coaching.** Sixty-five percent of companies routinely conduct performance feedback sessions between official performance reviews. Supervisors check in with their employees to monitor progress and provide feedback and coaching to help employees make any adjustments needed to achieve their goals.
- **Summarize and document accomplishments.** Nearly all companies (95%) conduct final reviews at the end of the year and 63% include midyear or quarterly reviews as well. Supervisors and employees formally review and document performance during these sessions.
- **Evaluate employees.** More than 90% of companies use some form of performance ratings to evaluate employees. These ratings are typically made by supervisors and include ratings of individual objectives and behaviors/competencies as well as overall performance.
- **Distribute rewards and other consequences.** Eighty-two percent of companies link individual compensation decisions to performance ratings, and well over 90% have some form of a pay-for-performance philosophy. Performance ratings typically serve as inputs to other decisions as well (e.g., staffing, promotion, identification of potential, and termination). This is the way it works for everyone; 77% of organizations use a one-size-fits-all approach to PM.[3]

These are the "guts" of PM 1.0: Individuals set objectives, get feedback along the way, and get a rating at the end of the year that affects them financially.

PM 1.0 is Woefully Ineffective

PM 1.0 gets failing grades in most companies. If Red Lodge Manufacturing were a real company, they would have a task force working on their process right now. Chances are your company doesn't like its process either. A recent report by Deloitte consulting shows that only 8% of companies report that their PM process "drives high levels of value." Reports by The Conference Board also paint a bleak picture.[4] Only 20% of companies were pleased with their PM process and only 35% felt the process helped them improve their business performance. Survey results showed PM was ranked 20th of 24 job satisfaction-related factors (average score of 2.8 of 5). In a separate survey, respondents rated the effectiveness of their PM system in accomplishing 11 objectives. The average effectiveness rating across the 11 factors was only 28% favorable. We expect a lot from PM and it underdelivers impressively in all areas.

Employees don't like PM either. Only 35% feel their goals are aligned with the company's objectives, and only 35% say they have been given useful feedback from their manager. Less than half (49%) see their performance reviews as accurate, only 47% say they motivate them to work harder, and only 40% say that when they do a good job their performance is rewarded.[5]

I don't need benchmarking reports to tell me employees don't like PM. Early in my career I had been assigned to work on a taskforce to redesign PM. I was mowing my lawn on a Saturday afternoon when my neighbor (who worked for the same company) walked down the street to talk. After exchanging the usual pleasantries, he asked me if I had anything to do with PM in our company. Of course I lied and said "No." It didn't really matter; he knew I worked in HR so he unloaded on me anyway. An hour later I put my lawnmower in the garage and stayed in the house the rest of the weekend. It doesn't matter if you are in church, at a school PTA meeting, at the grocery, or mowing your lawn people will tell you what they think of PM.

Despite the failure of PM 1.0, companies still believe in it and are searching for something that will make a difference. In 2014 more than 70% of the companies surveyed by Bersin were considering a redesign and simplification of their process.[6] Sixty-eight percent of companies surveyed by the Conference Board said they were planning to make major changes to their PM process.[7] Companies are "spinning the wheel," searching for a combination of practices that works. Those of us working on PM in organizations have tried everything. We've tried SMART goals and cascading goals. We have separated development from evaluation to get supervisors to spend more time on feedback and coaching. We've trained supervisors and then trained them again. We've tried building better rating scales and educating supervisors by teaching them about bias and errors. We've gotten more people involved by crowdsourcing feedback and implementing 360-degree feedback questionnaires. We've started rating competencies instead of traits and behaviors. We've added calibration sessions and implemented forced distributions to compensate for the inadequacies of our supervisors. We've tried a myriad of different types of reward and incentive programs to motivate employees. Finally, we've implemented technologies to make this failing process more efficient.[8] None of this has worked. There has been no magic bullet, no magic elixir leading to better results over the long term. Seventy years of research, constant tinkering, and no improvement. Reasonable people would have given up years ago.

I cannot understate the importance of this point: Companies continue to tinker with PM 1.0 because they still believe it can work. Like the software advertisement I quoted in the Introduction, most of us believe that success is just around the corner. If we can just get the right combination of practices, with big enough merit and bonus budgets and capable enough managers with the right amount of discipline and courage, it will work. In a perfect world it will work. We don't have a perfect world and we never will. No amount of tinkering at the margins will improve PM 1.0 because it is flawed at the core. PM 1.0 fails for four reasons: purpose, practices, paradigms, and propaganda. We expect too much from it, our ineffective practices are based on outdated paradigms and are held in place by propaganda coming from powerful constituents. I deal with purpose in the remainder of this chapter, take up paradigms in Chapter 2, and propaganda in Chapter 3.

PM 1.0 Is Too Expansive

We ask PM 1.0 to do too many things. Those of you who have tried to change it know this. In your project team meetings you end up with dozens of flipchart pages full of expectations, key stakeholders, and downstream processes tied to PM. Herman Aguinis, a noted expert and writer in this area, lists 23 distinct purposes across five general categories in his book about PM:[9]

- Strategic. PM aligns employee behavior with the organization's goals. It communicates important business priorities and initiatives to employees.
- Administrative. PM results are used to make decisions about people. Ratings are inputs to other downstream decisions like rewards, promotion, potential, recognition, development, and termination.

- Communication. PM communicates what is expected of employees and what they are supposed to do in their job. It signals the values and principles that are important to a company. It also tells employees how they are performing and how they need to improve.
- Development. Supervisors use PM to provide feedback and coaching to employees and to identify their strengths and weaknesses. Objectives can then be set to leverage their strengths and remediate their weaknesses, incorporating these objectives into development or career plans.
- Organizational maintenance. PM provides information on how the workforce is being utilized and how the organization is performing. It also helps identify training needs and is used to evaluate the effectiveness of HR interventions designed to improve performance.
- Documentation purposes. PM documents the basis for many administrative decisions. PM forms represent the paper trail to document the rationale for decisions, and they are also used as information sources in formal investigations and employment litigation.

This long list presumes a number of different stakeholders, each with their own unique (and potentially conflicting) needs and expectations:

- Employees. They want a system that gives them direction, helps them achieve their goals, and helps them earn appropriate rewards and other outcomes.
- Supervisors. They want a system that focuses employees on the right things and helps them achieve their goals. They also want a system that helps them differentiate performance and enables them to make administrative decisions about rewards, promotions, and succession management.
- Management and senior leadership. They want a system that differentiates performance to motivate, engage, and retain top talent. They also want a system that efficiently and effectively distributes rewards. Finally, they want a system that employees like with minimal "noise."
- Legal, HR, and compliance. They want a system that is defensible, that makes or informs decisions that will withstand future litigation.
- Compensation and benefits, talent management professionals. They want a PM system that is efficient to run and gives them the

information they need for their processes (rewards, staffing, talent identification, and succession management)

At the risk of stating the obvious, this is crazy. One process simply cannot meet all these objectives and please all these stakeholders. PM 1.0 has been doomed from the start. Why do companies expect so much from PM? The root cause of this problem is historical; PM 1.0 is a legacy of the past. A quick history lesson shows it has several historical influences, all of which are still represented in the systems of today.

A (Very Brief) History of PM 1.0

The first major influence on PM 1.0 dates back to the early 20th century and the "performance appraisal" era. The goal of performance appraisal was to measure job performance so companies could improve promotion decisions. Historically, promotion decisions were based on nepotism and familial ties, or on seniority. More concrete measures of performance were needed to provide a fairer basis for these decisions. These early systems typically included ratings of employees on traits such as judgment, integrity, attitude, and "presence" (my personal favorite). [10] As employment laws changed in the United States during the 1960s and 1970s, the legal defensibility of these decisions became an important consideration, and documentation became an important part of PM systems, which led to bloated PM forms, detailed documentation, and endless signatures back and forth. As we saw from benchmarking results, nearly every company uses ratings of performance to help make decisions about their employees.

The second influence on PM 1.0 was management by objectives (MBO). MBO emerged in the late 1950s and early 1960s and attacked the inhumane rating of employees in performance appraisals.

With MBO the focus moved away from rating traits to setting and measuring objectives. Quantitative targets were set and progress was measured against these targets. This practice was seen as more objective, fair, and reliable. Objectives and targets had the added benefit of aligning employee efforts with company objectives and its direction. [11] The influence of MBO on PM today is still strong. Most PM systems have an objective setting process that translates company and organizational objectives into individual objectives and assesses progress against them.

The final influence on PM 1.0 arrived with the emergence of the modern PM system in the 1980s. Modern PM systems addressed problems with traditional performance appraisals and MBO. They were forward-looking, focused on planning future performance versus measuring past performance. They focused on clarifying future expectations with employees, both in terms of what outputs and results were expected (the whats), but also how one was supposed to behave and what behavior would be rewarded and recognized (the hows). These systems also focused more on development, creating a development planning process, and separating the development review from the performance review. Modern PM systems also placed more emphasis on ongoing feedback, coaching, and evaluation throughout the year. Finally, modern PM systems developed more explicit links to rewards as pay-for-performance (P4P) philosophies began to appear in the 1980s.[12]

All of these influences were additive, like barnacles attaching themselves to a log, one on top of the other. Management by objectives added an objective-setting component to the measurement and evaluation focus of performance appraisal. Modern PM added a forward-looking and development focus, an emphasis on the whats and the hows, and an explicit linkage to rewards. PM 1.0 incorporated all of these features and purposes, with all the inherent conflicts they created. Few companies stopped to rationalize what they really needed from PM. All of these purposes created another problem for organizations: they made PM difficult to change. Leaders felt trapped; they didn't like their current process, but they couldn't change it because it was tied to everything they did in HR. I have been in the room for these conversations. Groups start looking at the downstream impact of making a change to PM (for example, getting rid of ratings) and they start listing everything that would be impacted by this change. The list is long. The last time I participated in an exercise like this there were 31 different items on the list. No one wanted to change a process that affected 31 other processes. I have seen groups talk themselves out of making a change to a bad PM process simply because it was tied to so many other things.

So PM 1.0 fails first and foremost because it has been saddled with a dizzying number of objectives and it tries to please too many masters. In designing PM 2.0, we start with purpose.

A Sensible Purpose for PM 2.0

PM 2.0 takes its cues not from history or from benchmarking, but from organization design. What purpose should PM serve in the design and function of an organization? How would PM add value to an organization? Like any organizational process, PM is situated within the specific context of the organization. This context is defined by the strategy of the organization and the architecture (organization design) that is put in place to execute that strategy. If we can understand how PM fits into an organization's architecture, we can better understand the role it should play.

An organization's architecture is designed to take the inputs available to an organization (environment, capabilities, resources, history, and deep culture) and transform them into outputs that are valued by key stakeholders, including customers. Architecture should be configured to operationalize the strategic decisions made by an organization. Architecture also describes how the organization will balance all the various demands made on it for time, attention, resources, and energy.

An organization's architecture is designed to affect the behavior and actions of employees. In fact, it is designed expressly to control and influence what employees do (and don't do) and what they pay attention to (and do not pay attention to). I use the word control here not in a derogatory way, but to convey the predictability an organization needs in ensuring employees' efforts are directed at things that will further the organization's long-term interests. An organization's architecture sends signals to employees about what is important and what is not important. In turn, it is these behaviors and actions by employees that produce the results the organization needs.

There are dozens of organization architecture models and frameworks available, each with their own set of design elements. [13] I am partial to David Hanna's model outlined in his book *Designing Complex Organizations*. I used this model and later iterations of it for many years for most of my organization diagnosis and design work, and it makes the most intuitive sense to me. Most of these models contain similar elements such as work processes, structure, technology, people, rewards, decision making, management processes, culture, and leadership. These elements need to be aligned with the organization's strategy, but they also need to be congruent with one another so they work well together to constrain behavior and action.

So, organization architecture is about alignment, influence, and control. Architecture aligns the efforts and attention of employees to the strategy and priorities of the organization. It constrains and controls what employees do and how they do it in order to maximize organizational performance. With this background, where does PM fit best? Most organizational models have an element that reflects the management, control, and governance processes of an organization. For me, this is where PM fits best. This element contains the technical work processes that convert inputs to outputs, but it also contains important management processes. These processes have less to do with the horizontal work flow and more to do with vertical governance and decision making that sits on top of the work flow. These decision processes allocate scarce resources (e.g., money and talent) and control what gets worked on and what doesn't. Business planning and budgeting are examples of these processes. PM is an extension of these processes. Once organizations finalize decisions about priorities and resources, individual departments make decisions about how to best use the resources available to address the organization's priorities. Supervisors then work with their employees to identify their individual priorities. This view of PM is very consistent with research on strategy deployment.[14] In order for a strategy to be implemented, decisions about strategy must affect decisions about architecture, and decisions about architecture must affect tactical planning. Strategy turns into action by creating a short-term map of priorities and allocating resources to those priorities. PM takes this to the individual employee level.

Most organizational models have a rewards element as well, and many people point first to this element in aligning PM since most reward systems use input from performance ratings. It would be a mistake to align PM with rewards, and I will begin to make my case against this in Chapter 2 when I discuss agency theory, one of the foundational influences on PM 1.0. According to this theory, the purpose of a reward system is to align the goals of employees with the goals of the organization and motivate employees to perform. Aligning PM with rewards is classic PM 1.0 thinking, and PM 1.0 thinking has not gotten us very far in improving PM. In Section 2 of this book (especially Chapters 5–7), I will make the case that PM should not be aligned with rewards. The best science shows this strategy isn't effective in producing the individual and organizational performance we need, and there are more effective ways to motivate employees and align their efforts with organizational goals.

Through the lens of organizational design, PM is a management process to identify and control what gets worked on, with what resources, and by whom. It helps the organization translate strategy and organizational priorities into individual priorities. It provides direction for employees, helping to align the efforts of employees to the goals and objectives of the company. It is a control system ensuring the right things get worked on, and that there is help and support available to ensure progress is being made against organizational objectives. It is also assigns accountability to work and tasks. PM 2.0 is about direction, alignment, control, and progress, in the service of organizational performance.

An important implication of this purpose is the key stakeholders for PM become the organization and senior leaders who have the responsibility for management processes. It may sound strange not to put employees and supervisors at the center of a PM system. I'm not saying you don't think about employees and supervisors when you design PM. I'm saying PM should be *designed* to accomplish a primary purpose. We shouldn't design PM to engage and motivate employees, because PM isn't the best way to accomplish this (hint: it's about the work!). The key is not to sacrifice the primary design by trying to accomplish other secondary purposes. For example, don't impose strict documentation requirements on every employee simply because your legal department insists on detailed documentation to support potential litigation, which only involves a few employees. Focusing PM on a singular purpose does not imply these other purposes and the needs of other stakeholder are not important. It simply means a PM process designed around direction, alignment, control, and progress may not satisfy these other needs, and I would argue it shouldn't have been designed around those other needs in the first place. Other solutions will need to be found to address these other purposes and expectations, and I will share plenty of good solutions for you to consider.

What PM 2.0 Doesn't Do

Now having said what PM 2.0 should do, let me turn to what it shouldn't do. What PM 2.0 doesn't do is nearly as important as what it does do. Focusing PM on direction, alignment, control, and progress leaves a void for most companies. How do we evaluate performance? How do we pay people? How do we defend ourselves against litigation? PM 2.0 gives up a lot and there will be strong objections to giving up these other purposes. I will provide answers to these questions throughout the rest of this book, but let me begin to address these concerns here.

Administrative decisions

PM 2.0 is not about making merit pay decisions, bonus decisions, promotion decisions, or termination decisions. This may come as a shock to many of you and understandably so. For most of your companies, this is the primary purpose of PM: to evaluate employees so you can make decisions about them. Focusing on these downstream decisions implies PM is a means to an end and not an end in itself. You *can* make these decisions without PM. It may be efficient to use the same overall performance rating as input to all these decisions, but I don't think you should use an efficiency lens in making these decisions. As we will discuss in Chapter 4, the overall rating produced by PM isn't good enough to support these high-stakes decisions. So, while it may be efficient to use a PM rating for all these decisions it probably isn't effective.

You can use other information to make these decisions, or you can collect performance information using specially developed performance evaluation processes. This information will probably be more accurate anyway. I don't think it makes sense to suboptimize the governance and management functions of PM because we want it to produce a rating that drives other HR decisions, especially when it won't do so accurately anyway.

Communication

PM 2.0 is not about communication. A planning discussion should not be the first time employees learn about expectations and job responsibilities. Employees will certainly get important information from PM (e.g., priorities, where expectations are being met or not met), but this shouldn't be why companies have a PM system. Similarly, PM should not be the channel we use to communicate everything that is important, mandatory, or required. This is a common mistake companies make because PM is an easy target: It's how employees are graded. PM becomes the vessel into which everything that is important is poured. Those of you who have been on the front lines of PM know this firsthand. If your company loves competencies, PM is the place where competencies are evaluated. If your company has specific expectations of leaders, PM is the place leaders are held accountable for these expectations. If your company has a new branding effort (and what company doesn't), PM is the place where important brand attributes get translated into employee and leader behavior. If your company has important values or operating principles that guide its actions, PM is the way employees and leaders are held accountable for living these values and principles. If it is important, we have to integrate it into our PM process. It goes on and on. You end up with a bloated, confusing mess. PM isn't the only way to signal something is important, and it isn't the only way to hold people accountable for things. In fact PM is a relatively weak lever for driving behavior change. Most organizations mistakenly use PM changes as lead interventions in their organization change efforts when it should probably lag other interventions.

If your goal is to create a more inclusive culture for example, fire all the leaders who don't behave this way and replace them with leaders that do. This is far more effective in driving organizational change than adding inclusive behaviors to your PM process.

Development

PM 2.0 is not about development, it's about performance. If an employee needs to improve, learn something new, or develop a skill in order to be able to perform some aspect of their job, this objective should be included in their PM plan. Working on this skill becomes part of their performance plan because performance will suffer without it. Development needs to be in the service of performance. This may sound like a subtle point, but designing PM for development will suboptimize it for performance. Longer term development and career development are important considerations. That's why they should not be a core part of PM. I favor developing a separate process to address these needs, independent of PM.

Documentation

PM 2.0 is not about documentation to support legal challenges. Legal challenges typically involve only a handful of employees every year. Why would we design a PM process that affects tens or even hundreds of thousands of employees based on the requirements of only a handful? Documentation is important for the 1%, but this should be managed outside of PM, e.g., as a part of a "performance improvement process" or formal discipline process. We should design PM for the 99%, not the 1%. If we disconnect PM from all these other administrative decisions, legal defensibility becomes much less of a concern anyway.[15]

So PM 1.0 is failing us and purpose is a key reason. PM 2.0 keeps only what is critical and what can't be accomplished in other ways.

Key Messages

- Most companies have similar PM processes. I call this last generation performance management—PM 1.0 for short.
- PM 1.0 is generally seen as ineffective, yet companies still believe in it and regularly make incremental changes looking for something that works.
- Contemporary PM was developed from three distinct roots. The effect of each new development was to add more functions to PM and make systems more complex.
- Companies expect a lot from PM. Modern PM processes are designed to meet too many different needs and satisfy too many different organizational stakeholders.
- Next generation performance management—PM 2.0—is a management process focused on direction, alignment, control, and progress.

■ PM 2.0 should not be designed to evaluate performance, differentiate rewards or support other downstream administrative decisions like talent identification, succession planning, staffing, or promotion. These decisions can be made more effectively in other ways.

2

Paradigms

The Natural Laws of Performance Management 1.0

It ain't what you don't know that gets you into trouble.
It's what you know for sure that just ain't so.
—Mark Twain

We cannot solve our problems with the same thinking we used when we created them.
—Albert Einstein

In 2010 Blockbuster declared bankruptcy and would soon vanish from the planet. In the year 2000 this fact would have come as quite a shock to all of us. At that time most of us drove to a Blockbuster store every weekend, rented a movie, and went home and watched it on a VCR or DVD player. Of course this seems ludicrous today; no one has VCR or DVD player any longer. In 2000, Blockbuster was wildly successful and dominated the video market. Their business model focused on brick and mortar stores and physical access to movies, and late fees for revenue. They never saw companies like Netflix coming. Actually that's not true. In 2000, Netflix CEO Reed

Next Generation Performance Management, pages 17–29
Copyright © 2017 by Information Age Publishing
17

Hastings proposed to Blockbuster's board that Netflix manage their online brand. He was laughed out of the room.[1]

Blockbuster suffered from what change experts Stewart Black and Hal Gregersen call a "failure to see."[2] Black and Gregersen cite three fundamental reasons why individuals and organizations fail to change: failure to see, failure to move, and failure to finish. People don't see what to do, they don't do it, or they don't stay with it. Blockbuster didn't see the problems with their current business model, and they didn't see how Netflix might capitalize on these problems. By the time Blockbuster saw the writing on the wall in 2004, it was too late. Actually it may not have been too late. Blockbuster CEO John Antioco proposed changes that could have saved the company, but the board of directors fell victim to Black and Gregersen's second failure: the failure to move. The company was unwilling to take the costly steps necessary to compete with Netflix. Blockbuster's board replaced Antioco and the new CEO went back to the old business model. They were out of business within 5 years. Today Netflix is a darling.

Management scholar Henry Mintzberg explained this problem very simply in his book *The Rise and Fall of Strategic Planning.*[3]

> Every manager has a mental model of the world in which he or she acts based on experience and knowledge. When a manager must make a decision, he or she thinks of behavior alternatives within their mental model.

Mintzberg made this statement after his work with Shell Oil Company. He worked with managers to shift their perspectives on important issues, altering their mental models, mindsets, and worldviews by enabling them to become more explicit about their key assumptions. He writes about their breakthroughs, quoting the managers themselves.

> From the moment of this realization, we no longer saw our task as producing a documented view of the future business environment 5 to 10 years ahead. Our real target was the mental models of our decision makers.

The problem we face with performance management (PM) is the same problem Shell managers had with envisioning new business models for the future. Our problem isn't with rating scales, SMART goals, incentive plans or other practices discussed in Chapter 1. Our problem is with the paradigms behind these practices and the mental models of the people who design, implement, and control them. Leaders have their own assumptions and beliefs about what works and what doesn't based on their education, training, and experience. Like the leaders at Shell and the leaders at Blockbuster many of our leaders suffer from a failure to see. They don't see alternatives to PM 1.0 because they are stuck in PM 1.0 paradigms. It is hard to see a PM 2.0 world when you are wearing PM 1.0 glasses. This is why all of our tinkering doesn't help; the alternatives we consider are all based on PM 1.0 thinking. To solve the PM problem and make real change, we need to confront these paradigms just like Shell managers needed to confront their mental models. This won't be easy; it requires "bucket work."

One of my favorite metaphors for individual and organizational change comes from the fairy tale *Iron Hans* by the Brothers Grimm. Robert Bly popularized the fable in his book *Iron John: A Book About Men.*[4] In the fable, a hunter answers a challenge from the king to go to a part of the forest that men don't come back from. The hunter goes into the forest, and his dog is taken by a hand that shoots out of a lake. Slowly draining the lake using a bucket, he finds at the bottom a hairy wild man with iron skin who is taken back to the town castle and imprisoned. The king's son is playing with his golden ball when it accidentally rolls into the cage holding the wild man. The prince does a deal in which he gets the ball back, but only after having released the hairy man in the cage. This deal marks the beginning of the boy's manhood and in the end Iron Hans turns out to be a pretty good guy. This is a story about maturation and self-examination, and it requires bucket work. When we empty the lake that is PM 1.0, our flawed paradigms are at the bottom.

Two Revolutions

In the 1950s a revolution was beginning. Actually it was a counterrevolution. A number of scientists in the fields of psychology, anthropology, linguistics, computer science, and neuroscience were creating a new field: the field of cognitive science.[5] This would be the beginning of the overthrow of behaviorism. Behaviorism as embodied by Edward Thorndike and B. F. Skinner was well-entrenched in psychology by the 1940s.[6] Behaviorism involved the study of observable behavior and held that behavior can be understood by looking at its consequences and need not involve the use of other explanatory concepts such as consciousness or other mental processes. This thinking was firmly entrenched in business as well, as evidenced by the piece-rate systems popularized by Fredrick Taylor and his principles of scientific management.[7] But by the mid-1950s, pioneering scientists in these diverse fields had made their case that the days of behaviorism were numbered, and the dogma represented by the principle that behavior was solely a function of its consequences began to crumble. T. A. Ryan at Cornell was attacking the concepts of consequences, drives, and instincts as explanations of behavior. He and others began using new terms like tasks, intentions, motives, and

needs to explain behaviors that never extinguished long after the reinforcements were gone, and activities that people engaged in apparently because
of their own intrinsic interest. He proposed that tasks were the causal explanations of most behavior, not reinforcements, consequences, instincts, or
drives.[8] Simply put, people have stuff to do and they do it. In Ryan's words:

> I am proposing, in fact, a hypothesis based upon the most unsophisticated
> common sense. Specifically, I assume that when I decided to write this pa-
> per, the decision actually influenced the movements of my fingers in typing.

Pretty heady stuff. By the 1960s, psychologists like Edwin Locke were
studying conscious factors like intentions, goals, or purposes in task performance and motivational theories like goal-setting were born.[9]

Twenty years after the beginning of the cognitive revolution, another
revolution was taking shape in economics. Richard Thaler was a graduate
student in economics at the University of Rochester. He began to keep track
of observations of behavior that classical economics could not explain. At
first this was simply to amuse himself. He observed that people ascribed
more value to things they own merely because they owned them. People
who owned a coffee mug required twice the price to sell it than they would
pay to acquire it. This was not rational. The mug had a fixed value and the
minimally acceptable buying and selling price should be the same. Owning
it should not change its value. Thaler called this effect the "endowment effect" and this was the beginning of behavioral economics.

By the time Thaler was logging the failures of classical economic models, Herbert Simon was already questioning the idea of the "rational man"
assumed by standard economic theory. He suggested that our minds must
be understood relative to the environment in which they evolved.[10] Decisions are not always optimal. There are limits to a human's knowledge and
their ability to process information, and as a result they make bad decisions.
He called this "bounded rationality."

Another force in the overthrow of classical economics came from the
work of Amos Tversky and Daniel Kahneman at Stanford.[11] They developed
prospect theory, which shows decisions are not always optimal and our
choices are influenced by the way they are framed or their context. Consider the classic decision problem:

> Which of the following would you prefer: (a) a certain win of $250, ver-
> sus (b) a 25% chance to win $1,000 and a 75% chance to win nothing? How
> about (c) a certain loss of $750, versus (d) a 75% chance to lose $1,000 and
> a 25% chance to lose nothing?

Tversky and Kahneman's work shows that responses are different if choices are framed as a gain or a loss. When faced with the first type of decision, a greater proportion of people will opt for the riskless alternative (a), while for the second problem people are more likely to choose the riskier alternative (d). This happens because we dislike losses more than we like an equivalent gain. Giving something up is more painful than the pleasure we derive from receiving it. This is not rational. By the late 1970s and early 1980s, behavioral economics had emerged as a discipline to explain many of these anomalies uniting economic and psychological principles.[12] The exclamation point to the overthrow of classical economics would come some 40 years later when the financial crisis reduced the financial world to a pile of ash. Human beings are not rational and markets are not capable of regulating themselves and protecting their own shareholders. People, and markets and institutions, are flawed. Michael Lewis placed the blame for the financial crisis squarely on the shoulders of incentives and classical economic thinking, and on the culture they created in these institutions.[13] If it was not apparent before, it should have been apparent after the financial crisis that we cannot control behavior using classical economic and psychological principles, not without dire consequences.

These two revolutions pointed out the flaws in classical principles from psychology and economics. You cannot motivate and change behavior by rational appeals, incentives, and punishments. The problem is no one told the business community. These principles remain the foundation of how leaders today are trained to motivate their employees and manage their behavior and performance. The 1940s are alive and well in modern organizations, and these principles are still at the core of many human resource practices, including PM. This book attempts to bring PM into the 21st century by exposing and rejecting these principles in favor of new ones based on better science. A deeper understanding of these principles and how they shape our thinking is essential to any PM change effort.

PM 1.0 Paradigms

The bedrock of PM 1.0 comes from a handful of theories from economics and psychology that prescribe how leaders motivate and control employee behavior in organizations. Their principles form the "natural laws" of PM 1.0, and they have a strong effect on the mental models of leaders and HR professionals. These theories dominate the education leaders and HR professionals receive in business schools; they form the basis for much of the management and HR training they receive in organizations. They affect how HR managers and compensation professionals develop systems, processes, and interventions to control behavior and how they train line managers to operate these systems. Leaders and HR professionals also develop their own ideas and beliefs (and ways of justifying them) based on their own experience. Let's face it, designing PM systems is not like splicing genes. Leaders and HR professionals think they know what needs to be done.

The problem with paradigms is they rarely get examined. PM 1.0 paradigms are accepted as truths, and when people get together to fix PM, they talk about practices not paradigms. The famous organizational scholar Chris Argyris wrote about this problem back in the 1960s and 1970s looking at how individuals and organizations learn. He and colleague Donald Schon argued that people have mental maps and these maps guide their actions. He also argued that few people are aware of the maps or theories they use to guide their actions.[14]

Compounding this problem is the penchant organizations have for "single-loop learning."[15] For Argyris and Schon, learning involves the detection and correction of error. When something goes wrong, we try something different. If a three-category performance rating doesn't work, we try four or five categories. If a forced-distribution process doesn't work, we relax the requirements and provide "guidance" on the expected distribution and allow some exceptions. When faced with failure, like Henry Mintzberg says, we stay within our theory or mental model. We question our tactics, we don't question our thinking. Argyris and Schon argue that we need double-loop learning. When things don't work like we expect, we need to step back and examine the assumptions, beliefs, and values that underlie our practices. Instead of asking how many rating categories to use or if we should force a distribution across those categories, we need to ask if we should evaluate employee performance at all. Can we really measure performance well enough to tie big rewards to it? Instead of debating the right mix of variable pay elements, we need to ask if we should have variable pay at all. These questions simply don't get asked when organizations redesign PM. Double-loop learning requires reflection, it requires bucket work, which is not a strength of most leaders. Business leaders get paid to act, and talking about assumptions and beliefs when the clock is ticking on a project seems like a waste of time. Teams working on PM tend to jump right in and start designing their new process. Moving from PM 1.0 to PM 2.0 will require reflection and double-loop learning. It will require bucket work.

Homo Economicus

Economics classes are required of nearly every business school student, and economic principles are staples of nearly all basic management philosophies and training. The primary economic influences on PM 1.0 come from classical economics and labor economics. Most of you could recite classical economic assumptions in your sleep: self-interested, motivated by money, maximize gains and minimize losses, rational and efficient.

These beliefs lead organizations to emphasize compensation and reward systems to motivate employees. The way to an employee's heart is through his wallet—"show me the money." Incentive pay and the role of financial inducements have rich histories in economics dating back to Adam Smith in the late 1700s.[16] The impact of standard economic principles on PM, however, goes beyond a focus on money. People are self-interested. They look at their own costs and their own benefits. Organizations design reward systems that reward individuals for their own efforts (versus the results of teams or the organization as a whole). Organizations are meritocracies; they look at fairness through the lens of individual merit. Rewards are earned; individuals with the biggest contributions receive the largest rewards. Meritocracy also assumes supervisors are endowed with certain superpowers: the ability to discriminate who has contributed the most; the ability to separate fact from fiction in people's contributions; and the power to suspend any biases and tendencies that may interfere with their judgments. We will have much more to say about meritocracy in Chapter 9.

These theories explicitly caution us against making rewards contingent on group or organizational performance, believing that self-interested, utility-maximizing individuals will slack off under these conditions and "free ride" on the group's efforts. Finally, standard economic principles also assume people are rational. They assume people will always do what is good for them and they can accurately assess costs and benefits. This principle requires employees to have their own superpowers, such as the power to be dispassionate and objective, the power to suspend and hold at bay any and all biases they may have, and to recognize when they are making mistakes that will limit their own outcomes.

Labor economics has also had a major influence on PM 1.0 practices. Labor economics looks at patterns in wages, employment, and income as a function of supplies of labor (workers) and the demands of labor (from employers). One theory with a strong influence on PM 1.0 practices is agency theory.[17] As it applies to PM, the agency relationship involves a principal (a company) delegating work to an agent (an employee) who performs the work. Principals and agents need to cooperate in order for each of them to get what they want. Agency theory describes the relationship between these two parties using the metaphor of a contract. As you can imagine, when two self-interested parties come together there are problems inherent in the relationship, and this theory is frequently framed as "the principal-agent problem."

- Consistent with standard economic theory, it assumes agents are self-interested and their goals will not be aligned with the goals of the principal. As a result, other mechanisms are needed to align the goals of agent with those of the principal (e.g., rewards, incentives, monitoring, and fear of being fired).

- Principals are assumed to have difficulty verifying the agent is upholding their part of the bargain. Principals and agents are assumed to have "asymmetric access" to information. This means employees could slack off and do poor work and the principal wouldn't know. This creates costs and risks for principals reinforcing the need for the monitoring and surveillance of agents.

- Finally, it assumes the two parties have different attitudes about risk and may prefer different actions because of this. Agents, for example, are assumed to prefer less risk and more certainty (e.g., more stability in their wages).

The solution to these problems is presumed to be good contracting between the principal and agent, and effective monitoring of performance. Agency theory's influence on PM 1.0 practices shows up in a number of ways. First, there is a heavy emphasis on individual rewards and incentives to bring employee goals and efforts into alignment with company goals. Agency theory uses external contingencies like rewards to motivate employees to perform and to align their efforts with the goals of the company. Second, feedback in an agency relationship is primarily about monitoring employees and catching them doing things that maximize their own utility but subvert the company goals. Third, according to agency theory goal setting isn't a process to engage and motivate employees, it is a process to spell out the terms of a contract and specify the reward contingencies for successful fulfillment of the contract.

Agency theory epitomizes the tenor of PM 1.0. The relationship between employees and their supervisors is not assumed to be collaborative and trusting. You don't use terms like moral hazard, conflict of interest, and agency costs to describe a collaborative, mutually beneficial relationship. The relationship between employee and employer is assumed to be adversarial with an embedded structural tension, especially from the employer perspective: "Employees don't share my goals" (conflict of interest); "I bear all the risks and incur all the costs of employee misbehavior" (moral hazard); and "I incur the costs of preventing employee misbehavior" (monitoring and surveillance). Even the framing of the theory is telling: the principal-agent problem. The relationship between an employee and a manager is assumed to be problematic at the outset, and the goal is to put in place practices to mitigate these problems. These principles don't leave you with a warm and fuzzy feeling as you enter an employment relationship; they make you want to put on your combat gear.

Another labor market theory with a strong influence on PM and other HR practices is tournament theory. Tournament theory was developed to explain flaws in classical economic thinking, such as when differences is wages are not based on how productive someone is or where pay is not proportional to one's skills, abilities, experience, or qualifications.[18] For example, think of a golf tournament with 100 participants. Tiger Woods receives $1,000,000 for winning it and the last place finisher receives $1,000. Is Tiger Woods 1,000 times better than the last place finisher? Probably not. The premise of tournament theory is that in some cases, performance is judged relatively and not based on some objective evaluation of performance.

Another implication of the theory is that a certain amount of wages from employees at a given level are withheld and given to employees at higher levels. In a golf tournament, for example, the lower finishers give up prize money to the higher finishers to motivate players. In organizations, for example, the salaries of vice presidents are high not to reward them, but to motivate those toiling at the bottom of the pyramid to work hard so they too can someday become vice presidents. These salaries also motivate current vice presidents to work hard to stay on top. The idea is that employees compete in "tournaments" with the prizes being promotions, higher salaries, or top prizes in a sales contest. Tournament theory has several important implications for PM. First, ratings and relative comparisons are essential so employees know where they stand. Second, competition among employees and transparent feedback on performance are important elements of motivation. Finally, differentiation of rewards is critically important; more differentiation translates into high levels of motivation and performance.

These two theories add resolution to the principles behind PM 1.0. Employers see their relationship with employees as problems that can be solved by clear contracting, surveillance, performance measurement, and competition, and by differentiating individual performance and rewards based on performance.[19] PM 1.0 feels a lot more like the movie *The Hunger Games* than it does the movie *Hoosiers*.

Carrots and Sticks: The Psychological Man

PM 1.0 programming of leaders and HR professionals goes beyond the business school. Many aspiring leaders and HR professionals take introductory psychology classes (usually to satisfy a science requirement). Here they learn the principles of motivation and control from a psychological perspective. A handful of psychological theories have influenced PM practices: reinforcement theory (the law of effect and operant conditioning), expectancy theory, and control theory.

Thorndike's law of effect holds that responses that are followed by satisfying outcomes become more likely to occur, and responses that are followed by an annoying state of affairs will be weakened. Similarly, operant conditioning (popularized by B. F. Skinner) holds that individual behavior may change in form, frequency, or strength as a function of the consequences of the behavior.[20]

These theories have two important implications for PM. First, behavior is externally mediated. What people do is based on external factors not internal desires, motives, or goals. Second, behavior can be modified by its consequences. If you want to change behavior, modify the consequences of that behavior. If you want to understand a behavior, understand the consequences holding that behavior in place. These theories have been applied in organizations for decades to motivate and control employee behavior, primarily through feedback and the use of rewards, incentives, and recognition.

Expectancy theory sees motivation as a function of two factors: People must see their efforts lead to a successful performance (expectancy), and successful performance must lead to outcomes they value (instrumentality). Expectancy theory has influenced PM in three important ways. First, motivation is seen primarily as an individual phenomenon and individual outcomes should be based on individual performance. This reinforces the view of organizations as meritocracies. Second, expectancy theory further reinforces the point that it is external contingencies that matter; effort and behavior are functions of what happens after that behavior, which puts a premium on extrinsic rewards. Finally, while expectancy theory allows for a variety of outcomes to motivate employees, not surprisingly most attention is paid to financial outcomes.[21]

Finally, control theory has influenced PM practices primarily in the area of feedback and coaching. According to control theory, feedback is essential to resolving discrepancies between a goal or target (e.g., the speed set on a car's cruise control) and the actual performance of the system (e.g., the car's actual speed). When a discrepancy is noted (the car is faster or slower than the target speed by some margin), the appropriate action is taken (engage or disengage the engine). An important implication of control theory for PM is that feedback is primarily focused on gaps: discrepancies between demonstrated performance and expected or target performance. In a missile guidance system, for example, feedback ha[anytime there is a gap between the trajectory and the target. When we apply this thinking to PM, feedback is something that happens when employees get "off course," and it places a strong emphasis on delivering negative feedback. In fact, many of the associations we have with feedback are negative. Feedback in a sound system when an open microphone is too close to a speaker is clearly negative; the sound is loud and obnoxious. When you look up the word feedback in a thesaurus, many of the associations have negative connotations (e.g., criticism, evaluation, assessment).

Summary of PM 1.0

So our bucket work is done and the lake that is PM 1.0 is drained. On the muddy bottom we can now examine the assumptions, beliefs, and principles that govern it (see Table 2.1).

TABLE 2.1 PM 1.0 Paradigms, Assumptions, and Beliefs	
PM 1.0 Element	**Paradigms, Assumptions, and Beliefs**
General	• The relationship between a company and an employee is adversarial, with inherent structural problems, conflicts and risks • The optimal relationship between a company and an employee is contractual • Motivation is externally mediated
Planning	• Alignment of employees with company priorities is externally mediated by contracts, contingencies, consequences, and threats • Goals are specific contracts that specify what needs to be done • Goals only have instrumental value. They are important only insofar as rewards and outcomes are tied to them. They specify what accomplishments will be rewarded
Feedback	• Monitoring and surveillance is necessary to hold employees accountable and ensure they are fulfilling the terms of the contract • Keeping score is important; employees need to know the score and where they stand • Feedback is primarily negative, correcting employees when they get off track
Evaluation	• Employees want and need to be evaluated and compared with others • Ratings and rankings motivate • Competition and relativity are important for motivation • Supervisors can evaluate performance
Rewards	• Money motivates • Behavior and performance are best controlled by external reward contingencies • Rewards need to be contingent upon individual performance in order to motivate • More differentiation of performance and rewards is better for motivation

These assumptions and beliefs represent the biggest barrier to change for PM. The mental model they create blinds us from seeing suitable alternatives. Leaders and HR professionals don't second guess them, they don't engage in double-loop learning. If you are not convinced of the power of these mental models, tell your chief HR officer you think the company should abandon performance ratings or individual performance-based pay. Look into their eyes.

I had a memorable conversation like this at a conference with the person in charge of PM at a very large company that everyone reading this book would recognize. I had challenged her earlier in the day when she reported the percentage of employees who fell into each of the five buckets of their performance ratings—to the second decimal point. I told her the decimal points probably weren't needed, that there is nowhere near this level of precision in supervisor ratings of performance (a point I will come back to in Chapter 4). During my presentation I was openly critical of the practice of tying individual rewards to mostly inaccurate performance ratings. At a break she challenged me asking the question I have been asked dozens of times: "If we don't pay people based on their performance, what *do* we pay them for?" She pressed me for an answer and I flippantly responded, "For showing up." This got a laugh from those eavesdropping on our conversation, and she seemed pleased with herself, as if I had neatly fallen into the trap she set. She felt she had exposed the flaw in my logic, that we couldn't possibly pay people for simply showing up since this violated all the natural laws of PM. Like I said, failure to see.[22] This exchange has stuck with me and suggests we have two problems with PM, not one. Our first problem is it doesn't work and our efforts to fix it have failed. Our second problem is we can't fix the first problem unless we fix our thinking, and this exchange reinforces the fact that the second problem is going to be the harder one.

As Black and Gregersen discuss in their book, the solution to a failure to see is high-contrast, high-confrontation experiences. We need to show leaders examples of organizations that do it differently to confront their beliefs and assumptions. The problem with this strategy for PM is there aren't many organizations that do it differently. Everyone does it the same way. Organizations that do things differently are usually small companies (mostly technology companies), companies with unions, government agencies, or international organizations working under different labor laws. These are not the types of organizations that are benchmarked or imitated by large multinational organizations. What's worse many of these organizations don't necessarily like their own practices and would rather adopt the "modern" practices of large private-sector organizations. It is hard to benchmark an organization that doesn't like its own practices.

So we are prisoners of our paradigms and our mental models. If we have any chance at real change, this is where we need to start. In Section II, I hold these paradigms and principles up to the harsh light of scientific scrutiny. Spoiler alert. They don't fare well. The world has changed since Adam Smith authored *An Inquiry Into the Nature and Causes of the Wealth of Nations* and since the thinking of Edward Thorndike, Fredrick Taylor, and B. F. Skinner ruled the day. The revolutions in cognitive science and behavioral economics have ushered in new paradigms and new thinking that should guide us in designing PM. While I will argue the science is on our side in overthrowing these paradigms, it won't be easy. There are strong forces holding them in place.

Key Messages

- The key problem with PM is flawed paradigms and mental models.
- Our outdated paradigms and mental models have roots in classic theories from psychology and economics that have long since been discredited as sufficient explanations of complex behavior in organizations.
- These paradigms and mental models never get examined or debated in the face of every new failed PM practice.

3

The Forces Against Change

Mock on, mock on, 'tis all in vain. You throw the sand against the wind,
and the wind blows it back again.

—William Blake

No shepherd and one herd! Everybody wants the same, everybody is the same:
whoever feels different goes voluntarily into a madhouse.

—Friedrich Nietzsche

There are lots of reasons to abandon performance management (PM) 1.0. It doesn't work and everyone hates it. It tries to do everything for everyone and pleases no one. It is based on paradigms rooted in outdated theories overthrown in the 1950s and 1970s. We have known for decades these paradigms are suspect, and yet human resources practices like PM are based on them and persist in organizations. Why? Why do companies stay on the well-worn path of PM 1.0 despite its failure?

My conversation with the woman from the regional hospital system mentioned earlier illustrates a big reason PM 1.0 remains popular despite

Next Generation Performance Management, pages 31–42
Copyright © 2017 by Information Age Publishing
All rights of reproduction in any form reserved.

its failings: ~~Companies do what other companies~~ do. Companies imitate the practices of other companies and these practices become accepted as the standard. She was there to learn what other companies were doing so she could apply the learnings in her organization. These and other forces exert a gravitational pull on PM practices keeping them in the orbit of PM 1.0 and its flawed paradigms.

The Scourge of Benchmarking

I don't need to tell you benchmarking is big business. Most of you probably do it regularly. A survey by Bain and Company shows benchmarking is the fourth most popular management tool used by large companies and the second most popular tool in North America.[1] In it's heyday in the late 1990s, upwards of 80% of companies used benchmarking and most were very pleased with the value it provided. Usage has moderated of late, perhaps due to cost pressures faced by large companies after the financial crisis, but satisfaction with the tool remains high.

In a nutshell, benchmarking involves talking to someone who does well what you want to do, presumably because doing it has contributed to their success. There are different forms of benchmarking from rigorous 12-step processes popularized by Xerox and Robert Camp to more "social" benchmarking where you simply call people on the phone and talk to them about what they are doing.[2]

There are firms whose sole purpose is to conduct benchmarking studies and maintain repositories of such studies. Consulting firms and HR think tanks have increasingly made benchmarking an important part of their business models. They regularly conduct surveys of their clients and members asking them about their practices and how they feel about them. They produce benchmarking reports highlighting best practices of top companies. They host meetings, webinars, and conferences where companies come together and discuss their practices. They write articles and blogs highlighting case studies from specific companies. They make it easy to find out what other companies are doing.

Don't get me wrong, I have no problem with benchmarking. I like to know what other companies are doing as much as the next person. However doing things simply because other companies do them is dangerous. First we have no idea why other firms adopt certain practices. Did they pick them because they are effective? Not likely. It's more likely they adopted their practices because others had adopted them (the "Dante's inferno" of benchmarking). Second, even if the companies being benchmarked are successful, we don't know if their success has anything to do with these specific practices. This is not likely to be the case for PM. No company can attribute their success to their PM process. A PM process does not give a company a competitive advantage. At best, a well-designed PM process enables the strategy the company has chosen or at least doesn't interfere with it. If you have a bad strategy, a world-class PM process isn't going to save you.

The influence of consulting firms and business think tanks has grown dramatically in the past several years. Upwards of 85% of Fortune 500 companies are members of the Corporate Executive Board, a leading business think tank. The Conference Board, another business think tank, has more than 1,200 public and private companies as members. The Institute for Corporate Productivity (i4cp), a leading HR think tank, has experienced record growth in their membership roster the majority of which are Fortune 500 companies.[3] These firms are growing at a time when HR staffs are shrinking as companies cut expenses and outsource many HR functions.[4] Thin HR staffs are increasingly reliant on these firms for expertise and insight. They have a virtual monopoly on information channels to HR practitioners and business leaders as a result.

These firms also help business leaders and HR professionals sort the wheat from the chaff in the information being published about a particular HR practice. There has been an explosion of information available on business and HR practices today. There are more business communication media and channels available than ever before, from books, magazine articles, and webinars to blogs and social media posts, all pushed directly to leaders and HR professionals. The rapid growth of the Internet and social media has dramatically reduced the cost and effort to communicate. This has dramatically increased the quantity of information hitting the desks of business leaders and HR professionals, but has also decreased the quality. There is more garbage being communicated today than ever before, and all of it spreads at amazing speeds through social media and other formal and informal professional networks. As a result, business leaders and HR professionals have a bewildering amount of information at their fingertips and they have little time to digest it. They rely on their consultants and HR think tanks to sort it all out for them and this puts them in a powerful position. When a company wants to redesign PM, they simply call up their consultant or HR think tank.

Our companies imitate the practices of top companies like teenagers who buy the jeans the popular kids or celebrities are wearing. This "institutional envy" is facilitated by the adoration top companies receive in the business press. Companies like GE, Google, Apple, and Disney become media darlings and other companies imitate their practices. Those of you who grew up on farms may know the concept of the bell cow. The bell cow is the leader of the herd. You put a bell around its neck, and if you want to know where the herd is, you listen for the bell. In the 1990s General Electric (GE) was the bell cow. They were very successful and many companies adopted their practices simply because GE (and their CEO Jack Welch) did them. The diffusion of forced ranking systems throughout large companies in the 1990s and the early 2000s was due in large measure to the emulation of GE's practices. In fact, as I write these words GE has recently announced they are eliminating performance ratings, a practice beginning to spread among large companies. General Electric's adoption of this practice will likely accelerate the move by other companies away from performance ratings. In Chapter 4 I will have much more to say about this practice and the dangers inherent in mindlessly following GE's lead.

Forces like benchmarking, imitation, and the increased reliance on these external firms has led to a homogenization of business practices across companies. Practices become institutionalized and other companies imitate them in order to achieve legitimacy.[5] Stanford professor Jeffrey Pfeffer has written about this phenomenon and cites a number of business practices that research shows are adopted simply because others are doing them (e.g., poison-pill anti-takeover defenses, mergers and acquisitions, downsizing, and the adoption of matrix organization structures).[6] PM practices like forced distributions and pay-for-performance programs are adopted for similar reasons. Forces like benchmarking and imitation have an "entraining" effect on practices, pushing and pulling them toward the mode. This is why PM 1.0 persists; its practices are the standard. If everyone does them how can they be wrong?

A friend of mine told me a story about PM reform efforts at his company that perfectly illustrates the tendency to blindly follow what has always been done. In this particular company they had embarked on a PM redesign project and were midway through it at the end of the year. Employees in this company did not like the PM process, nor did the leaders. Because the design wasn't completed, they gave organizations within the company the option of not doing PM for the upcoming year. They gave them a "hall pass." They could opt out of the process they hated. Most did it anyway. They continued with a process they hated because, "It's what companies do" (and they couldn't think of what else to do).

What Passes for "Research" Has Changed

Benchmarking has had another more subtle effect on the discourse around HR practices. When consulting firms and HR think tanks conduct their benchmarking surveys and summarize the results in a report, this is labeled research. Many companies base their actions on this information and believe their actions are research-based. I don't mean to parse words and debate the meaning of the word research; however, we need to distinguish this kind of research from research based on theory, hypotheses, and rigorous experimentation and control.

The evidence-based management movement (which I will say more about here) argues we should adopt practices based on *evidence* that they are effective.[7] In evidence-based management language, the standard for evidence is getting weaker. If a report from a consulting firm or HR think tank documents that a particular practice is common among companies and those companies have been more successful, this is evidence the practice must be effective. Doing something because it is popular is different than doing something because it is effective. We need to clean up our language. I propose the following terms:

- **Common practices.** These are observed frequently in companies. This is the standard output from most benchmarking studies. Common practices are frequently labelled "best practices" because everyone does them. We believe in the wisdom of the crowd that if everyone does them they must be effective. The use of performance ratings is a good example.
- **Unique practices.** These are observed less frequently in companies. Practices can be unique for many reasons. They can be novel and not yet widely adopted, or organizations adopting them may be unique or in unique circumstances. Practices can also be unique because they are risky and few companies have been willing to try them. Abandoning performance ratings is a good example. Finally, practices can be unique because they are stupid and no one in their right mind should be doing them.
- **Effective practices.** These have been shown by rigorous scientific research to be associated with important outcomes organizations value (e.g., performance, productivity, retention, engagement, innovation).
- **Best practices.** This term should be abolished.

Information that reaches HR professionals and business leaders is more likely to be about common and unique practices than effective practices. When leaders look around at other companies, it is PM 1.0 as far as the eye can see. Why would they make fundamental changes?

Fatalism and Rationalization

There is also a feeling of resignation that leaders and HR professionals adopt with respect to PM. You can't blame them. They have tried everything to improve it and nothing has worked. Things get better for a short time but it doesn't last. You hear it in their language; they assume the PM problem is simply intractable and every solution has a down side, and they begin to rationalize. I have heard comments like these many times and I'm sure you have as well. In fact I have said many of these things myself in the past.

- All PM systems have warts; you simply have to pick your warts. No process will please everyone. There will always be noise. Every few years companies trade one set of warts for another.
- Good medicine tastes bad. An effective PM system tells employees what they don't want to hear and they won't always like it. Certain employees will always be unhappy.
- The world isn't fair. PM systems come with tough messages and employees need to hear them. It won't always seem fair, especially to those on the losing end.
- Our employees are big boys and girls. We shouldn't have to tell employees everything they need to know and we can't hold their hands all the time. We pay them a lot of money; they should know what to do.
- We pay our employees well. Employees should quit complaining about the little things and be grateful for what we give them.
- Not everyone can get a trophy. (This is my personal favorite.) Some people come out on top and some don't. That's life. Corollary: "Not everyone can get a ribbon."
- A good baseball hitter gets out 7 times out of 10. If we can hit .300 with our PM system we are doing OK. We can't please everyone (evidently, if we are successful we can only please three out of 10 employees).

You could probably come up with your own list. Comments like these are discussion killers when talking about PM reform. Organizations are good at rationalizing the noise that comes with poor-performing PM systems and inertia develops around them. It's easy to tolerate a poor performing PM system since they typically aren't fatal. Most companies don't go out of business because they have a terrible PM system. It is more like having a pebble in your shoe: while it can be annoying, you can still function pretty well.

These attitudes make the complaints from employees more tolerable and lead companies to stay with practices that are not working. It takes a full-scale revolt by employees or some really bad press (in Microsoft's case for example) in order to get organizations to do anything different, and when they do it usually involves making incremental changes. I am a volleyball player and former coach. Deciding to change a PM process feels a lot like deciding to replace a volleyball coach (or a coach in another lower status sport) in middle school. Almost no athletic director wants to go through this hassle. In most schools in the United States, for example, volleyball is not central to the school's athletic program. It doesn't bring much money in and it doesn't attract a lot of fans. Athletic directors will tolerate a lot of problems and poor performance from a volleyball coach before they justify the hassle of conducting a search and replacing one. It takes seriously bad behavior and a full-scale revolt (usually by parents) to force the issue.

Six Sigma to the Rescue?

Many of you may work in or consult with companies that have adopted Six Sigma or a similar business and quality improvement methodology. These methods have been successfully implemented at many companies and have been associated with great improvements in efficiency and effectiveness. These methodologies make liberal use of data and analysis. One would think more disciplined methodologies like these might force organizations to be more rigorous in looking at the evidence of effectiveness. This hasn't been the case in my experience. These methodologies typically emphasize understanding the "voice of the customer" and the "voice of the business" in driving improvement. Few of these methodologies make use of content expertise or "voices" outside of the business (e.g., voice of the expert or voice of science). There aren't explicit steps in these methodologies where team members consult with experts or examine research evidence to see if the expectations of customers or the business are reasonable, and which of many solutions might be the most viable. These improvement methodologies have penetrated deeply into large companies, and much of the organization improvement-related energy is channeled into these projects (including PM projects) using these methods and tools. Well-meaning teams of insiders carry out these projects without ever asking questions about the effectiveness of potential solutions.

Even popular techniques and methods in my own discipline contribute to this problem. Techniques like future search conferences and large group interventions bring groups of people together to diagnose and solve problems. These methods are high-involvement techniques that bring the energy and talents of those in the room to address a problem. These techniques have certain advantages (high probability of follow-through and implementation), but also have liabilities (do we have the right people in the room?). When these methods are applied to problems where there is a base of scientific research and evidence, this information is typically not represented in the room. Complete PM systems can be designed using these techniques without ever consulting research on which PM practices are effective.

Science to the Rescue: Evidence-Based Management

PM 1.0 is held in place by very powerful forces and overcoming those forces won't be easy. So how do we get out of this mess? Science. We need to use rigorous scientific evidence to inform our decisions about PM. Experts call this evidence-based practice (EBP). Evidence-based practice is concerned with making decisions about practices (medical, management, and the like) by integrating the best available evidence from research. In this case, research means more than finding out what other people do. It means the systematic collection of data through observation and experimentation, the formulation of questions, and the testing of hypotheses.

The problem the HR profession faces with PM is not new. The EBP movement began in medicine in the 1980s when it became clear that much of what doctors were doing was considered inappropriate when considered against the expert standards of the times.[8] I don't know about you, but the prospect of managers and HR professionals not using evidence-based practices is frightening enough, but physicians? If there was ever a place where research evidence should prevail one would think it would be in medicine. It turns out physicians are no different than practitioners in other professions: they trust their gut and their experience.

The evidence-based management movement began in the late 1990s. While it has many vocal proponents, most experts agree the track record of applying scientific evidence in the field of management is abysmal.[9] Part of the problem is structural. Management isn't a real profession (like medicine) with common training and standards, and you can't sue a manager for malpractice like you can sue a physician (this is regrettable). However, many of the other problems that plague HR professionals and managers are the same ones that plague physicians (e.g., laziness, overconfidence, narrow-mindedness).

Some management experts argue there simply isn't the same volume of research on the effectiveness of management practices that there is in medicine. While this may be true for some practices it isn't the case with PM. There is a lot of good research available to guide leaders and HR professionals, we simply need to get them to pay attention to it.

Barriers to Evidence-Based Management

There are several reasons business leaders and HR professionals don't use rigorous scientific evidence to make decisions about HR practices. Let's start with some of the easy ones. First, scientific research is hard for leaders and HR professionals to find. It is not as readily accessible to them as other sources of information. Business blogs, articles, and popular management books are pushed directly to them; scientific research is not. Finding it requires effort and they simply don't take the time. Less than 1% of HR practitioners read academic journals.[10] There are also thousands of academic journals that publish scientific research. There are dozens of journals that publish research related to PM. For this book I read research from close to 50 different academic journals across a half-dozen different disciplines.

Even if a business leader or HR professional makes the effort and finds a relevant scientific article, it's likely they won't be able to understand it. Academic research is typically heavy on theory, methodology, and statistical analysis, and light on intelligible results and practical implications. Those of you who have read academic journals, especially in economics, know they can bring you to your knees. There may be nuggets of gold in there, but finding them is difficult even for those trained to read this research.

Finally and perhaps most importantly, leaders and HR professionals don't look at academic research for insight because they rely on their own judgment and intuition. The same is true for physicians. They rely on their own training, experience, and judgment, which can be out of date or simply wrong. Leaders didn't get to be leaders by being unsure of themselves. They trust their judgment, and they all have personal experience with PM and with motivating and managing a staff of employees. A study by Sara Rynes and her colleagues illustrates the scope of this problem for HR professionals. They surveyed members of the Society of Human Resource Management, the largest professional HR organization in the world. They asked participants about their beliefs related to effective HR practices. They presented participants with 39 statements about HR practices, some of which were true and some of which were false. All of the statements had a body of scientific research supporting them and so were obviously true or false based on the weight of scientific research evidence. On average HR professionals only got about half of the questions right. Note these were HR professionals. Clearly there are many areas where HR professionals' beliefs diverge from research-supported practices.

I can't make this point any better than Jeffrey Pfeffer and Robert Sutton did in their book *Hard Facts, Dangerous Half-Truths and Total Nonsense.* [11]

> Business decisions...are frequently based on hope or fear, what others seem to be doing, what senior leaders have done, and believe has worked in the past, and their dearly held ideologies—in short, on lots of things other than the facts.

A final point I will make on this subject has to do with accountability and the culture around HR. Leaders don't demand to see evidence of the effectiveness of their HR practices the way they do their marketing practices or R&D programs, for example. Evidence that other successful companies engage in these practices seems to be good enough.

Counteracting These Forces

Changing PM isn't going to be easy; these forces are powerful. You need to go into a PM redesign effort with eyes wide open. Here are my suggestions for managing the restraining forces of PM 1.0:

- Minimize your reliance on outside partners like consulting firms and HR think tanks and educate yourself on the information they are giving you.
- Ask your outside partners to review and summarize the academic research related to specific PM practices. Ask them to find you organizations that do it very differently, to provoke your team and your stakeholders.
- Contact reputable graduate school programs and pay their graduate students and professors to conduct literature reviews and prepare summaries for you. Ask respected academics to conduct research briefings with your team.
- Immerse yourself in the science. Dedicate time to discussing assumptions, beliefs, paradigms, and scientific evidence. Involve outside experts and your key stakeholders in these meetings.
- Expose your team and stakeholders to the science early in your project so they get comfortable asking questions about effective practices early in the project. Use a scientific lens regularly throughout your project.

- Educate your stakeholders on the science and push back if they have expectations for PM that are unreasonable.
- Invest heavily in change management as a part of your project. Introduce scientific evidence into your business case and into your analysis. Plan how you will influence your key stakeholders.
- Staff your team with people who are more open to different ways of looking at business and HR problems and who may be more receptive to an evidence-based lens.
- If you are using a Total Quality Management or business improvement methodology like Six Sigma to drive your project, make sure you have experts in PM on the team or as adjunct members. Use them to educate the team on scientific research up front.
- Focus your benchmarking efforts on companies that are engaging in practices supported by rigorous scientific research. Delay benchmarking activities until later in your project, after you have digested the scientific research evidence and after you have educated your stakeholders and team members on how to use a scientific lens to look at PM practices.
- Find organizations to benchmark that are truly doing things differently. Talk to organizations outside of your industry that are dealing with similar issues (e.g., healthcare and education on the topic of pay-for-performance).
- Listen for and confront rationalizations and fatalistic attitudes in your team meetings and in your interactions with your stakeholders.

Key Messages

- Companies rely on external benchmarking to guide them on which PM practices they should adopt. This causes them to focus on common practices instead of effective practices.
- Companies are increasingly reliant on advice from consulting firms and business think tanks to guide them on which PM practices to adopt. These firms control the information channels to business leaders and HR professionals, and they have made external benchmarking a key part of their business practice.
- Common practices become institutionalized and companies imitate them to achieve legitimacy. This leads to a homogenization of practice and makes practices difficult to change.
- Companies tend not to look at rigorous scientific research to guide them in redesigning PM. It is difficult to find and difficult

to digest. The voice of the science tends not to be represented in PM redesign projects.

▪ Business leaders and HR professionals have their own ideas about how to fix PM that are based on their own judgment, intuition, and personal experience.

What to Stop

A quick review of Section I reveals most companies do PM the same way (PM 1.0) and no one seems happy with it. Our practices are ineffective because they are based on flawed paradigms that no longer fit today's organizations or workers. Little changes because we rely on benchmarking information from consulting firms and HR think tanks that reinforces common practices and practices of top companies. And because PM is focused on so many objectives and affects so many HR decisions, it is difficult to change in any fundamental way.

There is good science available to inform PM design efforts, but it has had little effect on actual practice. Leaders and HR practitioners trust their outside partners or their own judgment and their own experience to guide them in reforming PM, which causes them to make tactical changes within the tight orbit of PM 1.0. The solution to this problem is a narrow, well-defined purpose for PM and science-based practices based on more defensible paradigms (PM 2.0).

Moving to PM 2.0 requires that we (a) dismantle many PM 1.0 practices and abandon the objectives behind those practices and (b) implement new practices based on new paradigms and better science. The first of these will likely be the more difficult task. Section II makes the case for stopping these practices and helps you see different ways to accomplish the objectives behind them. I can't get you comfortable with what to *start* (new practices) until I convince you that you can stop practices you feel you can't live without. These practices include quantitative evaluation of performance (Chapter 4), the use of money (Chapter 5), and pay-for-performance programs (Chapter 6) to motivate and control behavior and performance in organizations. This is where we turn next.

4

Evaluating Performance

A Fool's Errand

All perceiving is also thinking, all reasoning is also intuition,
all observation is also invention.
—Rudolf Arnheim

There are no facts, only interpretations.
—Friedrich Nietzsche

In 1936 social psychologist Musafer Sherif conducted what is now a classic experiment on social factors and perception. He put subjects in a totally dark room and showed them a pinpoint of light on a wall. After a while many subjects reported the light moved. This has come to be called the autokinetic effect.[1] This occurs because people have flawed perceptual machines: when they close their eyes, they lose their frame of reference for the position of the light. When they reopen them, they have a new frame of reference causing the perception of movement. Sherif found it was even more fun to put three people in a room and have them estimate how far it moved. Over successive trials, groups of three would converge on some

Next Generation Performance Management, pages 45–62
Copyright © 2017 by Information Age Publishing
All rights of reproduction in any form reserved.

estimate and there was wide variation in that estimate across groups: some settled on larger estimates, some smaller estimates, and some in between. When one person's flawed perceptual machine collided with the flawed perceptual machines of others, normative forces developed that affected their judgments in lasting ways. Groups converged on their own social norm and this happened without any coercion, discussion, or prompting from group members or the experimenter.

This phenomenon is quite remarkable. People see something move that doesn't and their estimate of how far it moves is dependent on how far other people say it moved. For those of us creating measurement and decision-making processes that rely on people's judgments, like performance management (PM) for example, evidence like this does not bode well for us.

Even the judgment of experts can be suspect. Music competitions are the launching pad for careers in classical music and increasingly in popular music with shows like *The Voice* and *American Idol*. Professionals judge these competitions based on their experience and specialized expertise. Researcher Chia-Jung Tsay at University College in London conducted a series of experiments to understand how judges picked the winners in these competitions.[2] She shared clips of the performances of the top three finalists at 10 prestigious international classical music competitions with nearly 1,200 participants across many different experiments. Some of the experiments used novice subjects with no particular musical expertise and some used accomplished musicians.

For each experiment Chia-Jung manipulated the information available to participants and examined whether or not participants could predict the winners picked by the professional judges. She assembled 6-second clips of each competitor. Some subjects heard only the sound of the competitors. Other participants saw only the video with no sound. Finally, some participants had available both the audio and the video. The results were eye-opening. The participants who had video information only were the best at picking the winners. Yes, that's right. Those who had no sound did the best. Those who only had sound did the worst. This happened in experiment after experiment and happened regardless of whether subjects were novices or professional musicians.

These findings sound absolutely ludicrous, but they have been replicated in other domains as well predicting elections, teacher evaluations, and company profits (from CEO appearances).[3] As my kids would say, "This is messed up." More accurately it seems people are messed up; they don't use the information they should when making important decisions. In PM we trust supervisors to judge the performance of their employees accurately, and we put hundreds of millions if not billions of dollars in rewards at risk based on these judgments. Based on this research it seems prudent to wonder if they are up to the task.

Ratings Are a Way of Life

You can't monitor, motivate, and reward if you don't measure. PM 1.0 requires organizations to monitor employee performance and measure whether or not they are delivering on their contracts. Evaluation and monitoring are essential because rewards are tied to evaluations and because transparent evaluations motivate employees. Supervisor ratings of performance are the default performance measurement choice for most companies, and PM 1.0 assumes these ratings can be made accurately. Most supervisors are very confident in their ability to finely discriminate between different levels of performance—just ask them! PM 1.0 also depends on ratings to motivate; employees want to know where they stand. They want to be rated. They want to be compared with others. They thrive on the competition for top ratings and rewards. A low ratings doesn't discourage them, it "stokes their motivational fires" driving them to work hard for a top rating next year.

Ratings Are Not Going Away

Performance ratings have been a popular topic of conversation in the business press over the past 2–3 years. Many writers are calling for companies to abandon ratings and some are heeding the call.[4] Despite these calls it looks like ratings are here to stay. Well over 90% of companies use performance ratings, and in a 2012 study of 100 companies by Ed Lawler and his colleagues at the Center for Effective Organizations (CEO) none had abandoned ratings. That's right, none. Other sources show only 3% of companies plan to remove ratings in the near future.[5]

Employees Expect to be Rated

The world is full of ratings especially with the explosion of social media. We rate our friends on Facebook, we rate our colleagues on LinkedIn, we rate our restaurants on Yelp, and we rate our service providers on Angie's List. We get graded in school and we get graded at work. Asking people if they want to be graded or rated is like asking the fish if it likes the water. People don't know any different. And why wouldn't we rate people and compare them with one another? People compare themselves with one another.

This fact is well-known in psychology.[6] Video and computer game designers know this as well. Players want some sense of reputation and games use ranks and levels to indicate a player's level of accomplishment.[7]

People Think They Are Above Average

People don't mind being rated because most think they will be rated highly. People have an incredible capacity to delude themselves about their own talent. Researchers call this an illusory superiority bias. Garrison Keillor calls it the Lake Wobegon effect, where "all of the children are above average." Ninety-three percent of U.S. drivers feel their driving skills are above average.[8] In a study of self-assessments of performance, psychologist Herbert Meyer found that more than 40% of participants put themselves in the top 10%. Only 2% put themselves below the 50th percentile. Apparently the most biased are high-level professional and managerial employees (over 80% placed themselves in the top 10% category) and those with the least amount of talent.[9]

Science Shows Our Assumptions About Ratings Are Flawed

PM 1.0 assumes supervisors can and will accurately evaluate the performance of their employees, and it assumes that these ratings will motivate employees to work hard. The scientific evidence supporting both of these assumptions is weak.

Ratings Don't Necessarily Motivate People

Contrary to our assumptions, telling people where they stand isn't motivational magic. Wharton economist Iwan Barankay studied the impact of relative ratings, a common occurrence in the two-thirds of organizations using forced or guided distributions.[10] He recruited 330 workers via Mechanical Turk, Amazon's crowdsourcing Internet marketplace. Before the experiment began, Barankay asked them if they wanted their performance to be compared with others and as expected the majority (74%) said they did. In the first stage of the experiment, Barankay posted two identical jobs: one that offered feedback on accuracy and one that didn't. Despite the subjects' preferences and in contrast to the assumptions under PM 1.0, 77% picked the job without feedback.

In the second stage of the experiment, he asked workers to come back and do more work. Half were told they would get feedback on their performance and half were told nothing. The promise of feedback scared off returning employees; those promised feedback were 30% less likely to come back for more work. Even more interesting, those who were promised relative feedback and returned to work were 22% less productive than those who returned to work and didn't get feedback. Even those who were told they were the "cream of the crop" (top 10%) were not more productive when they returned to work and received feedback.

Other studies have shown similar results: relative feedback can negatively affect performance and can lead employees to behave in counterproductive ways like sabotaging others and artificially inflating their own output.[11] Poorer performers get demoralized by their ratings and give up, while high performers "let off the gas" and reduce their efforts.[12] Ratings create special problems where strong norms of collegiality and reciprocity exist: people don't want their own performance to negatively affect their peers.[13] Finally, relative feedback is more damaging to motivation and performance in collaborative work environments when ratings are tied to differential rewards. While some studies find relative feedback and rankings improve performance, research shows they hurt more often than they help.[14]

I want to revisit the video and online gaming context again because many have used gaming to make the case that if ratings motivate in the gaming world they will motive in the business world. Gaming practices are based on different paradigms than PM 1.0. Video games use ratings, rankings, and levels to indicate mastery. The need for mastery is a powerful motive, one that Dan Pink discussed at length in his book *Drive*. Gamers want to get better, and the scores, levels and ranks they achieve are indicators of their level of mastery. They will stay up all night trying to get to the next level of Mortal Combat, Halo, or Destiny. It is this same motive that leads gamers to help those they play against. Helping others get through a level reinforces their sense of mastery ("I must be pretty good if I am helping others get there"). Video games are designed so individuals and teams compete against the game and the enemies, not each other. This is not what happens in organizations. While many games have people compete against each other, the goal is to achieve the next level, and having achieved it gamers frequently turn around and help their competitors get there as well.

How Ratings Are Made

To understand the problems with performance ratings we need a simple model of how supervisors make rating decisions to see where things can go wrong (Figure 4.1). Employees' achievements (the flag on top of the mountain) are a function of their "talents," which comprise their

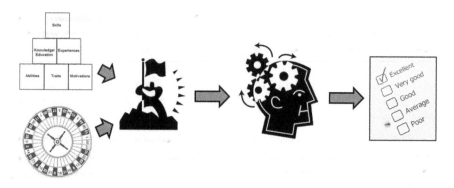

Figure 4.1 A simple model of the rating process.

knowledge, skills, abilities, traits, experiences, etc. There is also a certain amount of luck and randomness involved in what employees achieve (the roulette wheel). A supervisor considers an employee's achievements over the past year and assigns a rating to the employee. Technically it is more complicated than this since other people frequently get involved (supervisors may solicit feedback from others and higher level leaders can review and change a supervisor's rating).

Now let's introduce the concept of error. Let's define error as anything that affects the final performance rating that shouldn't. There are a couple places where error affects this process. First, factors can affect a person's achievements that have nothing to do with their talents (the roulette wheel in our model). For example, an employee can get lucky and get assigned to the big project with strong sponsorship and all the resources they need. They can also be unlucky; their project can be killed, their budget cut, they lose key people on the project, and other bad things occur over which they have no control.[15] If supervisors don't accurately account for these factors in their ratings, they can overrate or underrate the performance of their employee.

Errors also happen when factors affect ratings that have nothing to do with employee achievements. Like the music competition judges, supervisors may overvalue the wrong things and undervalue the right things. They may also have other ulterior motives for the ratings they assign. Lastly, the errors individual supervisors make are compounded when we aggregate the ratings of employees made by hundreds or thousands of supervisors, each of whom uses a different "calculus" for arriving at their ratings.

Figure 4.2 illustrates the impact of these errors. Imagine a continuum of performance from *high* (5) to *low* (1) and a frequency distribution of ratings. Imagine the performance of two employees we will call Red and Green, both

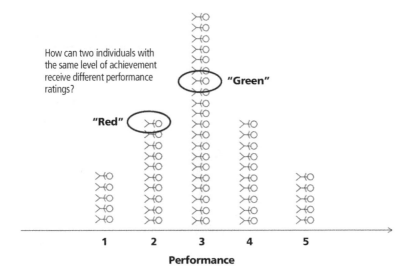

Figure 4.2 Performance ratings for 2 individuals with the same underlying performance.

of whom have comparable achievements and the same underlying performance for the year. You can see they received different performance ratings. Now that we understand the concept of errors and the impact they can have on ratings, we can discuss why supervisors are so prone to making them.

Performance Is a Function of More Than Talent and Hard Work

As Figure 4.1 shows, an employee's achievements are affected by factors that have nothing to do with them. Edward Deming was famously critical of performance ratings for this reason.[16] Deming maintained that 94% of individual performance outcomes are attributable to the system in which employees work. The design of work processes and the availability of resources, support, and information can all affect an individual's performance independent of their efforts. People can also simply get lucky and draw good projects while others can be unlucky and draw terrible projects. Deming and others argued that it simply wasn't practical or possible for supervisors to account for all these other factors when they made their ratings. It didn't make sense to evaluate people on performance that was mostly outside their direct control.

People Are Flawed

Supervisors are human beings (at least most of them are) and human beings are flawed. The research we reviewed in the beginning of this

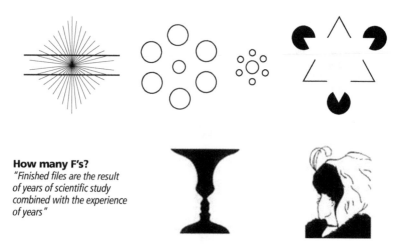

How many F's?
*"Finished files are the result
of years of scientific study
combined with the experience
of years"*

Figure 4.3 Common illusions.

chapter confirms this. Human beings have difficulty observing accurately, reporting what they observe accurately, and making judgments about what they observe. If you have doubts about this consider what happens when you show people the images in Figure 4.3.

- People observe and report things that are not really happening (Sherif taught us this).
- People's judgments are influenced by extraneous factors. They report curvature of the parallel lines in the upper-left image. They report that the interior circles in the two upper-middle images are different sizes.[17] Contextual factors cause them to get it wrong.
- People see things that are not there and they don't see things that are there. People naturally fill in the blanks. Gestalt psychologists call this closure. They see lines and triangles in the figure at the top right.[18] People also miss things. They frequently miss the letter "f" in the word "of" in the sentence at the bottom left. A powerful illustration of this point is an experiment in which six people (three in white shirts and three in black shirts) pass a basketball around. A subject is asked to count the number of passes by people in white shirts. A gorilla walks into the middle of the action and half of all subjects in the experiment don't report seeing it.[19]
- Individuals actively interpret what they see. Two people exposed to the exact same information can see two different things. Some people report seeing an old woman in the image at the lower right; some report seeing a young woman. While some can see

both, some cannot. Some individuals see a chalice in the illusion at the lower middle, while others see two faces.[20]

▪ People can't remember the details of things they see every day. On average people can recall only three of eight features of the U.S. penny.[21] Similarly, only about a third of subjects correctly recalled the layout of the 10 digits on the keypads of push-button telephones.[22]

While these examples are fun, other examples from social psychology and criminology show our flaws can have significant consequences. Eyewitnesses can be influential in the outcome of a criminal trial, yet evidence shows they can be very inaccurate and what they recall is easily shaped by direct and indirect influence efforts.[23] People can even be convinced they committed a crime that never happened.[24] We also know eyewitnesses are not always motivated to be accurate and tell the truth. Those of you who watched the *60 Minutes* report on the attack on the U.S. embassy in Benghazi on September 11, 2012, (aired on October 27, 2012) saw this play out in the national spotlight. Their story depended on a supposed eyewitness account of the attack. This person later reported not being there at all, which caused the people at *60 Minutes* quite a bit of heartache.

It turns out we come by some of these flaws honestly. Research by Northwestern University psychologists Donna Bridge and Ken Paller suggest recalling a memory often makes that memory less accurate, like photocopying successive copies of a picture degrades the quality.[25] This happens because instead of time traveling back to the original memory, we are recalling the memory of the last time we remembered it along with any inaccuracies included in that memory. In subsequent recalls, mistakes can build on one another over time leaving out details and introducing more mistakes. A memory of an event can grow less precise even to the point of being totally false, and people will swear it happened that way.

It's easy to see how all these flaws can affect how a supervisor evaluates the performance of their employees. Two supervisors can view the same achievements differently. Frame of reference matters; an executive can see a supervisor's performance very differently than his/her direct reports. A mediocre performer in a weak group can look better than a mediocre performer in a strong group. Supervisors can go beyond the data and fill in the blanks to tell a more coherent story of an employee's performance. They can also ignore, forget, or misremember things about an employee and their achievements. Supervisors are the same "species" as participants in all of these experiments. People who can be convinced they committed a crime when they didn't, or who didn't notice a gorilla in the middle of a group of people passing a basketball, are evaluating the performance of their employees every day in organizations.

People Are Biased and Lazy

Psychology and economics research show people are biased and they use unconscious shortcuts (heuristics) when they make decisions. While heuristics can make things easier on the brain, they can lead to serious mistakes and errors. Psychologist Daniel Kahneman received the 2002 Nobel Prize in economics for his work in this area, and his book *Thinking, Fast and Slow*, which describes many of these findings should be required reading for everyone who makes decisions in organizations.[26] Examples of these biases and heuristics will follow here and it is easy to see how they can affect supervisor ratings of job performance:

- **Anchoring.** Individuals give more weight to the first information they receive. Initial impressions anchor subsequent thoughts and judgments. Individuals who start strong but fade may get higher ratings than they deserve. Impressions based on last year's ratings can also be hard to change.
- **Status quo.** People become attached to the status quo. Once a person is labeled a poor performer it may be hard to change this perception.
- **Sunk costs.** We make choices in ways that justify past choices even when past choices no longer seem valid. You may try to improve the performance of an employee despite the lack of progress.
- **Confirmation.** People seek information that confirms what they suspect and ignore information inconsistent with current beliefs. Employers may ignore negative feedback about an employee they like.
- **Failure to learn.** People fail to correct their beliefs despite strong evidence they should. Individuals who make mistakes early may not be able to change opinions about their performance.
- **Recency.** People anchor on information that is readily available, vivid, or recent. A strong (or weak) performance late in a performance period can carry additional weight.
- **Fundamental attribution error.** People attribute good outcomes to skill and bad outcomes to other circumstances or bad luck.

Biases like these and ratings tendencies like halo (failing to differentiate), leniency (too positive), severity (too negative), and central tendency (failure to use the extremes) are well-established in performance appraisal research and they negatively affect the accuracy, reliability, and validity of performance ratings.[27]

Athletic competitions have always been fertile ground for illustrating these biases. Even the expert professional judges used in these competitions display these biases. It is well established, for example, that going first or last in a competition can lead to different outcomes. Performing a gymnastics routine with a higher difficulty level can also lead to higher scores. Judges tend to be inconsistent with one another and even inconsistent with themselves over time.[28] These same biases affect other competitions outside of sports.[29] For example, research on wine competitions shows judges are inconsistent in their ratings of the same wine and exhibit significant inconsistency with other judges. In one study, only 10% of judges replicated their score for the same wine.[30] There were also order effects in wine judging; judges scored wines presented first higher.[31] If expert judges are biased and make mistakes, how can we turn loose millions of amateur judges every year to rate the performance of their employees and expect them to get it right?

People's Motives Are Questionable

To this point I have been indicting a supervisors' ability to make accurate ratings, and most of the problems highlighted so far tend to be unconscious and unintentional. This is only part of the problem with ratings, and those of us working in organizations know supervisors can have their own agenda when it comes to the ratings they give employees. Experts in this area acknowledge that deliberate distortion is more prevalent in affecting ratings than unintentional error.[32] To quote psychologist Steve Kozlowski and his colleagues: "Rating an employee's performance is best viewed as a discretionary, motivational, and political process that managers use to reward and punish subordinates and influence organizational decision making."[33]

Again, sporting competitions provide abundant examples of this problem.[34] A fascinating study by economist Brian Callahan and his colleagues looked at the results from the 2009 World Gymnastics Championships. Using execution and difficulty scores, they found that gymnasts who were scored by trading partner countries realized a greater return in terms of execution score for each increase in difficulty than did gymnasts from nontrade partners. Because of this they found gymnasts performed less difficult routines when being scored by judges from countries that shared a trade agreement with the athlete's country. Research on figure skating from the 2002 Olympics reaches similar conclusions. Judges showed strong nationalistic tendencies and concerns about their own careers were partially to blame.[35] Remember these were *professional* judges; it takes years to reach the highest levels of judging in these competitions. Despite this level of professionalism and skill, they are not immune to the biases, errors, and temptations to distort that affect the masses of our amateur supervisors.

These Flaws Significantly Reduce the Quality of Supervisor Ratings

Psychologist Thomas O'Neil and his colleagues summarized the results from studies looking at the quality of performance ratings (Figure 4.4).[36] Only about a quarter of the variation in performance ratings can be explained by differences in the employees doing the performing (ratees) and their achievements. Some individual studies put this figure as low as 8% to 9%. The majority of the variation in ratings is explained by differences in the people doing the rating (the raters). This means a distribution of performance ratings like the one shown in Figure 4.2 says more about the different rating tendencies of the supervisors than it does the performance of the employees. To employees PM must feel a lot like a lottery: They press a button and a ping pong ball comes out with a number on it. These findings aren't surprising if we think about the flaws we just discussed and the task facing supervisors:

- Review a year's worth of employee effort, behavior and accomplishments.
- Appropriately consider other factors that should and should not affect the evaluation.

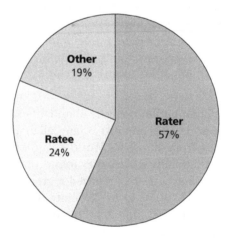

Figure 4.4 Summary of variation in supervisor ratings attributable to specific sources (O'Neil et al., 2012).

- Boil this all down to one number that is objective, fair, comp
  accurate, and honest.
- Adjust the number for how this person's accomplishments compare to his or her peers.
- Rate the employee using the same process, criteria, and standards other supervisors use.

As the title of this chapter suggests this is a fool's errand. When you look at a distribution of ratings for your organization like that displayed in Figure 4.2, you need to think about the margin of error. This error could be substantial, so employees who received a 3 on a 5-point scale may have truly performed like a 4 or a 5 (or a 1 or 2). Despite the massive amount of error in these ratings, I have seen organizations report the percentages of their workforce by rating category to the second decimal point.

There Is Little Hope Ratings Can Be Improved

Despite the magnitude of this problem and the complexity of what we are asking supervisors to do, we have not given up on ratings. We have tried everything to improve their quality.

Build a Better Rating Scale

We have tried to develop better ratings scales and rating formats, and these efforts have largely failed to improve the quality of ratings.[37]

Fix the Raters

We have tried training raters on errors and the rating process to im-prove their skills. These efforts have led to, at best, modest improvements in the quality of performance ratings.[38] Even if training was effective, if su-pervisors are not aware of their own biases or aren't motivated to make ac-curate ratings in the first place, training won't help.

Add More People

We have tried involving other raters (360-degree feedback) and making raters more accountable by holding calibration sessions with other raters and executives. Both of these strategies seem wrong on the face of it: let's get more flawed human beings, with their own questionable motives in-volved in the process. Neither seems to help. Ratings of the same person by

if they share the same perspective (e.g., two bosses,
...ply don't agree very much (correlations from .30 to
...sychologists Jerry Palmer and James Loveland showed
...es can actually make things worse. In an employment
...they found group discussion combined with raters' pre-
...ons made ratings more extreme and less accurate.[40] Super-
...el pressured in these forums to conform to norms (e.g., about
...ed rating distributions) or to defer to the opinions of higher level
...aders regardless of how their employee is performing. This process also
turns supervisors into advocates, making an employee's rating more dependent upon the influence skills, abilities, and personality of the supervisor
instead of the achievements of the employee.

Force Supervisors to Distribute Their Ratings

Another popular solution has been to acknowledge supervisors are
biased and to force them to distribute their ratings according to a prede-
termined distribution.[41] This solution is typically designed to prevent le-
nient distributions with too many high ratings. This is a practice GE and
Jack Welch made famous in the 1990s and represents PM 1.0 at its finest.
While statistics show the more extreme form of this practice is on the wane
(forcing a distribution and firing the bottom 10%), two-thirds of companies
still provide guidance to supervisors to distribute their ratings according to
some target, usually a bell curve.[42]

Proponents argue this process is more efficient and fairer and is more
consistent with a meritocracy. Critics say it creates a "zero-sum game" producing a competitive atmosphere undermining collaboration and teamwork. Supervisors struggle with these systems; they can interfere with providing meaningful feedback and can lead to dysfunctional behavior like
carrying poor performers so they have someone to put in the bottom rating category. They can also create legal liabilities like early followers of GE
found out (e.g., Ford, Goodyear, and Sprint).[43] Even if you assume the ratings are accurate, after firing the bottom 10% for a couple of years the
math works against you and sooner or later and you end up firing decent
performers (unless you do a terrible job of hiring). Finally, it also isn't clear
whether the distribution it forces is any more accurate than a nonforced
distribution, and the shape of the distribution it forces (bell curve) may not
be the correct shape to begin with.[44]

Steve Ballmer implemented this practice early in his tenure at Microsoft. In 2012 *Vanity Fair* editor Kurt Eichenwald implicated this practice in
Microsoft's 10 years of famine.[45] Those Eichenwald interviewed all cited

Microsoft's stack ranking system as one of the destructive forces within the company, killing collaboration and innovation. Microsoft would later abandon this process (and Ballmer along with it). In an ironic twist, one week prior to the announcement that Microsoft was abandoning their forced ranking system, Yahoo CEO Marissa Mayer announced she was implementing a forced ranking process causing 600 people to lose their jobs. She must not have reviewed the research. The irony of these two tech companies moving in completely different directions was not lost on the business press.[46]

Despite our best efforts, we have not succeeded in improving supervisor ratings of performance enough to make them useful for HR decisions. There is a classic formula for understanding the drivers of performance used in applied psychology, attributed to Victor Vroom:

$$\text{Performance} = \text{Motivation} \times \text{Ability}$$

For someone to perform some task well, they need to have the ability and skills to accomplish the task and they need to be motivated to perform the task. When you look at the task of evaluating the performance of an employee, the evidence suggests supervisors fail on both counts.

Abandoning Ratings. It Probably Won't Help

Consultant David Rock reports that as of this writing at least 52 large companies have shifted away from traditional ratings-based PM processes.[47] While it is early, Rock reports these companies are seeing a number of benefits, mostly from reducing the administrative burden and focusing less on ratings and more on other things (e.g., better manager-employee conversations and feedback and more conversations about goals, growth and development).[48] Two high-profile companies recently threw their hat in the no-ratings ring: GE and Deloitte. Of course it is ironic to see GE abandon ratings since they were the "poster-child" for more "draconian" rating practices like forced ranking.[49] They are also making other changes like opting for more feedback via a new PM app called PD@GE (Performance Development at GE). It is clear, however, that while companies have abandoned ratings they have not abandoned differentiation of rewards. This creates a dilemma for companies like GE. Susan Peters, GE's head of HR, I'm sure speaks for many HR executives when she says GE wants to get rid of ratings yet they still want to maintain their culture of meritocracy, pay-for-performance (P4P) and differentiation. She acknowledges she doesn't know what the answer is yet. I predict she will be disappointed with the answer.

The dilemma GE faces is the principal barrier most companies face: their employees don't like ratings but they use them to make merit pay adjustments (90%), promotion decisions (76%), bonus allocations (64%), and succession planning decisions (63%).[50] This is a classic dysfunctional dependency relationship: Companies stay with flawed ratings because so many other decisions are tied to them. A bad relationship is more comfortable than an alternative we cannot see, because we are blinded by our current paradigms. Most companies simply can't stomach trying to solve this problem for all the reasons we highlighted in Chapter 3. They continue to "whistle past the graveyard" hoping and praying their incremental improvements will give them higher-quality ratings, and ignoring the complaints from employees that they're not.

Deloitte is an interesting case because they actually highlight the problems with performance ratings in their business case for PM reform.[51] Deloitte replaced overall performance ratings with a series of questions asking supervisors about future actions they might take with employees (presumably based in part on knowledge of their performance). Supervisors answered four questions about an employee:

- Given what I know of this person's performance, and if it were my money, I would award this person the highest possible compensation increase and bonus (5-point scale from strongly agree to strongly disagree).
- Given what I know of this person's performance, I would always want him or her on my team (same 5-point scale).
- This person is at risk for low performance (Yes/No).
- This person is ready for promotion today (Yes/No).

Supervisors answered these questions quarterly and the data were aggregated to provide an annual "performance snapshot," which was used as input for compensation and other decisions. Deloitte's solution made some of the same compromises GE made. They were still differentiating rewards and simply replacing one rating with another. It isn't clear whether their new rating is any more accurate than their old rating.

Susan Peters' comment about GE's journey highlights another problem with the no-ratings movement. Companies are frequently making the right decision for the wrong reason. Companies are getting rid of ratings to stop the noise from employees, not because they see fundamental flaws in the ratings they are making. Companies are saying supervisors shouldn't rate employees, not that they can't. GE and Deloitte are abandoning ratings but they are not abandoning PM 1.0. They are still committed to P4P, meritocracy, and differentiation of rewards, all hallmarks of PM 1.0. They are simply pushing the "rating" downstream, and judgments about rewards will suffer from many of the same problems and biases I described earlier. Companies will experience short-term benefits and goodwill from employees by simplifying processes, reducing the burden, and by showing employees they are paying attention to their concerns. But these solutions will not solve the underlying problem. You can't abandon ratings and keep PM 1.0 and be successful in the long term. I predict many of these companies will come back to ratings in the near future.

PM 2.0: A Way Out

The way out of this mess is to go "all-in" and abandon PM 1.0. PM 2.0 begins with the premise that supervisors cannot measure performance accurately, consistently, or fairly and declare that ratings and rankings (as well as money, P4P, and differentiation) don't motivate employees. You don't need a rating to communicate direction, align employee efforts with company goals, or communicate that performance needs to improve or to celebrate progress. Not having to "keep score" frees supervisors to recognize and leverage strong performance, and coach and improve weaker performance. Getting you to move toward PM 2.0 will require convincing you that you can make the decisions that depend on ratings without them. There are three solutions to living without PM ratings.

Stop Using Performance Information as Input to Other Decisions

We shouldn't be using PM ratings as input to many of these decisions in the first place. For example, replace your current merit pay and bonus programs with programs that are market-based and based on group and firm performance instead of individual performance (I will say more about these options in Chapters 5, 6, and 9).

Use Other Information in Place of PM Ratings

Use objective assessments to help make staffing, promotion, talent identification, and succession decisions. Assessment tools like 360-degree feedback surveys, personality tests, interest inventories, ability tests, skills assessments, and assessment centers can provide valuable information to help you make these decisions. These assessments can be developed and validated specifically for the decisions you need to make.

Develop Special Performance Evaluation Procedures

If you can't live without a performance input to a decision, measure it specifically for the decision you are making. If you are staffing a job or making a promotion decision, for example, ask the supervisor of each candidate to complete a simple performance evaluation form. Use it along with other information to make the decision and then throw it away. This rating will be more accurate since the information isn't shared with employees and it isn't affecting other decisions about the employee. You could use a similar process for talent assessment. Ask supervisors to rate the performance of their employees in the same way they evaluate other criteria, making a simple overall judgment. If you want something more rigorous, develop a simple performance evaluation form and ask supervisors to complete it before talent review meetings so results can be discussed along with all the other information. Again, this performance information should be more accurate since the information isn't shared with employees nor does it have other far-reaching consequences for the employee.

Key Messages

- Almost every company uses performance ratings despite significant problems with them.
- Human beings are flawed and have a number of biases and other motivations that affect their judgments and decisions including decisions about performance.
- Performance ratings have considerable error in them; they say more about the supervisor doing the rating than the employee doing the performing.
- Attempts to improve ratings and their quality have largely failed.
- While people say they want to be rated and compared with others, their actions suggest otherwise.
- It is not clear that ratings or rankings motivate employees to work hard.
- Relative ratings can be counterproductive and get in the way of collaboration and teamwork.
- PM 2.0 acknowledges the serious flaws with performance ratings and abandons them, proposing alternative ways of making decisions linked to them.

5

Money: It's a Crime

*Money never made a man happy yet, nor will it. There is nothing in its nature
to produce happiness. The more a man has, the more he wants.
Instead of filling a vacuum, it makes one.*

—Benjamin Franklin

Enough no more; Tis not so sweet now as it was before.

—William Shakespeare

In 2011 scientists were struggling to decode an AIDS protein. To be specific, scientists had been working for 15 years to solve the crystal structure of M-PMV retroviral protease by molecular replacement. Who do you turn to when you have a difficult biology problem and you can't solve it? Gamers of course. Scientists put this problem on a site called Foldit, an online computer game designed in 2008 by University of Washington's Center for Game Science in collaboration with the University of Washington's Biochemistry Department. The site is designed to help scientists solve protein problems. It turns out computers are not that adept at visualizing structures in three dimensions, something people with their spatial, pattern-matching

---

Next Generation Performance Management, pages 63–74
Copyright © 2017 by Information Age Publishing
63

and reasoning skills can do more easily. The game allows players to fold the protein structures using tools provided in the game in an attempt to predict the correct protein structures. The different solutions are then evaluated by scientists to see which can be best applied in the real world. It took the gamers 3 weeks to solve the AIDS protein problem—that's right, 3 weeks. And they did it despite the fact that very few of these players had any background in biochemistry.[1]

Foldit gamers have solved a number of scientific problems, and they do it for free. No money changes hands. There was no bounty for the best protein structure. They held no contests where the winner got an all-expense paid trip to Las Vegas or received a million-dollar prize. Why would people, who already have jobs, work for weeks on other people's puzzles without being paid for their work?

Money Is Central to PM 1.0

Each year corporations spend billions on noncash and cash incentives. In 2015 this figure was $90 billion, just in U.S. corporations alone, up 17% from 2013.[2] Companies make massive investments in cash and noncash incentives and almost no one questions this investment; they assume it provides a suitable return.

As I said in Chapter 3, money and economic theories and principles are central to performance management (PM) 1.0. People are rational and self-interested, and they need the promise of a payoff to be motivated to do the work.

Benchmarking data confirm this. Most companies connect PM results to financial rewards.[3]

- 91% of companies tie pay to performance to at least some extent
- 82% of companies link individual performance ratings and compensation decisions
- 79% of companies tie bonuses to performance
- 68% of companies tie salary increases to performance

It is also clear why they do it. Ninety percent of companies say they have a pay-for-performance (P4P) culture in order to attract, retain, and reward talented employees, with 69% saying their goals are to retain top performers.

Money plays a central role in other talent management practices as well from attraction and engagement to retention. The practice of using money to motivate is completely institutionalized in large corporations. In fact most organizations see it as *the* motivator. Over the past 15–20 years financial rewards and incentives have become the de facto strategy for controlling behavior, motivating performance, and driving change in organizations. We assume that virtually anything can be accomplished if we get the incentives right. And if our changes don't go exactly as planned, we assume we didn't get the incentives quite right and we adjust them.[4] There is little discussion about alternative levers for driving performance or organizational change. When I learned organization design principles 30 years ago, compensation and reward systems were seen as one of many levers for aligning behavior in organizations. Now they are the only lever. In the past incentives were necessary but not sufficient; now they are sufficient.

Even the word reward has changed. In the past rewards meant many different things: a pat on the back, a promotion, an interesting job, a high-profile project. Today the word reward is synonymous with financial payment.

People Are Not Motivated By Money

Testing the assumption that people are motivated by money is tricky. What do we mean by motivated? Motivated to do what? What behavior, outcomes or decisions do we want to influence? Attract? Join? Engage? Perform? Stay? How important is money in influencing this behavior or these decisions? The science provides reasonable doubt as to the validity of this assumption.

People Don't Just Work for Money

I once heard Ed Lawler say that if we didn't think money was important to people we should try not paying people and see how many of them showed up for work the next day. It is obvious money is important. People who work typically get paid for it and they wouldn't if they didn't. However, as we noted at the beginning of this chapter, there are many practical examples where this principle seems to break down.[5]

- People willingly work hard for no pay as volunteers giving their time, energy, and even their money away. Twenty-five percent of the U.S. population volunteers. This is 63 million people.[6] Are there really 63 million exceptions to this principle?
- People willingly work in industries, professions, and jobs where they know the pay is relatively low (e.g., nonprofits, teaching, and government). It is likely many of the people in these jobs have higher-paying options.

▪ Many people willingly work hard for no pay as a part of larger community efforts (e.g., Wikipedia, Linux, community gardens). For example, thousands of citizens helped the Florida State University's herbarium by helping catalogue their collections. Thousands of good Samaritans willingly scoured satellite images to help find Malaysia Airlines flight 370, which disappeared without a trace on Saturday, March 8, 2014. So many volunteered it brought down the servers of the firm hosting the images. These people received no financial payment for their efforts.[7]

▪ Legions of students go to work every year in companies for no pay in unpaid internships.

Working for weeks to solve a protein problem on Foldit without getting paid is not rational. In fact this behavior confounds economists.

> Under certain conditions, employees are prepared to undertake a task for immediate need satisfaction or for its own sake, and that some tasks will be performed without monetary payments. This is contradictory to the standard economic assumptions of agents being self- interested and the disutility of labor.[8] (Herpen, Van Praag & Cools, 2005)

I love the use of the word disutility in this quote. Economists literally see what gamers do on Foldit as counterproductive. This behavior is seen as a labor market failure. Gamers could have been doing something productive with their time.

People Are Not Rational

Practical examples like these suggest economic models are insufficient to explain people's behavior. Research on decision making provides additional compelling evidence. For example, consider the concept of loss aversion. Loss aversion refers to people's tendency to prefer avoiding losses to acquiring gains. Research suggests losses are psychologically more than twice as powerful as gains. We feel more depressed at losing $100 than we feel elated by winning $100. Economically this does not make sense. One hundred dollars is $100 whether you win it or lose it. However this is not how we behave.[9] We hold onto a flagging stock longer than we should because we can't bear to take the loss.

Using money and economic principles to control behavior can also lead to unexpected outcomes. For example, at the time of this writing Minneapolis and Miami were experimenting with a concept called "dynamic tolling" for regulating traffic flow on freeways. Here is how it was supposed to work. You raise the price of admission to the commuter lane during peak periods and fewer drivers would drive in that lane. Traffic congestion should decrease. When the engineers raised the toll, they were telling the drivers not to go there. This is economics 101: raise the price and fewer people consume the good, and economically self-interested individuals should obey. That was not what happened. In Miami, the tolls were maxed out on the I-95 express lane and record numbers of drivers were willing to pay it. Similar results were seen with Minnesota's MnPass system.

What was happening was people saw travel in those lanes as "premium goods" and were willing to pay more for them, and for the time saved. Commuters interpreted the toll price as an indicator of congestion and when it was high they flocked to the commuter lane to save time. In Minnesota, drivers were willing to pay $1–$2 per minute ($60–$120 per hour) of time saved to travel in those express lanes. This was far more than conventionally estimated values of time saved.

Maybe it isn't money that motivates maybe it's time. As is typical, single-loop learning reigns supreme; when an incentive system doesn't work, we tinker with it (instead of questioning it). At the time of this writing, Miami was scheduled to increase the maximum toll to $10.50 to reduce congestion.[10]

Money Attracts

There is strong support for the notion that pay drives attraction and job choice.[11] Higher pay can attract people to an organization. There is also evidence (as I will discuss in the next chapter) that having a performance-based pay philosophy can help attract talent to an organization. My own research confirms this. When we ask job candidates what factors are important to them in considering which company to work for, pay shows up at the top of the list. When we empirically look at which factors drive applicant decisions to join a company, compensation is the most important driver. Money is a big part of the overall employment value proposition.

However, relying too heavily on financial rewards and attracting more extrinsically-minded people can have consequences. In their book *Hard Facts, Dangerous Half-Truths and Total Nonsense*, Jeffrey Pfeffer and his colleague Richard Sutton discussed research by Donald McCabe and Linda Trevino who studied cheating at universities.[12] They found that students who were in college for more instrumental or extrinsic reasons (e.g., for the degree) cheated more than students who were more intrinsically motivated. The ends justified the means. What's worse, in their study they estimated that 85% of students came to college for instrumental reasons. They also found business students cheated more than students in other majors, a frightening finding for those of us hiring lots of business school graduates who will someday be running our companies.

Hiring more extrinsically oriented employees might hurt both employees and companies in the long run. Research by Christopher Niemiec and his colleagues at the University of Rochester found that for students with more extrinsic career aspirations (e.g., making a lot of money), achieving them did not make them happier. In fact, compared with students who had other more intrinsic career aspirations (e.g., purpose-related) students with extrinsic goals had higher levels of anxiety, depression, and other negative indicators.[13] While its clear money attracts, those of us in organizations should carefully consider how prominent a role we want money to play in our employment value proposition and who we are attracting with it.

Money Does Not Make People Happy

In the early 1970s economist Richard Easterlin observed that despite a steadily growing economy in the United States happiness had not improved.[14] Getting richer did not make Americans happier. This finding has come to be known as the Easterlin paradox. Easterlin has observed this phenomenon in other countries as well. For example in China, South Korea, and Chile per-capita incomes have doubled over the last 20 years with no significant rise in happiness over that period.[15] The fact that this finding was labeled a paradox tells us something about the state of economic thinking at the time: more money should make people happier. This is economics 101 and is the central premise of PM 1.0. Almost none of us believe the adage that "money doesn't buy happiness." The fact that one out of every two people in the United States play the lottery is testimony to this fact. People play the lottery despite the fact that lottery winners aren't more satisfied with their life that the rest of us.[16]

Easterlin's findings in the 1970s stimulated a wave of research on this question, and as is typical with many things in the social sciences, the answer to this simple question was anything but simple. While this research can be very complex, in the end there was little support for the hypothesis that money can buy happiness. Money had little sustained impact on happiness; other factors appeared to be much more important.[17] Research by Angus Campbell and his colleagues looked at 10 different "resources" in explaining happiness (e.g., income, number of friends, religious faith, education, income). They found that all 10 together only explained 15% of the variation in happiness.[18] Satisfaction may have more to do with personality and temperament (genetic factors) than with an individual's personal or financial situation.[19] Aside from genes, there are two other important reasons why money does a poor job of predicting happiness, both of which are important to those of us involved in PM, compensation and talent management to understand: adaptation and status.

Adaptation

The fact that money doesn't drive happiness does not mean that if you give someone a lot of money they won't be happy; or conversely, if you take away their money they won't be sad. They will. Differences in income between individuals are different than changes in income for a given individual. Individuals adapt quickly to these changes and they become the norm. In a classic article, Phillip Brickman and Donald Campbell said people labor on a "hedonic treadmill" and that major positive or negative events or life changes don't seem to have a lasting effect on their happiness. Humans have a "set point" for happiness and they quickly return to that set point despite the major events that happen to them. As they accomplish their goals and as they accumulate possessions, their expectations also rise. They soon habituate to the new level and it no longer makes them happy. Conversely, setbacks make people unhappy but again they soon adapt. Brickman and Campbell proposed that people were destined to "hedonic neutrality" in the long run.[20] In the end, all the resources people accumulated (e.g., income, friends) had little to do with their happiness.[21] This happens at the country level as well; emerging economies go through "bursts" of GDP growth and the happiness of their citizens remains the same. Psychological theories like Helson's adaptation theory provide a similar explanation for this paradox. Judgments of experience are relative to a reference point that shifts with experience. One's judgment or evaluation of an outcome is a function of all the previously experienced outcomes. As soon as an individual gets a pay increase, it is quickly psychologically "spent" losing its satisfying value.[22]

Status

People are social creatures and individuals compare themselves with others. This is the foundation for the equity theory of motivation. It isn't how much money you make that is important. What is important is that you make more money than your neighbor. Relative income is at least twice as important as actual income in driving happiness, and most of the effect of income increases is due to status effects. This is why when everyone makes more money (e.g., during a booming economy), people are not necessarily happier ("a rising tide raises all boats"). Status is a zero-sum game. More money can also change your comparison group. When you make more money, you move into a bigger neighborhood and you are now comparing yourself with a higher-status standard.

This phenomenon is observed with animals as well. A very powerful illustration of this comes from biologist and primatologist Frans de Waal's research on the social behavior of capuchin monkeys.[23] Capuchin monkeys live in groups in the wild and they have a very organized and social society. In one of his many experiments, two monkeys were in cages, side-by-side, in full view of one another. They had a very simple task; they gave a rock to the experimenter, and they got a reward, a piece of cucumber (evidently a suitable reward for a capuchin monkey). Next, the researcher changed things. The partner monkey did the same task and received a grape. It seems grapes are a far better food than cucumbers for capuchin monkeys. This created inequity and it was very evident. The first monkey, seeing its partner get a grape for performing the same task, again performed the task and again got a piece of cucumber. To say the monkey was unhappy is an understatement. It did not eat the cucumber. It became outraged throwing the cucumber, screaming, and pointing at the experimenter. Rewards that had once been satisfactory become unsatisfactory when others around us get something better.

The effects of adaptation and status conspire to severely limit the power of additional money to increase happiness. It has been said that the half-life of a pay increase is 10 minutes. Researcher Andrew Clark and his colleagues estimate that less than 15% of the effect of a salary increase will survive in the long run. They add further this is probably an overestimate because new generations or cohorts may start with higher aspiration levels than older generations.[24] We see similar findings in organizational research. Meta-analysis research shows pay has a very low-level relationship to overall satisfaction.[25] So while money is one of many levers to increase happiness, it doesn't seem to be a very potent one.

People Are Biased to Think Others Are Motivated by Money

There are other reasons why companies over-rely on money and other extrinsic motivators. People overestimate how much other people care about extrinsic features of a job such as pay, and underestimate how much people are motivated by intrinsic job features (e.g., challenge, purpose). Psychologist Chip Heath analyzed responses to the General Social Survey (a representative sample of people in the United States) and found people rated "important work that gives a feeling of accomplishment" as the most important aspect of their jobs. Pay typically ranked third. When people were asked about others, however, 73% thought that large differences in pay were necessary to get people to work hard, and 67% agreed with the statement that people would not be willing to take on extra responsibility at work unless they were paid extra. People believe that others are more motivated by money, while they report being less so.[26]

This holds true for executives as well. Michael Beer and his colleague Nancy Katz surveyed executives about rewards and incentive systems.[27] They found that 68% reported their companies had executive bonus plans because senior management believed they motivated executives. These same executives reported their day-to-day behavior and decisions were not based on how they would affect their bonus or the bonuses for their staffs. So executives believed bonuses motivated others, but they didn't affect their own behavior. Interestingly, Beer and Katz also found that executives didn't really believe incentives worked that well. Their companies had them because other companies had them. Executives believed their company couldn't attract executives unless bonuses were part of the package.

These findings suggest executives implement P4P programs because of their own "lay" theories about their value, or because they are simply responding to competitive labor market practices and they use motivational rhetoric to justify their decisions. These biases along with the effects of benchmarking, "institutional envy," and labor market dynamics may go a long way to explaining the overuse of incentives (and the underuse of other methods to motivate), despite reservations about how well they work.

Money Changes People

Psychologist Kathleen Vohs has studied the effect of money on people's behavior for the better part of 10 years. Her research showed focusing too much on money had negative consequences for organizations. Much of Voh's research involved "priming," exposing experimental subjects to stimuli related to a specific subject (in this case money), but usually at the unconscious level. In one experiment, for example, Vohs and her colleagues had subjects play Monopoly. After the game was over, subjects experienced one of three conditions related to money priming. In the high-money condition, $4,000 in Monopoly money was inadvertently left out on the table. In the low-money condition, $200 was left out. In the third condition, no money was left out on the table. The experimenters next staged an accident in which a confederate walked across the lab and dropped a box of pencils. Participants in the high-money priming condition helped less, picking up fewer pencils than subjects in the other two conditions. Vohs and her colleagues have conducted dozens of experiments like these and find that while money-primed individuals tend to work harder, they also tend to be less cooperative and helpful to others. Money-primed subjects prefer to work alone, play alone, and put more physical distance between themselves and others. Money-primed individuals focus more on themselves, a point I will come back to in Chapter 9 in discussing meritocracy. This effect even happens with children who have a very limited understanding of money's purpose.[28]

Focusing too much on money can also make money more important to people. Researchers Sanford Devoe from the University of Toronto and his colleagues studied survey data from the United Kingdom and conducted their own experiments looking at the importance people placed on money after performing various experimental tasks. Their results showed that the more money people earned (especially based on their own efforts and labor), the more important money became to them.[29]

I will come back to this point in Chapter 6 when I talk about performance-based pay systems. Experts believe these systems are actually changing people—changing their values and consequently changing their behavior. Organizations may be creating their own problems with compensation programs; organizations that "live by the sword" may "die by the sword." Those that put a lot of emphasis on money as a part of their value proposition (financial services and investment banking for example) may create environments where they need to continuously "up the ante" as money becomes more important, which may have downstream negative consequences for teamwork and collaboration.

Money Doesn't Retain

Companies believe money helps them keep their best people. I have heard this statement countless times from executives and senior HR leaders, and benchmarking statistics show this is why most companies have performance-based pay programs and high levels of reward differentiation. The science tells a different story. A meta-analysis study by Rodger Griffith and his colleagues showed pay and satisfaction with pay were only weakly related to turnover.[30] They found many other factors had stronger relationships with turnover than pay (e.g., supervision/leadership, co-worker relations, stress, and job satisfaction). To quote the authors: "Interestingly, effect sizes for pay and pay-related variables are modest in light of their significance to compensation theorists and practitioners." Indeed, the popular opinion among practitioners and researchers that "employees don't leave companies, they leave bosses" supports this view of the muted effect of pay on retention. My own research supports this as well. Pay is far down the list of factors associated with turnover.

But this isn't how organizations behave. Human resources and compensation practitioners are all too familiar with the "fire-drills" that occur when top talent announce they are leaving the company. Organizations typically throw more money at them to get them to stay. More than half of the companies in a recent survey reported they used retention bonuses and this number is on the rise (as is the amount).[31] What do organizations get in return for these investments? They typically get what they pay for: retention. The vast majority of these bonuses come with strings attached: they forfeit the money or a portion of it if they leave within a certain period of time. These bonuses work because they make it hard for people to leave, not because they make people want to stay.

Organizational researchers distinguish between "continuance commitment" and "affective commitment." Continuance commitment is when people stay because the cost of leaving is higher than the cost of staying. Affective commitment is when people stay because they like the company and what it stands for. My colleague David Futrell uses a marriage metaphor to differentiate these two and sums it up this way: "People with high affective commitment stay married because they love each other; people with high continuance commitment stay married because they don't want to lose half their stuff." Affective commitment also has benefits that continuance commitment does not, namely higher motivation and performance.[32] If you rely on money to retain, you don't get these benefits. Organizations rely on money to retain because it's easy and because of the PM 1.0 programming of their leaders and HR professionals. Other factors are more effective. Our research shows that engagement (affective commitment) is twice as effective as money in retaining top talent. The problem with using engagement to reduce retention is it's hard. Top people want interesting and challenging work, more responsibility, and opportunities to be promoted. Throwing money at people is easier than improving these factors.

So it's clear that people aren't rational and they don't just work for a financial payoff. People can and do work hard without any financial contractual arrangements in place. I'm not saying "homo economicus" is dead, but the role money and rewards play in people's work lives is more complex and does not necessarily align with PM 1.0 principles. I am not suggesting that you to abandon all focus on money and rewards. Money attracts. You need competitive compensation to get people in the door. Rewards and compensation are big parts of a company's employment value proposition, and candidates are attracted by competitive salaries and by a P4P philosophy. However it's also clear that PM 1.0 principles and overemphasizing money and incentives can cause problems and have unforeseen negative consequences for organizations. I will explore this in more depth in the next chapter.

If Not Money, What?

I will hold off on answering that question here. In the next chapter I will finish my attack on the role of money and rewards as motivators in PM 1.0, and I will start to explore more deeply the "myth of meritocracy" and the fallacy that individual differentiation drives motivation and high performance. Chapters 4 and 5 make the case that you should abandon PM 1.0 practices. In Chapters 7 through 9 I will develop PM 2.0 more fully and show how you can fill the void left by abandoning a focus on money and rewards to motivate. PM 2.0 starts with the premise that people are motivated by factors other than money, such as challenging work, making a difference, making progress, and the need to belong. This isn't rational, but it works and it may be more sustainable than the worship of money.

Key Messages

- Companies believe strongly in the power of financial rewards to motivate employees.
- People have an extrinsic motivation bias. They assume most people are motivated by extrinsic rewards like money.
- While money is important, there is ample evidence that people work hard for low pay or no pay at all.
- Compensation is important for attracting people to a company and getting them to join.
- There is little evidence that money makes people happy at work or in life, or that money plays a strong role in engagement and retention.
- Organizations would be better served by looking beyond financial rewards and investigating other ways to motivate by focusing on—work and career growth as well as strengthening work relationships.

6

A Pleasant Death
of Performance-Based Pay

So long as a man rides his hobby horse peaceably and quietly along the
King's highway, and neither compels you or me to get up behind him—
pray, Sir, what have either you or I to do with it?

— Laurence Sterne

To every complex question there is a simple answer and it is wrong.

—H. L. Mencken

In the late 1990s the City of Albuquerque had a problem. It was spending too much money paying its garbage truck drivers overtime. The city needed to reduce its costs. The solution? Incentives. If drivers finished their routes early, they could go home early and still get paid for eight hours.

It worked.

Kind of.

Next Generation Performance Management, pages 75–92
Copyright © 2017 by Information Age Publishing
All rights of reproduction in any form reserved.

Overtime decreased but audits revealed several problems. Drivers were exceeding the legal weight limit because they didn't take time to go to the dump. They were speeding. They were having more accidents. They weren't picking up all the trash, and customers were complaining. They didn't do the necessary maintenance to their trucks and repair costs went up. To quote the *Albuquerque Journal*, "The unintended results of the incentive program could be an increase in safety risks, cost of operations, legal liabilities and customer dissatisfaction."[1]

Incentives seemed like an obvious solution: pay people for the behavior you want. Recall the question my colleague asked me at a performance management (PM) conference: "If you don't pay people based on their performance, what do you pay them for?" PM 1.0 is so institutionalized in organizations people can't conceive of any other way. Organizational scholar Herb Meyer captured this sentiment 40 years ago: "It seems logical to base pay upon performance. In fact, the principle of merit pay is so logical that it seems almost ludicrous to criticize it."[2] Pay for performance (P4P) and the use of rewards to motivate and control is the hobby horse of large, global corporations; we mount them and we ride them. Company leaders obsess over getting the incentives right, and leaders like those in Albuquerque thought they had it right. As mentioned in Chapter 5, corporations spend billions of dollars on rewards and incentives every year. No one questions this investment or the value it returns; many companies think they should invest more.

The use of P4P programs by corporations increased dramatically in the 1980s driven by the idea that the role of company leadership was to maximize the interests of shareholders. The strategy to accomplish this was to increase accountability by tying the rewards of the CEO and other senior leaders to measures of shareholder value (e.g., stock price via options and grants). The result? Research showed the percentage of executive compensation contingent on stock price increased from 10% in the 1990s to 70% by 2003.[3] Over time this principle has cascaded down in organizations, and benchmarking statistics reveal the widespread use of P4P programs as well as the high levels of dissatisfaction with these programs.[4]

- 91% of companies link pay to performance to some extent.
- In the United States variable pay is becoming a larger percentage of total pay for more people.
- Most companies (71%) differentiate rewards based on performance and many (69%) think they should be differentiating more.
- 90% say their goal with P4P is to attract, retain, and reward talented employees.

- Less than 20% say their plans are effective and/or their objectives are well met. Companies report a number of challenges with their programs.
  - 63% say managers lack the skills or motivation to carry out these programs.
  - 74% say their budgets aren't big enough to differentiate sufficiently.
  - 50% say inconsistent administration is a problem.
  - 45% blame the fit of their program with the company's culture.
- Most companies (70% to 75%) have made or plan to make major changes to their programs to address these challenges.

P4P Isn't the Panacea We Assume

P4P is the heart of PM 1.0. Agency theory says employees are self-interested and their goals and objectives will not be aligned with those of the company. Companies need specific contracts with financial incentives to align the interests of employees with the company's. Virtually no one questions this principle. Compensation textbooks talk about how to do it, not whether to do it. Even employees don't question it; they want their pay to be based on their performance.[5] How else would we do it? Unfortunately, the scientific evidence shows P4P doesn't have the broad benefits we think it does.

P4P Doesn't Broadly Improve Performance and Productivity

Hundreds of studies have been done on this topic, and several meta-analysis studies have analyzed the results of the individual studies.[6] Many proponents of P4P cite these meta-analysis studies to support the effectiveness of these programs. Despite what line managers and HR professionals believe, and what compensation consultants and HR think tanks so often tell you, scientific evidence isn't compelling:

- P4P and incentive programs can work although the improvements are modest (institutional research puts the improvement in the 5% to 10% range).
- These programs work mostly in laboratory settings and for low-level, low-complexity jobs (e.g., production, industrial, retail sectors). They work better for boring or noxious tasks where it may be difficult to get people to perform them and for tasks where

paying attention and working harder can improve performance (think about the person picking up road kill on the highways).

- Even when these programs work, increased motivation gets only part of the credit. These programs work in two different ways: by attracting better people (sorting effects) and by getting more effort and performance from existing employees (incentive effects). At least half of the benefit of these programs is attributable to sorting effects.
- Benefits tend to be short-lived and disappear when incentives are removed.
- Much of this research looks at piece-rate reward systems and is focused on improving quantitative performance measures. There are few jobs in most organizations where piece-rate reward systems can be implemented and where good quantitative performance measures are available.
- In many of the studies proponents cite, it is difficult to give full credit to P4P for benefits realized because other changes were frequently made at the same time (e.g., process improvements associated with the introduction of incentive systems) that could have also improved results.
- Alternative solutions carried out in some of these studies frequently worked as well as or better than P4P (e.g., feedback, social recognition, goal setting, internal labor markets).
- Even when they work, many P4P programs have side effects and unintended consequences that can significantly reduce or vanquish any value they return (more on this later).
- Some of this research (especially the institutional research) has a number of serious flaws that significantly limit the conclusions that can be drawn.[7]
- P4P has not worked well in other sectors (healthcare, education, and public sector management) for many of the same reasons it fails in the private business sector.[8]

The "poster child" for proponents of P4P is the classic research study by economist Edward Lazear at Safelite AutoGlass.[9] This study is referenced by nearly every writer in this area to support the effectiveness of P4P. Lazear worked with the management at Safelite to introduce a piece-rate system to replace hourly pay for auto glass installers. This program was wildly successful improving productivity by 44%. Researchers Jeffrey Pfeffer and Robert Sutton commented on the characteristics of this study that made it so successful and suitable for a variable pay program.[10]

- The job was easily learned.
- Employees worked independently, requiring no coordination with other employees.
- It was easy to measure and monitor quality, so working faster and taking shortcuts wouldn't work. If there was a problem with a windshield, it was easy to identify and it was easy to identify who was responsible. If there was a problem, the installer had to re-install the new windshield on his own time and pay the company for replacement glass before getting any new jobs.
- The company already had a sophisticated, computerized work-monitoring system. Adding the incentive system didn't require additional investments in technology to monitor or measure employee productivity.
- Goals for these employees were unambiguous and one-dimensional: install windshields quickly with sufficient quality.

Lazear himself was careful to explain why this setting was so ideal for using individual incentives: "Output is easily measured; quality problems are readily detected; and blame is assignable." There are few jobs where these criteria can be met in most large organizations.

Differentiating Rewards Doesn't Necessarily Lead to Higher Performance

If P4P is the heart of PM 1.0, differentiation is the soul. Companies strive to reward their top people handsomely and give those at the bottom of the distribution little or nothing. Most organizations subscribe to the belief if you aren't differentiating you aren't motivating.

Wage inequality is growing in the United States with no signs of slowing. P4P programs accounted for 21% of this growth between the late 1970s and the early 1990s, and for almost all the growth for higher wage earners. Economists like Thomas Lemieux and his colleagues applaud this trend, assuming inequalities in wages reflect real differences in the skills, performance, and value contributed by workers.[11] This assumption should be disputed. The most frequently used measure of job performance in organizations is supervisor ratings. Pay-for-performance in most companies means pay for performance ratings. If you are differentiating rewards based on performance ratings (and let's face it most of us are), then you have error in your performance measures, and lots of it. Research from Chapter 4 shows the differentiation we get based on performance ratings isn't likely to be high in accuracy and validity.

The default assumption from PM 1.0 is that more differentiation is better for people and organizations. A review of the scientific evidence casts doubt on the validity of this assumption.[12] Economist Benoit Mahy and his colleagues reviewed this research and called the evidence inconclusive.[13] Sometimes more differentiation is bad for productivity, sometimes it's good, and other times it depends on how much differentiation there is and what the differentiation is based on (legitimate or illegitimate factors). Management researcher Jason Shaw recently did a similar review and found the same wide variation in findings.[14] Many psychologists and management researchers argue that wage inequality and differentiation—even for legitimate reasons—can harm social functioning and group performance, especially in more collaborative environments.[15] The more collaborative the environment, the more damaging differentiation is likely to be. Charlie Trevor and his colleagues looked specifically at the effects of pay differentiation in more collaborative settings and found it to be beneficial in only about a third of the studies.[16]

Matt Bloom, a University of Notre Dame economist, studied the effects of pay differentiation in one of the more interesting settings: major league baseball. Baseball is a good laboratory for looking at the impact of pay differentiation since a number of good measures are available for both player and team performance, and because it is the ultimate in meritocracies. Bloom studied player and team performance from 1985 to 1993.[17] He found that across all measures individual player performance was negatively related to pay differentiation. The more variation/differentiation in the team's payroll, the worse individual players performed. Teams with a few high-priced players that skewed the salary distribution tended to have players who performed poorly. The same was true for team performance: more variation in the team's payroll meant poorer team performance, including financial performance. The story is similar in other sports.[18]

Spending a lot of money on high-priced talent doesn't always work in baseball and it may not work for business either, especially when people need to work together. Larry Page and Sergey Brin discovered this at Google. The problem with Google is they hire smart people, make them wealthy, and then they get restless and run off and start their own companies. Quentin Hardy from *Forbes* wrote about this in 2007. Like city leaders in Albuquerque, Google turned to incentives to solve this problem. They created a Founders Award for people who made significant contributions. These awards were made in cash, and the idea was to replicate the kind of financial windfall that people can get with start-ups. For example, there were a handful of Google employees responsible for the unusual Dutch auction public offering in 2004 that shared an award of $10 million. This kind of money can dramatically change the distribution of wealth within a company. Hardy reported this practice angered a lot of people at Google because they were left out. Founders' Awards are rarely given now, replaced by smaller awards augmented with more personal recognition, such as personal visits by Page and Brin.[19]

P4P Does Not Improve Retention.

Despite the fact that retention of top performers is a key reason most companies have P4P programs, there is surprisingly little testing of whether it does so. Determining if P4P retains top talent requires that we first understanding the relationship between performance and turnover. Such research can be complicated, but most of it shows top performers are generally less likely to leave.[20] This makes sense; better performers tend to get more of everything, more rewards, more challenging assignments, more responsibility, more promotions, and more attention in general. So if top performers are less likely to leave, to what extent should P4P get any of the credit?

Once again our commonly held assumptions don't hold up. Having pay tied to individual performance does not reduce voluntary turnover, controlling for other important factors (industry, occupation, size of company, and tenure).[21] Top performers tend to stay with their companies but not because they have rewards tied to their performance. In fact there is some evidence that having pay linked to performance may even increase voluntary turnover, especially in certain occupational groups with certain P4P programs (e.g., commission sales). Research on pay differentiation reaches similar conclusions: more differentiation is associated with higher turnover and lower tenure.[22]

P4P Can Hurt Creativity and Innovation

Innovation is vital for the long-run success of most large corporations. I already mentioned the case of Microsoft where their PM process was seen as a barrier to innovation. Activities that drive innovation in companies differ from traditional activities aimed at efficiency. They are risky, unpredictable, long-term oriented, and labor-intensive, and they tend to be idiosyncratic in nature. Innovation requires different incentive structures than those that encourage investment in traditional activities and projects.[23] Teresa Amabile and her colleagues at Harvard University studied the conditions under which creativity and innovation flourish.[24] She identified a number of "creativity killers," many of which are associated with PM 1.0 practices.

- **Risk aversion**. Taking risks means tolerating and accepting failure. Failure is typically penalized in traditional PM and reward systems.
- **Strong focus on evaluation**. The expectation of a threatening, highly critical evaluation can undermine creativity. A supportive, informative evaluation can enhance intrinsic motivation, which is important for creativity. PM systems in most organizations get low marks on being supportive and informative.
- **Surveillance**. Being watched and monitored can lead to lower levels of creativity. Most PM systems involve frequent reviews, check-ins, and feedback to ensure performance is on track. The more intrusive this feels, the more it can negatively affect creativity and innovation.
- **Contracted-for reward**. Working for a reward versus working for your own enjoyment can have a detrimental effect on creativity. Most traditional PM systems have explicit contracting to document objectives and specify reward contingences for successful performance. The more "contractual" this feels and the less control employees feel, the more it can undermine creativity and innovation.
- **Competition**. Competing for prizes can undermine creativity. Most PM processes focus heavily on relative performance, which leads to competition for top ratings and rewards.
- **Extrinsic motivation orientation**. People who are focused on the extrinsic reasons for engaging in an activity tend to be less creative than those focused on intrinsic reasons. Most organizations have an explicit P4P philosophy with a prominent focus on extrinsic rewards.

Researchers Pierre Azoulay and Gustavo Manso from MIT and Joshua Graff Zivin from the University of California at San Diego studied different funding streams for scientific exploration and looked at their impact on the creativity and innovation of scientists.[25] Their hypothesis was that different funding models create different incentives in scientists and produce different results in terms of creativity. They hypothesized that less-traditional, longer term funding models that are more tolerant of failure and less onerous in terms of structure, rigor, and surveillance produce more innovation. They looked at two different funding sources: the National Institutes of Health (NIH) and the Howard Hughes Medical Institute (HHMI). NIH has a funding model with traditional incentives, more similar to a classic P4P (and PM 1.0) model.

- Funds projects not people
- Documentation of detailed planning for experiments and deliverables to be specified in advance
- Rigorous surveillance, monitoring, and review
- Lower tolerance for failure in renewal
- Shorter funding timeframes
- Focused on concrete deliverables
- Minimal feedback from reviewers.

HHMI's model is seen as less traditional and more innovation friendly.

- Longer funding cycle, including 2 years of continued funding after termination
- Looser expectations about concrete deliverables and plans
- Looser reviews, monitoring, and surveillance
- High-quality feedback to investigators
- Allowance for the reallocation of resources when researchers want to shift direction and approaches—funds, people, not projects.

Azoulay and Manso's results were clear. Research contracts that were based on more-traditional, performance-based incentive models led to less scientific creativity, fewer breakthroughs, and lower scientific productivity. Scientists from HHMI produced high-impact articles at a much higher rate and changed directions more often than NIH researchers. Publication rates were 39% higher, 96% higher for top percentile citations. HHMI scientists also had more early failures than NIH researchers: they placed more risky bets. Finally, their work was characterized as more novel and was cited by a more diverse set of journals. Economists studying pay differentiation reached similar conclusions. They found that creativity and innovation were higher with lower levels of pay differentiation and suffered when differentiation went above a certain threshold.[26] The moral of this story seems to be that if you want to kill innovation, put a bounty on it.

P4P Can Have Toxic Side Effects

As the City of Albuquerque learned, even when P4P programs work they can cause problems. This should not surprise us. Management scholar Steve Kerr warned about this more than 40 years ago in his famous article "On the Folly of Rewarding A While Hoping for B."[27] Although this article has been widely read and widely cited, business leaders and HR professionals still believe deeply in PM 1.0 and are convinced their programs won't suffer these consequences. Yet few days go by before we read another news article about companies, schools, hospitals, or healthcare systems getting more than they bargained for with P4P.

We Get Manipulation Instead of Improvement

Sometimes we get the right outcome but in the wrong way. A study of enterprise software salespeople revealed they manipulated their quarterly commissions by concentrating deals into a single quarter and offering discounts to customers who went along with their timing. These manipulations cost the company 6% to 8% of their revenue, about the value of the salesperson's commission. One especially poignant example of this problem was reported by Adam Grant and Jitendra Singh. At one of Green Giant's plants, frozen peas were accidently being packaged with insect parts. To address this problem, the plant created an incentive program in which employees received a bonus for finding insect parts. Employees responded by bringing insect parts from home, putting them in packages of peas, and "finding them" to boost their bonus.[28] Education and healthcare are full of examples like this. Educators in Birmingham, Alabama, schools manipulated two measures at once in 2005. They asked 500 of their poorer students to leave school before standardized testing began but after the school was evaluated for funding, which was based on enrollment. Doctors and hospitals with incentives to keep costs down and improve outcomes treat only the healthiest patients.

Sometimes these programs have more serious consequences. Researcher David Denis and his colleagues looked at the relationship between securities fraud allegations and executive stock options among 358 companies between 1993 and 2002. Firms that made more stock options available to executives faced more fraud allegations. Economists Sumit Agarwal and Faye Wang studied the behavior of banks during the financial crisis. During the run-up to the crisis, many banks encouraged loan underwriting with incentives for loan officers. The incentives led to a 47% increase in the loan approval rate and a 24% increase in the default rate. They concluded banks lost money by switching to incentive pay.[29]

Sometimes P4P and incentives cause employees to focus on what's being rewarded and ignore other responsibilities (economists call this multitasking). In a widely cited P4P study, Canadian tree farmers planted more trees under an incentive plan, but more trees died (quantity improved, but quality suffered). Physicians working under incentives to increase cervical cancer screening, spent less time on mammography and hemoglobin A1c testing. Teachers devoted less attention to science, social studies, art, music, and physical education because math and reading were the subjects covered in standardized testing (and their incentives were tied to test scores).[30]

We Get More Competition and Less Collaboration

Collaboration and helping behaviors are important to the effective functioning of organizations, and employees working under individual P4P programs are less likely to display these behaviors.[31] This seems to have been Hewlett Packard's (HP) concern with incentive programs in the mid-1990s. Harvard researcher Michael Beer reported on HP's P4P experiments in 2004. In 12 of 13 cases the programs did not survive, in part because they didn't fit with HP's high-commitment culture. Its programs had unintended consequences. Managers eventually decided that performance could be more effectively improved through alternative managerial tools such as good supervision, clear goals, coaching, and training.[32] Beer concluded by saying, "The implementation costs and risks of these programs appear to be higher in high-commitment cultures like HP where trust and employee commitment is crucial to long-term success."

A study with bicycle messengers by Stephen Burks and his colleagues reinforced these findings and highlighted a deeper and more profound impact that P4P may be having on our employees. They found bicycle messengers at firms that had adopted P4P were less cooperative in the laboratory, on the job, and off the job. What was alarming was this wasn't simply a selection effect with more individualistic, egoists being attracted to firms with these programs. Working under P4P schemes actually causes an increase in more self-serving, egoistic behavior among people who are not otherwise oriented this way, and it does so very quickly.[33]

These Programs Are Changing Our Employees

The implication of Burks' study is important: A P4P program can actually cause people, who may otherwise be cooperative, to be less cooperative. Michael Lewis, author of the best-selling book *The Big Short* makes this same point in his discussion of the financial crisis of 2009.

> Incentives are at the bottom of it all. Part of this is a moral problem that grows out of the change in structure of Wall Street. When there were partnerships and people's money was on the line ... they were encouraged to behave in ways that were to the long-term benefit of the organizations they belonged to. Long-term behavior is just much different from short-term behavior—it encourages a different morality. And for several decades on Wall

Street, the short-term sensibility has been encouraged and compensated very highly. The incentive system has changed and changed the values of the people who work there.[34]

Others agree. Jean-Francois Manzoni suggests the use of short-term financial incentives makes pay more important to people, which in turn makes their use more necessary and creates a vicious cycle of increased reliance on them.[35] Uri Gneezy, Stephan Meier, and Pedro Rey-Biel discuss many examples of how contingent rewards change people's frames of reference and the rationale for their behavior.[36]

A fascinating example of this is a study with an Israeli daycare center. Gneezy and fellow economist Aldo Rustichini found the center had trouble with parents showing up late to pick up their children, forcing staff to stay late. As a deterrent, the center started fining late parents (about $3). After the fine was implemented, the number of late parents actually increased. Even after the school canceled the fine, the parents' behavior did not improve; it remained stable at the same levels as when the fine was in place. The two economists said the fine changed the frame of reference for parents. Before the fine, parents wanted to arrive on time to be considerate of the staff, who also had families to get home to—a" pro-social" frame of respecting, not abusing other people's time. After the fine, the relationship took on a "market" frame in which the cost of "extra time" was about $3 (a fairly low price), and parents had to decide if they wanted to buy this additional service. After the fine was removed, the market frame did not change; the price simply went down for the extra service.[37]

Focusing too much on contingent pay and incentives reinforces an economic PM 1.0 frame. Others go even further arguing that economic principles and theories themselves can be self-fulfilling, shaping management practices and actually creating the behavior they predict.[38] It is this point that should frighten you the most. Are we actually changing the values of our employees by implementing these programs, creating the behavior we want, further reinforcing the need for these programs?

People Work for the Money, Not Because They Enjoy It

People who do things because they are inherently interesting and enjoyable are intrinsically motivated. People who do things in order to attain some separate outcome or reward are extrinsically motivated. These two sources of motivation are not independent. Researchers argue that P4P and extrinsic motivation can "crowd out" or undermine intrinsic motivation.[39]

The original research in this area was done by psychologist Edward Deci. He suggested that people had a set of inherent growth tendencies and innate psychological needs that were the basis for their self-motivation. These needs were mastery (competence), autonomy, and belonging. For Deci, the effects of rewards on intrinsic motivation depended on how they affected feelings of mastery and autonomy. If a reward was perceived as controlling (e.g., a piece-rate system) it would negatively affect the need for autonomy and undermine intrinsic motivation. However, if rewards were perceived as informational (e.g., you won the Nobel Prize), they satisfied the need for mastery and would enhance intrinsic motivation.[40] Research shows extrinsic rewards can negatively affect intrinsic motivation, especially when the work is complex and interesting to begin with, when it requires creativity and innovation, when incentives/rewards are explicit and expected, and when they come with extensive, intrusive monitoring.[41]

P4P Can Be Hazardous to Your Health

Even when these programs work, they can be hazardous to employees. Programs like piece-rates always involve time pressure because the average rate is determined by time and motion studies. Time pressure causes psychological distress. Piece-rate systems have been associated with higher levels of stress hormones, higher blood pressure levels, and higher anxiety than time-based systems. Longitudinal research shows these programs may be implicated in elevated levels of several physiological risk factors for cardiovascular heart disease. Arie Shirom and his colleagues studied the health impact of different pay systems (time-based, piece-rate, combination, and group incentives) on workers in 21 different factories in Israel. They found being on a performance-contingent pay system was associated with higher levels of depression and somatic complaints, even after controlling for other factors. This was true for all performance-contingent pay systems, but even more for piece-rate systems.[42]

After looking at the science it is clear P4P programs are not motivational magic bullets. In fact, far from it. There is little evidence these programs have generalized, widespread benefits for performance, productivity, retention, and innovation in organizations. Even in the narrow circumstances in which these programs might work, the side effects of the treatment may be worse than the disease. These programs also cost organizations a lot of money to design and run, and they consume a lot of management time and attention. Organizations need compensation staff, consulting resources, and management time to design, administer, track, evaluate, and redesign these programs. Managers and employees need to be trained and retrained as changes are made. Fog Creek Software estimated their sales reps spent 20% of their time keeping track of what money was due them under their commission system.[43] It is not clear these programs are worth the investment, and their cost continues to rise as organizations tinker with them every year.

PM 2.0: Life Without P4P and Differentiation

As would be the case with eliminating performance ratings, abandoning reliance on money and P4P will leave a huge void for most companies. How do you just stop? How do you motivate without money as an incentive? What happens to your compensation philosophy and strategy? How do you reinforce culture and behavior change?

The journey starts by abandoning PM 1.0 thinking. We need to replace the outdated economic and psychological principles behind PM 1.0 with new principles that are better supported by scientific research. There are two approaches to filling this void: (a) Find other ways to motivate employees, and (b) replace traditional, individually based compensation programs with other programs. We will talk more about these strategies in Chapters 7 through 9, but I will provide a brief overview of these strategies here.

Motivate Employees in Other Ways

Deci's research (mentioned earlier) can be a helpful guide in thinking about other ways to motivate employees. Dan Pink popularized his research in his book *Drive*. Recall Deci identified three innate needs that people must satisfy for optimal functioning and growth:

- ▪ Competence. People have a need to gain mastery of tasks and learn different skills. Employees want to be good at the work they do. They like work that plays to their strengths and will work hard to improve and master new things.
- ▪ Relatedness. People need to experience a sense of belonging and attachment to other people.
- ▪ Autonomy. People need to feel in control of their own behaviors and goals.
- ▪ Purpose. People need to be part of something bigger than themselves (this was Pink's addition to Deci's three needs).

Appealing to these needs is not always as straightforward as throwing money at people, but in the end it is likely to be more effective and longer-lasting. Here are suggestions for tapping into these needs.

Use Jobs to Motivate

The work people do every day is the strongest source of engagement and motivation. The research to support this couldn't be any clearer.[44] If you have only one motivational bullet, look at the work people do. Organizations and supervisors should do all they can to make jobs more interesting, challenging, and fulfilling. Make the work more meaningful by adding a wider variety of tasks so employees use more of their skills and talents. Give employees and workgroups whole pieces of work to do so they feel they are making a contribution to something significant. Provide employees with more responsibility and autonomy by delegating important work to the lowest possible levels, and give them as much freedom, independence, and discretion as possible in carrying out the work. Make sure employees get feedback so they see how their work is making a difference. Another helpful strategy is to allow employees discretion in crafting their own jobs.[45] Allow them to create more meaning by reshaping the boundaries of their work. They can look for other ways to expand their current responsibilities by developing new skills on their own, acquiring new knowledge, and taking advantage of other development opportunities. They can volunteer for special opportunities and short-term assignments. Both supervisors and employees should be on the lookout for these opportunities and do a better job of matching employees to jobs in the first place, so that employees are doing more of what they like to do and are good at.

Create More Opportunities for Promotions and Job Transfers

Employees are motivated by the opportunity to take on additional responsibilities. Organizations should structure job families and job levels so more meaningful promotion opportunities are available. Even lateral job moves can be meaningful to employees who want to be exposed to different areas of the company and who want to learn and leverage different skills.

Leverage Relationships

Individuals are energized and motivated by the relationships they have at work. Ensure supervisors know how to create strong, productive relationships with their staff and within their teams. This starts with hiring the right supervisors, promoting the right people into supervisory roles, and training supervisors well on how to establish trust and create effective teams with productive working relationships. Employees like being a part of a team, working with colleagues whom they trust and respect and who support each other. I will have much more to say about this in Chapter 9.

Create a Compelling Purpose

This will be the lesson from Chapter 7. People want to be a part of something bigger than themselves. Day-to-day motivation at work has more to do with the work people are doing and the higher-level purpose the work serves than it does with a paycheck or bonus. Having a regular dialogue about the work employees do and how it contributes to important objectives can energize them. Make sure people feel they have something important to contribute.

Replace Individual P4P Programs With Other Programs

Abandoning P4P doesn't mean organizations don't need competitive compensation programs to attract talent and keep talented employees from being attracted away by better offers. There are lots of options beyond individual P4P programs.

Focus More on Base Pay

To attract people to your company, consider putting more money in base pay and less in bonus. Pay above the market. Target salaries at 75% or 90% of the market instead of at the median, especially for top talent or for employees with critical skills. Instead of using merit pay to increase employees' base pay over time, use market-based adjustments. Your company probably already does this in markets with explosive growth, high inflationary pressures, or hyper-competition.

Use Team- and Organization-Based Incentive Programs

Instead of individual P4P, consider implementing bonus programs that are based on team or organizational performance or other outcomes like profit-sharing, gain-sharing, employee ownership, or stock ownership plans. These programs are more flexible and have productivity benefits without the side effects of individual P4P programs. I will have much more to say about the benefits of these plans in Chapter 10.

Promote Employees More Frequently

You can also use promotions to motivate employees and increase their pay over time, especially for top talent. This practice may require that companies abandon the compensation practice of broadbanding in favor of more differentiated job structures and ladders, with more levels that allow for more frequent promotions during an employee's career. In studies that examined the effectiveness of robust internal labor market solutions like these, they were frequently more effective than P4P programs in increasing motivation, performance, and productivity. There is nothing more discouraging to employees than discovering they only have one or maybe two promotion opportunities in their entire career. Top talent will frequently leave a company in search of more responsibility elsewhere.

Use Other Mechanisms to Control Employee Behavior.

Financial rewards are frequently viewed as the key leverage point for aligning and reinforcing company culture and employee and leader behavior. They can still be used this way at the group and organizational level in the form of gain-sharing programs with metrics tied to important organizational priorities (e.g., expense control, cost reduction, quality improvement, or innovation). However you need to look at the full range of strategies for institutionalizing culture and behavior change. For example, if you want more innovation in your organization instead of introducing an individual incentive program to reward innovation, use your recruiting, hiring, onboarding, training and development, promotion, and recognition processes to reinforce this direction. Make innovation a key part of your corporate performance scorecard and create internal support organizations to champion new ideas and remove the bureaucracy and red tape that get in the way of innovation.

Making the Change to PM 2.0

I realize this all sounds idealistic and "utopian" and you are probably saying to yourself there is no way this will work in the real world. Not very many years ago I probably would have said the same thing. At the same time, I have lived in the real world of PM 1.0 for 30 years and it doesn't work. It can't work. We need to do something different, and it starts by admitting the world has changed and key elements of PM 1.0 are no longer effective, namely evaluation and the use of money and P4P to motivate.

Filling the void left by abandoning traditional evaluation and reward practices will require a number of changes, from the types of compensation programs used and the way they are designed to the way jobs are structured. It will also require you to hire, promote, and train your supervisors differently. These changes will also require a lot of effort from your HR organization at a time when there are fewer HR people around and those that are around are busy with tactical and operational responsibilities. There will also be significant resistance to these ideas that will take time and energy to overcome. I am not naïve, and I don't want you to be either; this transition won't be easy. Traditional evaluation and reward systems are firmly entrenched in big corporations and there are no signs this is changing. However, this doesn't mean it can't be done. Companies like Netflix, Atlassian, and Fog Creek Software have moved strongly in the direction of PM 2.0 and have not suffered for it. They abandoned individual pay-for-performance programs in favor of alternative strategies like market-based pay, paying at the top of the market, employee ownership, and other team and organizational incentive programs. I will have more to say about what these companies are doing in Chapter 9.

Finally, while I am recommending that you abandon your P4P programs, I am not advocating that you abandon your P4P philosophy. You can aggressively manage poor performance, reward performance over time as employees experience success, promoted employees faster into higher-paying positions, make liberal use of "rewards" other than money, and leverage team and organizational reward programs. You can still have a P4P philosophy without basing pay increases and bonuses on year-end individual performance ratings.

Key Messages

- Nearly every company has made a major commitment to P4P programs despite their lack of effectiveness and despite the problems these programs create for companies.
- Companies believe deeply in the economic and psychological principles behind P4P programs and they remain optimistic the flaws can be fixed.
- These programs and the differentiation they create tend not to improve productivity, performance, engagement, retention, or innovation. They are effective in a narrow range of circumstances and even when they work they are expensive, time consuming, and have serious side effects.
- Other more effective options are available for motivating employees and growing their pay over time.

What to Start

So let's take stock of where we've been and where we're going. In Section I we learned that PM 1.0 doesn't work and that its practices are based on outdated paradigms held in place by powerful forces. It has an expansive purpose: trying to please too many masters and failing to please any of them.

In Section II we learned that moving toward PM 2.0 requires that we first abandon ineffective PM 1.0 practices like quantitative evaluation and the use of money and pay-for-performance to motivate. We will also need to abandon the paradigms behind these practices and the economic and psychological principles on which they are based. But if we don't focus PM on evaluation, differentiation, and financial rewards, what *do* we focus it on?

In Section III we "burn the PM 1.0 ships in the harbor" and rebuild PM based on new paradigms that are better supported by scientific research. We introduce PM 2.0 new practices based on a new motivational foundation and new principles that are better supported by scientific research:

- Meaningful direction and purpose (Chapter 7)
- Progress (Chapter 8)
- Teamwork and Collaboration (Chapter 9)

7

Purpose, Meaning, and Direction

*If you want to build a ship, don't drum up people together to collect wood
and don't assign them tasks and work, but rather teach them to long
for the endless immensity of the sea.*

—Antoine de Saint-Exupéry

It is not enough to be busy. So are the ants. The question is: what are we busy about?

—Henry David Thoreau

In 1983, Steve Jobs wooed Pepsi executive John Sculley to Apple with one of the most famous lines in business: "Do you want to spend the rest of your life selling sugared water or do you want a chance to change the world?"[1] He used another famous line in an interview with David Scheff in *Playboy* magazine.[2]

> At Apple, people are putting in 18-hour days. We attract a different type of person—someone who really wants to get in a little over his head and "make a little dent in the universe." We are aware that we are doing something significant. We're here at the beginning of it and we're able to shape how it

Next Generation Performance Management, pages 95–109
Copyright © 2017 by Information Age Publishing
All rights of reproduction in any form reserved.

goes. And no, we don't know where it will lead. We just know there's something much bigger than any of us here.

Who wouldn't be excited about working at Apple when you get to "make a little dent in the universe?" Steve Jobs knew how to paint a compelling picture of the future and capture the hearts and minds of people. John Kennedy knew how to do it as well, as he did it in his speech about going to the moon to a joint session of Congress on May 25, 1961.

> First, I believe that this nation should commit itself to achieving the goal, before this decade is out, of landing a man on the moon and returning him safely to the Earth. But why, some say, the moon? We choose to go to the moon in this decade and do the other things, not because they are easy, but because they are hard; because that goal will serve to organize and measure the best of our energies and skills; because that challenge is one that we are willing to accept, one we are unwilling to postpone, and one we intend to win.

Nearly everything you need to know about the power of goals, direction, and purpose to motivate people is represented in John Kennedy's speech to Congress and in the *Playboy* interview with Steve Jobs. This is why goals and purpose and meaning embodied in them are at the center of performance management (PM) 2.0. Kennedy's speech and the goal of going to the moon was a rallying cry for a nation and gave purpose and meaning to the work of hundreds of thousands of people. The philosophy underlying PM 2.0 is simple: Give them something worth working for and they will. This lies in stark contrast to the philosophy underlying PM 1.0: Make it worth their while to work hard and they will. Just over 8 years after Kennedy's speech on July 20, 1969, NASA's Apollo 11 mission landed Neil Armstrong and Buzz Aldrin on the moon. It wasn't contracts and incentives that landed a man on the moon, it was purpose and meaning.

Make no mistake, NASA didn't go to the moon and back just on the wings of a presidential speech. It took people, planning, and effort. This is what goals do: they get people moving. Landing a man on the moon required the most sudden burst of technological creativity and the largest commitment of resources ($24 billion) ever made by any nation in peacetime. At its peak, the Apollo program employed 400,000 people and required the support of more than 20,000 industrial firms and universities.[3]

NASA didn't go to the moon without planning, and good things don't happen in organizations without planning. That's why PM 2.0 is a fundamental part of a company's management process. It translates big, hairy organizational goals into individual work activities. It directs employee efforts ensuring work gets accomplished in the service of those goals. It ensures employees work on things that matter and don't work on things that don't matter. It ensures employees understand what's important so they can make the right day-to-day decisions about their work. Finally, it ensures employees make progress against those important things. PM 2.0 is designed with this core purpose in mind because without it lofty strategies are doomed to fail. In fact most strategies and strategic planning exercises fail and they fail because they don't get implemented. They don't turn into specific plans and day-to-day responsibilities.[4] Strategy expert Arnold Judson accuses American business especially of not having the discipline and the will to manage the strategy implementation process over the long term. American business becomes too infatuated with quick fixes and fads. PM 2.0 is central to helping companies develop the discipline to turn their strategies into tactics and their tactics into real work by employees.

Every organization needs the equivalent of Kennedy's speech to Congress on some periodic basis. These "marching orders" for the organization need to get translated into clear goals and objectives for all the subordinate parts of the organization down to the department and workgroup level. Throughout this process it should be clear how the goals at the bottom of the organization serve and contribute to the goals of the larger organization and the firm. This process should not be a long, annual, bureaucratic, goal-cascading process. In fact most experts suggest these cascading processes don't work. They take too long and goals can change before they reach the bottom of the organization.[5]

Top down goals are not enough either. There are things that organizations, departments, and individuals need to do that are not captured under higher level goals, and higher level goals are not always clear and complete enough to drive action deeper in the organization.

The process of establishing direction is not linear or sequential either, it needs to be fluid, ongoing, and organic. Establishing direction in PM 2.0 is about context, it is about each employee understanding the context for their work. Context isn't achieved in a single conversation, it takes continuous, ongoing dialogue throughout the year. The more that employees understand the larger context for their work, the better decisions they will make when no one is around.

If your organization doesn't have a strategy implementation process or a local planning process, it is missing an important opportunity to motivate and engage employees. When I look at what leaders do that drives higher levels of engagement in their teams, one element consistently shows up at the top: making employees on their team feel like they are a part of something bigger than themselves. Steve Jobs knew how to do this. He knew in 1985 they were up to something bigger than any of them knew and one of his great gifts was conveying this to others and getting them to follow him.

Most Organizations Require Employees to Set Goals

The vast majority of organizations have some form of goal-setting as a part of their PM process.[6]

- 95% of companies set individual goals
- 80% have formal performance planning discussions
- 56% have a formal cascade of goals from company to business unit to department; 49% use an informal goal cascading process
- 41% set team-based objectives

While most companies go through the motions, they don't see the goal-setting process as the centerpiece of their PM process. PM 1.0 uses goals in an instrumental way. Goals and objectives are important because the stakes attached to them are important: rewards tied to goal achievement. This encourages employees to look ahead to the implications of goal achievement (or failure) instead of focusing on the meaning and value attached to the goals themselves. PM 1.0 sees the consequences of goal achievement as the source of motivation, not the goals themselves or the meaning behind them.

Other PM practices reflect this same philosophy. Several companies I know hold calibration meetings with their managers at the beginning of the year to discuss the goals and objectives of their employees. It is common to hold calibration meetings at the end of the year so managers can discuss the accomplishments of their employees and calibrate on the standards they will use to assign ratings (e.g., What does it take to merit a 1, 2, and so on?). Calibration at the beginning of the year has a similar purpose. Managers share the projects and goals they are assigning to their employees for the year anticipating which of these, if achieved, would merit top ratings and top rewards. This practice further illustrates my point; in PM 1.0 goals are contracts and play an instrumental role only. As an example, listen to how Oracle, a leading provider of PM software talks about how goals connect to PM.

> Goals are a contract between employee and manager. They provide the framework for accountability and promote conversations between the manager and employee to monitor progress throughout the year. Goals are also a contract between the individual and the organization.[7]

This statement represents PM 1.0 at its finest: contracts, accountability, and monitoring. Most of you are probably familiar with the fable of the three bricklayers. When asked, "What are you doing," the first replied, "I'm laying bricks," the second replied "I'm building a wall," and the third replied "I'm building a cathedral." The first bricklayer represents the essence of PM 1.0 thinking. We contract for a number of bricks and pay the bricklayer by the brick. The third bricklayer is the essence of PM 2.0. The daily goals of the number of courses of bricks to be laid are not contracts, but are the steppingstones or waypoints to a completed cathedral. Daily progress provides meaning and satisfaction beyond the wages earned per brick.

The Science Is Clear: Goals Work

The effectiveness of goal setting is among the most well-established findings from the social sciences. There have been hundreds of studies over five decades on the benefits of goal setting with several good reviews of this research (including three meta-analyses studies, the "gold standard" of research reviews).[8] Goals are central to motivation and they can be powerful tools in driving high performance and high engagement in organizations. Goals work their magic in four ways.[9]

1. They direct. Goals direct attention and effort toward relevant activities and away from irrelevant activities.
2. They energize. Challenging goals lead to more effort.
3. They affect persistence. People with challenging goals work longer and harder.
4. They require people to think, plan, and strategize. This is especially true if the goals require people to do something new and different.

The recipe for goal setting is clear from decades of research. Goals lead to high performance when they are specific and challenging, when people are committed to them, and when they get feedback on their progress.

Specific

Goals need to be specific. People who set specific goals perform better than those with no goals or general goals. Kennedy provided just enough specifics in his speech: "before this decade is out, landing a man on the moon and returning him safely to the Earth." Kennedy didn't say, "Hey, I'd like us to go to the moon before the Soviets and let's do our best to make this happen." The problem with do-your-best goals is people define them differently, which allows for a wide range of what passes for acceptable performance. Athletic trainers know this. Individuals typically don't know what they are capable of, and if left to their own devices they won't push themselves hard enough to continue improving. Specific goals lead to high performance for teams, too, which is important since work in organizations is increasingly being done by teams. We will revisit the topic of team goals in Chapter 9.

Challenging

People who set hard goals perform better than those who set easy goals. Hard goals activate all the motivational magic: They direct attention, they mobilize effort and persistence, and they encourage employees to develop specific strategies for attacking the work. Setting challenging goals is a delicate balancing act; however, if goals are too difficult employees may not have the ability to achieve them or they won't commit to them in the first place. It is clear going to the moon and back by the end of the decade qualified as challenging. Given the condition of the space program and NASA in the 1960s, it was not immediately obvious how they would accomplish it. At the time of Kennedy's speech, the United States had not put an astronaut into orbit and had only put one person in space. Even NASA employees themselves were not confident this goal could be achieved.[10]

Difficult, complex goals take planning, and the planning for the mission to the moon was extensive including a new mandate and expansion for NASA, repurposing the Apollo program and a new NASA Space Center in Houston. What the people at NASA and all of the contractor organizations did to accomplish this feat was nothing short of a miracle, and there were many dark days when it didn't look like it would happen (e.g., the Apollo 1 cabin fire in 1967 that killed the entire crew). But people with challenging goals persist and the United States ultimately prevailed.

Commitment

It's not enough for goals to be specific and challenging, people need to commit to them. Steve Jobs and John Kennedy got people committed, and NASA and Apple people invested heavily, sometimes 18 hours a day in the case of Apple employees. The science behind goals says that people don't make this commitment without three things:

- Something important to work on (purpose)
- A belief they can actually accomplish it (self-efficacy)
- A voice in deciding what to do and how to do it (participation)

The Power of Purpose

The power of goals to move people starts with what's behind the goals—purpose and meaning. People want something important to do. This context is critical for PM 2.0; if employees see their work in the service of something important, they are more likely to commit to that work.[11] Good leaders know how to use purpose to connect with employees. Steve Jobs asked John Scully if he wanted to change the world. Kennedy told Congress the United States needed to win the space race (and the Cold War) with the Soviet Union.

Over the last 10 years there has been a growing realization that purpose and meaning are important for people's work and personal lives. It is also clear companies have a ways to go in addressing this need. A recent survey by Deloitte shows 68% of employees and 66% of executives believe that businesses are not doing enough to create a sense of purpose and show people they are delivering a meaningful impact.[12] PM 1.0 thinking is part of the problem. Motivation doesn't require purpose it requires incentives—carrots and sticks. The positive psychology movement puts purpose and meaning at the center of people's personal and work lives, and a similar movement is taking shape within the business community devoted to putting higher order purpose and meaning at the center of a business' value proposition.[13] Dan Pink wrote about the power of purpose as a motivator in his book *Drive*.[14] Teresa Amabile wrote about the importance of "making progress in meaningful work" to employee engagement and productivity in her book *The Progress Principle*.[15] The research behind this movement is clear.

- People need meaning and purpose in their lives.
- When they have it they experience a variety of positive outcomes: motivation, engagement, performance, well-being, and health).
- When they don't have it they experience more negative outcomes: dissatisfaction, disillusionment, stress, and strain.[16]
- Leadership is critical. Leaders who foster and inspire a sense of purpose have employees who perform better and have better overall well-being.[17]

Employees who are able to fulfill these needs at work are better off than those who aren't, and those who aren't fulfilling these needs at work are searching for it outside of work.[18] Research by Jessica Rodell from the University of Georgia shows that employees who volunteer outside of work experience more meaning in their current jobs, and the motivation to volunteer is higher among people with less meaning in their current jobs. Apparently there are a lot of people looking for meaning. According to the Bureau of Labor statistics about 63 million people volunteered for an organization at least once in the past year.[19]

The realization that purpose is important dates back at least to the work redesign movement of the 1960s. The prevailing attitude toward work design prior to the 1960s was exemplified by the work of Fredrick Taylor and Scientific Management, a founding father of PM 1.0 thinking: simplify jobs to make labor interchangeable and maximize efficiency. What leaders discovered, however (not surprisingly), was employees hated working in these "simplified," "efficient" jobs. They were boring and monotonous and the efficiency and productivity benefits simply didn't materialize. There were many efforts to overthrow this outdated model of job design, notable among them were the efforts of Richard Hackman and Greg Oldham in 1975.[20] Their model of work redesign still holds today as the recipe for enriching jobs and they put purpose and meaning at the center of it: Employees should be doing whole pieces of work (task identity); their work should be connected to meaningful outcomes; and workers need to see how their work affects the well-being of others inside or outside the company (task significance). When employees work in jobs where these factors are present, they experience more meaning and they are happier and more productive as a result.

Companies like TOMS shoes and Patagonia understand the power of purpose and are reaping the benefits in the form of higher levels of engagement and retention among their employees. TOMS was founded in 2006 by Blake Mycoskie. The company sells shoes based on the Argentine *alpargatas*, a canvass or cotton fabric shoe with a thin flexible sole. Mycoskie saw these shoes while in Argentina in 2002 competing in the second season of the television show *The Amazing Race*. During that trip he also noticed that many of the children running in the streets didn't have shoes. He decided to develop a version of the alpargata for the North American market, but he also wanted to give back to Argentina and other developing nations by donating a pair of shoes for every pair sold ("One for One"). TOMS's business model had purpose in mind from the beginning. The company's partners distributed shoes where the need was greatest, and employees who had been there a year participated personally in the distribution. It's clear from the way TOMS talks about their employees (the "TOMS Tribe") they attract purpose-minded individuals.

A TOMS tribe member is someone who goes the extra mile for others in need, has giving back woven into their DNA and shares inspiration in order to start a movement to CREATE POSITIVE CHANGE. As a TOMS tribe member, you aspire to be part of something bigger–HELPING OTH-

ERS AND GIVING BACK–while letting inspiration guide your efforts and involvement. When people ask, share the TOMS Giving story. Let them know that you stand for creating positive impact, and influencing others to think about new ways that BUSINESS CAN IMPROVE LIVES and the world around us. (Emphasis in original)

Attracting and retaining employees is easier when people know what they're doing makes a difference in the world. Mycoskie attributes the high levels of employee satisfaction of TOMS employees to the fact that their socially responsible business model attracts superb employees. "I've been lucky enough to attract passionate, dedicated people who will do anything to make an impact on the world," he says. "They are all seeking something more than a 9-to-5 job." Mycoskie's first employee Candice Wolfswinkel, now chief giving officer, worked for free for a year before receiving any pay. Chief financial officer Caroline Zouloumian left her career in finance after paying off her loans from earning a Harvard MBA to go work for TOMS. In 2009, the company received more than 1,000 applications for 15 summer internship positions.[21]

Patagonia is another company leveraging the power of purpose with their employees. Patagonia is a U.S.-based high-end outdoor clothing company founded by Yvon Chouinard in 1973. Its roots are in clothing and equipment for rock and alpine climbing, a passion of Chouinard's. Their success is attributable to relentless technical innovation that produces products good enough to meet the demanding expectations of experts in sports like mountaineering, rock and ice climbing, surfing, skiing, snowboarding, kayaking, biking, sailing, and fishing. Patagonia's success is also attributable to a deep, abiding commitment to preserving the diversity, ecological integrity, and beauty of the natural environment. Social responsibility and environmental activism are critical components of their value proposition, evidenced by their mission statement: Build the best product, cause no unnecessary harm, use business to inspire and implement solutions to the environmental crisis.

It is clear Patagonia is different when you walk in their headquarters and see a surf report on the corporate message board. Located in Ventura, California, Patagonia encourages employees to pursue the sports about which the company is passionate, and they provide flextime to allow employees to take advantage when the surf is up. It is also clear what kind of employee they are looking for. "We're always looking for motivated people to join us. We're especially interested in people who share our love of the outdoors, our passion for quality, and our desire to make a difference."

Employees can't imagine being anywhere else. Patagonia doesn't compete on salaries or benefits. People join Patagonia because this is the lifestyle they want to support. Their human resources and environmental principles and practices have resulted in high employee commitment and retention compared to industry and retail averages. Their employment culture is directly linked to their mission. They first look for people with the passion and commitment to a cause, and then look for people with the technical skills, which can frequently be trained for and learned on the job. You can't train passion and commitment.[22]

Self-Efficacy and Self-Confidence

While a strong sense of purpose and meaning will go a long way toward getting employees to commit to their goals, it isn't enough. People need to believe they can actually do it. Researchers call this self-efficacy. The more employees believe they can accomplish their goals, the stronger the impact goals have on employee performance. If Kennedy said he wanted us to go to the moon and back within 2 years, no one would have signed up. Goals need to be achievable. Kennedy didn't just make up the goal of going to the moon within the decade. He knew the United States had an advantage in the space race despite the early successes of the Soviet Union. He knew this was a race the United States could win. To increase self-efficacy, employees need to have the training, skills, and experience to accomplish the work. NASA hired the best and the brightest minds for the Apollo program and contracted with the top experts outside of NASA. They had all the support and resources they needed. Having role models and seeing others who have done it can also increase self-efficacy. Kennedy and others at NASA knew what the Soviets had done and they also knew the United States had achieved smaller successes already. They had seen evidence they could solve some of the more difficult technical problems.

Experiencing early success can also help build confidence and increase self-efficacy, especially with something as difficult and complex as going to the moon.[23] Supervisors need to break big, complex projects into smaller pieces so they are more manageable. Short-term goals help employees get early feedback on whether or not their strategies are effective so they can make adjustments if necessary. If employees have both short-term and long-term goals they are more likely to be successful.

Sony used this approach when they proposed their goal of having a zero environmental footprint by 2050 ("Getting to Zero").[24] The pressure on corporations to become more environmentally responsible has intensified to address the enormous environmental sustainability challenges we face (e.g., climate change, poverty, water shortages). This is an enormous undertaking and no other company had been this bold or identified the path to make it happen. To attack this goal the company broke it up into four key subgoals and six product lifecycle stages. The subgoals included: curbing climate change, conserving resources (materials, waste, recycling, and water), promoting biodiversity, and controlling chemical substances. The product lifecycle stages included: R&D, product planning and design, procurement, business operations, distribution, and take-back and recycling.

The strategy they used was to find a path to zero in each of these areas using methods, tactics, and approaches appropriate for each. For example, in distribution they focused on smaller packaging, improved loading efficiency, and shifting distribution to rail and water. Sony then set specific interim targets. For example, they wanted to reduce greenhouse gases by 30% and reduce mass-per-product by 10%. They created a 4×6 matrix of the subgoals and product lifecycle stages and set goals for each cell in this matrix.[25]

Sony then put in place a governance system to manage these activities. They integrated these responsibilities within the formal management structure by putting in place headquarters environmental functions. They added environmental functions and audit functions in regional offices and business division headquarters and sites. They also conducted annual assessments to get feedback on progress to identify risks and opportunities. Individual business units and sites established their own annual plans as well. Awards were given annually to recognize outstanding activities. They also provided environmental education for employees tailored to the work they did and their specific work objectives. All these efforts took an exceedingly complex and lofty organizational goal and translated it into specific responsibilities that employees could understand and align with.

Participation in the Process

The final strategy to get employees to commit to goals is participation. The theory holds that if people are involved in the process of deciding on their goals, they should be more committed to them. The science is less clear here. Some studies show participation improves commitment and performance, while others show it has no impact. If people believe in the goal and have line of sight to why the goal is important, participation in the process may not be necessary. It wasn't necessary for all NASA employees to be involved in deciding on the goal Kennedy set to propel the United States back to technological superiority over the Soviet Union. However it seems very likely that the top team at NASA was involved in these deliberations since it was clear Kennedy had discussed this goal with top officials prior to his speech to Congress. He needed this goal to be achievable, and his top team helped ensure this was the case. While individuals may not need to be involved in setting their own goals in order for those goals to motivate them, individuals do want a say in deciding how to accomplish their goals. The science is clear here: Involvement in the formulation of strategies for accomplishing goals improves the probability of success.

So the secret to getting employees to really commit to their goals is a compelling purpose, confidence they can do it, a clear path forward, and a voice in the process.

You Can't Buy Commitment

Another strategy frequently discussed in the goal-setting literature for securing commitment to a goal is by tying rewards and incentives to goal achievement. This is classic PM 1.0 thinking. Having read Chapter 6 (hopefully) you know this strategy doesn't work very well. Some writers like Lisa Ordonez and her colleagues from the University of Arizona have been critical of goal-setting, accusing organizations of "over-prescribing" goals in order to boost performance. She and other writers point the finger at goals when the finger should really be pointed at incentives. Nearly all the examples she cites in her paper "Goals Gone Wild" (Sears and Enron for example) are classic failures of pay-for-performance and incentives.[26] There is no question too strong a focus on goals can create a "results-at-all-costs" mentality that can suboptimize the overall results for an organization.[27] This is more likely to happen, however, when something big is tied to the achievement of a goal. Tying goal achievement to incentives may increase commitment (more likely to be "compliance" masquerading as commitment however), but it may not necessarily lead to the performance your organization is looking for and may give you more than you bargained for.

Feedback

While specific, challenging goals that employees commit to are important for success, it's hard for employees to make progress without feedback. Employees need feedback in order to make necessary adjustments to their efforts and strategies. This is a critical point and most people involved in PM either miss it or confuse it. Feedback should not be divorced from goals. Most of us have heard people say that employees want feedback. The reality is feedback is only important insofar as it tells employees about the progress they are making against their goals. Employees don't really want feedback, they want progress. This point also explains why performance ratings don't motivate. Many companies justify the use of ratings by saying employees need feedback on how they are doing. Again, this logic misses the point. Employees want to know how they are doing, but this is in reference to a particular goal they have, like progressing in the company or earning more responsibility. I will come back to this important point in Chapter 8 when I talk specifically about feedback and coaching. When feedback becomes disconnected from specific goals, it becomes less effective and can even interfere with performance.

Who Is Doing It Differently?

While most companies have their employees set goals as a part of PM, few are fully leveraging the power of goals and few have made it the center-piece of their PM process. Most companies follow the recipe of PM 1.0 using goals as contracts, motivating employees by linking goals and goal achieve-ment to rewards. Companies like TOMS Shoes, Patagonia, and others have gone "all-in," creating value propositions for their companies that tap into the power of purpose and meaning in motivating their employees. Employ-ees see their day-to-day work and goals differently in these companies. Writ-er Aaron Hurst, author of *The Purpose Economy*, has taken an even stronger stand arguing the search for purpose and meaning goes beyond making employees happy and companies productive. He argues the purpose move-ment is giving rise to a completely new economic model, one where value lies in establishing purpose for employees and customers through serving needs greater than their own, enabling personal growth, and community building. He has highlighted companies like REI, Steelcase, and others that are grounding the everyday work of employees in a larger purpose for their companies.[28] Other companies are taking smaller positive steps to improve the way their employees set and manage their goals within PM.

The Gap Inc.: Ongoing Goal Setting

When The Gap redesigned PM, they acknowledged that some goals would be more long-term while others might be set and accomplished with-in a couple of months. In their PM application, the goal-setting module was separated from the other modules and it was open all the time. They had two codes for goals: active and complete. When goals were completed, they moved to the bottom of the list. An employee and a supervisor could add new goals at any time and new goals moved to the top of the list. Finally, the goal plan was not a documentation tool for them. Managers could put comments in the tool but it was not required.[29]

exible Goal Setting

10 Cargill embarked on a significant PM reform project. A key
ey made replaced their time-consuming formal goal-setting process (which cascaded goals throughout the organization) with a more flexible and streamlined process that fit the different kinds of work performed.
They acknowledged that for some roles where the environment was more
unpredictable, it was difficult to set goals that remained relevant throughout the year. They focused their training efforts on equipping supervisors to
have discussions with employees about expectations and how they aligned
with the organization's mission and objectives. This context allowed employees to make course corrections during the year as needed, but also
created an important line of sight to a higher-level purpose for their work.[30]

PM 2.0: New Paradigms and New Practices

So PM 2.0 represents a shift in the way organizations think about goals and
about motivation in general. PM 1.0 relies on contracts, incentives, and
rewards to motivate, and it uses goals to establish accountability and reward
contingencies. It uses goals in an instrumental way: If you achieve these
goals, you will get these rewards. Research reviewed in this chapter shows
organizations don't need to buy employee commitment or threaten them
with unpleasant consequences in order to get them to perform. PM 2.0 uses
direction and context—goals, purpose, and meaning—to motivate. Goals
are a path to purpose and meaning. They engage employees in a conversation about how their work matters, and they guide employees as they do
their work and make adjustments throughout the year. Table 7.1 summa-
rizes this shift in thinking from PM 1.0 to PM 2.0.

TABLE 7.1 The Paradigm Shift From PM 1.0 to PM 2.0	
From PM 1.0 . . .	. . . to PM 2.0
• Goals have instrumental value. They specify what accomplishments will be rewarded	• Goals provide purpose, meaning and direction
• Alignment of employees with company priorities is externally mediated by contracts, contingencies, consequences, and threats	• Alignment of employees with company priorities is internally mediated by objectives with clear links to outcomes that are meaningful and important
• Goals are specific contracts that describe what needs to be done and the consequences of fulfilling (or not fulfilling) the contract	• Goals are general statements about the work that needs to be done and the outcomes to be achieved

The power of goals and direction was driven home to me in a conversation with one of my colleagues at a recent analytics conference. She was working on project to predict who would quit their company by using a variety of demographic and organizational information. One of her most surprising findings was those who were missing performance ratings in their PM system were statistically the most likely to quit. When she dug deeper she discovered that most employees who left their company without performance ratings never had performance plans entered in the system. Most of these employees never met with their supervisors to discuss priorities and never had conversations about goals and objectives. Those employees worked for negligent supervisors who never engaged them in a conversation about their work and why it mattered. As a result, many of them didn't stick around very long. If you have a good story to tell to employees about how their work matters, tell it early and tell it often.

Key Messages

- Employees are looking for meaning and purpose in their work lives. They want to be a part of something bigger than themselves
- A goal-setting process that connects the work employees do to the organizations larger purpose should be an important part of your organization's management process.
- Goal setting works. People who set and commit to specific and challenging goals perform better.
- Be careful with goals. Don't overemphasize the achievement of goals or specific targets, which may create a "results-at-all-costs" mentality, and don't link incentives or rewards to individual goal achievement.

$$8$$

Feedback and Progress

I have yet to find the man, however exalted his station, who did not do better work
and put forth greater effort under a spirit of approval than under a spirit of criticism.
—Charles Schwab

Every day you may make progress. Every step may be fruitful. Yet there will stretch out
before you an ever-lengthening, ever-ascending, ever-improving path. You know you
will never get to the end of the journey. But this, so far from discouraging,
only adds to the joy and glory of the climb.
—Winston S. Churchill

In 2013 a total of 32,719 people died in motor vehicle crashes; 29% of them were speeding-related. Speed has been a factor in nearly one-third of crash deaths since 2004.[1] A number of different solutions have been tried to get motorists to slow down. Some of them are expensive, like stronger law enforcement crackdowns. Other solutions are less expensive like speed bumps, rumble strips, and more and better signage. One strategy that has gained popularity in the past 10 years is the radar speed sign that gives drivers feedback on their speed as they approach the sign. This seems like

Next Generation Performance Management, pages 111–126
Copyright © 2017 by Information Age Publishing

something that couldn't possibly work—let's tell people something they already know (and distract them with a large sign). People know how fast they are going; they have a speedometer in the car. There are no explicit consequences, no one is being penalized, no carrots or sticks. It couldn't possibly work.

But it does.

Law enforcement officials in Tigard, Oregon, were concerned about the safety of the streets around the city's high school where drivers were routinely cited for exceeding the posted 20 mph speed limit by more than 20 mph. City leaders turned to radar speed displays to solve the problem since other solutions either were too expensive or simply not practical on these streets. A company who makes the displays loaned them one for a 90-day trial. At the end of the trial period, posting one radar speed sign reduced citations and speeds dropped by 66%. Even 6 months after the trial speeds were still down.[2] Simply giving drivers feedback on their speed changed driving behavior. No one had to be pulled over, no one had to write tickets, no one had to go to court and pay tickets and fines. This simple feedback mechanism worked.

Most of you have a very a powerful feedback tool in your pocket or your purse or even on your wrist. The vast majority of American adults own a smartphone and these have become very powerful feedback devices.[3] Many of you who have a smartphone or other similar device probably have a health or exercise app on it that counts your steps and gives you feedback against goals you set. If you are like most people, you check it regularly and quietly celebrate when you receive the signals you are making progress. Smartphones and other devices are becoming important feedback tools to help people change their behavior. In the healthcare arena for example, smartphones and health apps help patients and healthcare providers manage their health through real-time monitoring and treatment. Smart pill bottle caps with sensors let you know when you need to take your medicine, and smartphone apps let you know when your loved ones with Alzheimer's have wandered off and help you locate them instantly. The availability of low-cost technology like accelerometers, GPS sensors, and radio frequency ID (RFID) chips are enabling a wide array of devices to provide important information to help users improve many different outcomes. Its clear feedback can be a very powerful tool to help people manage and change their behavior.

The goal of feedback is the same for performance management (PM)— provide information that helps a person achieve their goals. Avi Kluger at the Hebrew University of Jerusalem has studied feedback extensively in the context of PM and he defines it as "actions taken by an external agent to provide information regarding some aspect of one's task performance."[4] I like this definition for several reasons. First, it views feedback as an intervention: an action affecting another's affairs, a deliberate entry into a situation in order to influence events or prevent undesirable consequences. Second, feedback as an intervention is focused on affecting someone else's affairs. An intervention is not about you, it is about them. An intervention is not about someone "getting something off their chest." Finally, feedback is deliberate. It has a purpose. As I said in Chapter 7 that purpose should connect it to the person's goals. This means you should give some thought to what you are trying to accomplish when you provide feedback. An intervention is also intentional; it is not something you say "in the heat of battle," at least not if your goal is to make things better.

Most Companies Have Feedback as a Part of Their PM Systems

The majority of organizations have periodic reviews during the year where supervisors discuss with employees how they are doing against their goals.[5]

- 95% of companies conduct formal year-end feedback and review discussions
- 63% have formal midyear or quarterly progress reviews
- About two-thirds (63%) routinely conduct performance feedback sessions between official performance reviews.
- Less than half (48%) of employees are satisfied with the quality of the feedback and development coming out of the PM process

Most companies emphasize formal feedback events that are prescribed at certain intervals (e.g., midyear and the end of the year). In these meetings supervisors tell employees how they are doing and how they can improve. While many companies report they have more regular, ongoing feedback throughout the year, it is clear the quality isn't what employees are looking for.

Supervisors Are Not Like Radar Speed Displays

When you see your speed flash in front of you on a radar speed display, that information comes directly to you, in real time. You own it and decide if and how to take action on it. Feedback in PM 1.0 works differently than this.

We learned in Chapter 3 that monitoring and surveillance is a key principle of PM 1.0. Feedback is about catching people doing something wrong. Agency theory says people will goof off it you let them and control theory says that feedback is about "discrepancies" or "gaps" between what you want employees to do and what they actually do. The law of effect says that when these discrepancies occur, supervisors need to apply negative consequences so they don't happen again. In organizations, feedback comes from your boss and it is something that is usually done to you.

The monitoring and surveillance of PM 1.0 is also about keeping track. PM 1.0 establishes goals that serve as contracts with reward contingencies tied to goal accomplishment. Feedback involves delivering messages about the likelihood of these contingencies paying off. Too many discrepancies and your rewards are in jeopardy. In organizations feedback comes with consequences: the threat of poor performance ratings and meager year-end rewards. The mark of a good PM 1.0 supervisor is having the courage to deliver transparent and honest messages about poor performance and the consequences that come along with it (while making employees feel good about it). Under PM 1.0, feedback is less like a radar speed sign and more like the police. They sit on the side of the road waiting for you to make a mistake, and when you do they write you a ticket and your insurance company raises your insurance rates. Feedback is about telling you what you are doing wrong and explaining what will happen to you if things don't improve. How many of you have been pulled over for not speeding to be congratulated and told to keep up the good work? We need something different for PM 2.0, something more like the simplicity and elegance of the radar speed signs.

Feedback Doesn't Always Work

Many writers who argue that PM should be blown up or abolished, propose replacing it with continuous feedback and coaching. Several books have taken this perspective.[6] These authors assume feedback improves performance—it's a "no-brainer." There are hundreds if not thousands of books, articles, workshops, and training programs on how to provide feedback effectively. There have been several summaries of this research, including a handful of meta-analysis studies in the psychology and education literatures looking at the effectiveness of feedback in improving performance.[7] Fabricio Balcazar and his colleagues did the earliest of these reviews in 1985. They reviewed 126 applications of feedback in organizations and looked at the consistency of its effects in improving performance. They concluded, "The results of this review indicated that feedback does not uniformly improve performance...and some characteristics of feedback are more consistently associated with improved performance than others."

This means we have known at least since 1985 that the effectiveness of feedback in improving performance is not a no-brainer. There have been other reviews since then, the latest by psychologists Avi Kluger and Angelo DeNisi in 1996 reviewing the psychology literature and John Hattie in 1999 reviewing the education literature. They came to similar conclusions. Kluger and DeNisi summarized the state of the feedback research literature this way:

> Several feedback intervention (FI) researchers have recently recognized that FIs have highly variable effects on performance, such that in some conditions FIs improve performance, in other conditions FIs have no apparent effects on performance, and in yet others FIs debilitate performance.

It is not as simple as give feedback and performance improves. As was the case with the benefits of setting goals, there are certain factors that help feedback drive high performance and other factors get in the way and actually interfere with performance. A closer look at this research reveals PM 1.0 thinking is the problem with feedback.

Feedback Must Be About Goals

The first thing we learn about effective feedback takes us back to a critical point we made in Chapter 7. Feedback relative to a specific goal has a positive impact on performance. Goal-setting is at the center of PM 2.0 and feedback is only important insofar as it provides information on how we are doing against our goals. We don't get on the scale every morning because it's fun to see what we weigh. We get on the scale every morning to see how close we are to our goal of losing 20 pounds before our 30th high school reunion. Feedback should not be disconnected from goals. It is goals and progress against goals that motivate people, not feedback. This may seem like a subtle point, but it is frequently the root cause of how and why feedback fails to support high performance. I have participated in a lot of feedback training over the years, and I can't recall a single program that focused on providing feedback in the context of goals. Feedback training is mostly about delivery, and especially delivery of negative feedback. When a supervisor meets with an employee to discuss their work, they should focus on the employee's goals, what's getting in the way of progress, or celebrating the progress being made and the factors that are facilitating it. PM 2.0 positions feedback in the context of goals.

It's Not about Feedback, It's About Progress

Most of us probably hear leaders and HR professionals say, "Employees want feedback…they want to know where they stand." As I said in Chapter 7, this reflects a common misunderstanding of why feedback is important and how it works. Employees don't want feedback, they want to make progress and feedback gives them information on progress. It is progress that motivates not feedback.

Researchers Hanna Klug and Gunter Maier from Bielefeld University in Germany reviewed a number of studies investigating the relationship between goals and the pursuit of goals, and on the measures of how happy people are (something researchers call "subjective well-being"). They found people who achieve their goals are happier than people who don't (not a big surprise). Interestingly, they also found that progress toward their goals was more important than actually achieving goals in driving happiness. The relationship between goal progress and happiness is stronger than the relationship between goal achievement and happiness. It is progress that really matters for happiness. On the face of it this makes sense. People can experience a letdown after they achieve their goals before they set their sights on something new. Research by psychologist Gabrielle Oettingen reinforces this point. Her research suggests that thinking about goal achievement can actually lower your motivation. In a sense, thinking about goal achievement mentally transports you to the point where you have achieved your goal and can decrease your energy levels as if you've already achieved it.[8]

Other researchers have also identified progress as a key contributor to happiness, engagement, and performance. Researchers who study affect in organizations (e.g., emotions, mood) find that people's emotional responses to events that happen to them (for example positive or negative affect) are determined by how they see these events affecting their progress toward their desired goals. Goal progress leads to a positive affect and goal blockages lead to a negative affect.[9] This is important because affect drives success. People who display more frequent positive affect are more successful in work and in life—happier people tend to be more successful.[10] I know what you're thinking. Doesn't the causal arrow go the other way? Doesn't success (and all the trappings that come with it) make people happier? Research by Sonja Lyubomirsky and her colleagues show that happiness is associated with and precedes many successful outcomes. Many researchers see this as a kind of virtuous cycle where progress against our goals makes us happier and more engaged, and these positive emotions then in turn give us the energy to work harder and take on more goals all leading to success in both work and life.[11]

A focus on progress is the whole premise behind Teresa Amabile's research described in her book *The Progress Principle*.[12] She and her colleagues studied employees working in 26 different project teams in seven different organizations over a period of several months. She was interested in the psychological experiences of employees as they went about their daily work life, something she called "inner work life." Her hypothesis was that inner work life had a lot to do with the success people experienced in organizations. Employees completed diaries describing how they felt on a day-to-day basis and made ratings on how engaged they were each day. She asked them to describe their daily work activities and the emotions, perceptions, and motivations associated with these activities. When she compared employees' best and worst days, she found that when employees described their best days they tended to talk about progress they had made, and when they described their worst days they tended to describe the setbacks they experienced. She discovered the experience of progress was an important element of inner work life. She found other inner work life triggers that also contributed to best days and worst days. On their best days, people received the support, help, and encouragement they needed from others (which she called catalysts and nourishers). In contrast, on their worst days not only didn't people get the support they needed, but they frequently experienced events that actively hindered, blocked, or undermined their work (she called these inhibitors and toxins).

Like other researchers she found that simply making progress—even if it was small—affected all aspects of inner work life. When people made progress they reported more positive emotions, were motivated by the work itself, and saw the work and their teams in a more favorable light. The last point she made in her research, which reinforces a key message from Chapter 7, was these effects were more pronounced when employees were working on something meaningful. Employees were most engaged when they "made progress in meaningful work." Progress and meaning are a powerful combination. Unfortunately, her research also showed that progress was not on the radar screen of most managers in thinking about what motivated employees. Amabile and her team asked managers to rank the importance of five different factors that drove motivation, one of which was making progress on the work they were doing. Only 5% of managers ranked that factor number one and most ranked it last.

This research adds an important element to the emerging picture of PM 2.0: PM 2.0 emphasizes progress not feedback and feedback is in the service of progress. Supervisors don't just need to provide feedback, they also need to provide the information, resources, help, and encouragement that employees need. When we combine a focus on progress with a focus

ls, purpose, and meaning from Chapter 7 we have a powerful motivational combination. Amabile's tagline is an apt characterization of PM 2.0
to this point: The key to motivating high performance is ensuring employees make progress in meaningful work.

Feedback Must Be About the Work

I want to revisit the meta-analysis study done by Avi Kluger and Angelo DeNisi to illustrate another problem with feedback. Their study is one
of the best reviews available on the impact of feedback on performance.
They assembled more than 3,000 studies and narrowed their review down
to 131 high-quality studies where solid conclusions could be drawn (this
gives you an indication of how much poor research is out there potentially
misinforming leaders and HR professionals). As I mentioned earlier, it was
surprising to find that in one-third of these studies, feedback actually made
things worse. When they took a deeper look at the studies to understand
why they found it had a lot to do with the focus of the feedback.

Kluger and DiNisi described a hierarchy of feedback loops. The loops
at the top were more fundamental and related to how people looked at
themselves, their personal identity, and their overall goals. The loops at
the bottom were more tactical and related to the tasks and work people
were doing at the moment. They found when feedback was focused at the
bottom of this hierarchy, feedback was more effective; when it was focused
higher in this hierarchy it was less effective. This was especially true when
the feedback was negative, critical, or discouraging. When feedback gets
personal (focused higher in the hierarchy) employees stop thinking about
the work and start thinking about themselves, how they relate to the work,
and how the goals of the work relate to their own goals. We know from
Chapter 7 that self-efficacy is essential for goals to lead to higher performance. Feedback that is more personal in nature, especially if it is critical,
can threaten a person's self-esteem and damage self-efficacy, which will severely limit its effectiveness for improving performance.

Recent neuroscience research may provide clues as to why this happens.
People's brains respond to various stimuli from the environment, including
feedback. There are two primary regions of the brain that are of interest:
the prefrontal cortex and the limbic system. The prefrontal cortex is evolutionarily more recent and represents the thinking and reasoning centers of
the brain. This region operates mostly at the conscious level as you attempt
to reason and think through issues. The limbic system is evolutionarily more
distant and tracks your emotional relationships to thoughts, objects, people, and events. The limbic system very often operates unconsciously. The

brain classifies the world around us into two categories: things that might hurt us and things that might help us. As a result, everything we do is based on the idea of minimizing danger or maximizing reward. Our limbic system tells us to move toward the rewards and move away from threats. When the limbic system is engaged the prefrontal cortex is disengaged. When we are threatened (think of a bear chasing you in the woods) our limbic system kicks in immediately and we take action unconsciously without having to consciously think and reason through what we are seeing and feeling. Our ability to think, reason, and analyze is disabled. Our view is narrowed and we use fewer cognitive resources.

Research reviewed by David Rock and others suggest that when people receive feedback the brain perceives it as a threat.[13] This could help explain how and why feedback can hurt performance. Feedback that is more personal or critical is more likely to be perceived as a threat. Improving performance requires thinking and reasoning. If the brain believes it is responding to a threat, these centers of the brain have been disabled and people may not learn what they need in order to improve. This may also help explain why feedback that is delivered by less personal channels (e.g., email, audio, and video) is more likely to improve performance and achievement since it mitigates the personal impact and may be less likely to activate the threat centers of the brain. This research also suggests many of the newer social media and crowdsourced feedback applications may be useful since they are less personally charged. The key to PM 2.0 is to focus feedback on the work and the task at hand, not make it seem personal.

Positive Is Better Than Negative

I'm sure many of you in management roles have heard of the "feedback sandwich." This is a popular guideline for giving feedback. It says that if you want to deliver negative feedback you should set it up with some initial positive feedback and then follow it up with more positive feedback; so the sequence goes +/−/+. This guideline says a lot about how we see feedback: It is negative. Using a surgical metaphor, positive feedback serves as both the "anesthesia" and the "dressing," preparing a patient for the scalpel and then applying the salve to make the patient feel better after the cut. This rule represents the essence of PM 1.0 thinking; we think of feedback as primarily negative, catching people doing something wrong and correcting them. If you don't believe this do a quick Google search on feedback and look at the lists of tips for giving and receiving feedback. Most of them assume you are dropping a bomb on someone (prepare yourself, set the stage, objectively state the behavior, communicate the significance of the situation, talk about possible solutions). This is my experience having participated in countless feedback and coaching programs and having sat in on numerous discussions about problems with PM. These programs would have you believe the biggest problem we face in PM is that negative feedback doesn't get delivered and supervisors are too weak and soft to deliver them. Line managers and HR professionals invariably point to positively skewed performance distributions to support this point.

Like many areas of PM, the feedback sandwich and our obsession with the need for negative feedback isn't supported by scientific evidence. Researcher Emily Heapy from the University of Michigan and her colleague Marcel Losada looked at the impact of positive and negative feedback on the performance of leadership teams. They studied 60 strategic business unit leadership teams from a large information processing company. They sat with these teams and coded the verbal communication among team members along three dimensions: positivity/negativity, inquiry/advocacy, and other/self. They hypothesized that positivity and negativity interact to create different "emotional spaces" for individuals, reflected by the ratio of positive to negative (P/N) comments. They hypothesized that high ratios (more positive feedback than negative feedback, also called a "positive feedback offset") created expansive emotional spaces that opened possibilities for action, while low ratios (more negative feedback than positive feedback) created restrictive emotional spaces that closed possibilities for action.

They measured the performance of these teams using financial performance, customer satisfaction ratings, and 360-degree feedback ratings among team members. Using these performance measures they grouped the teams into high, medium, and low performance groups. Interestingly, of the three dimensions they investigated they found that the P/N feedback ratio was the strongest differentiator between high and low performing teams. In contrast to the feedback sandwich, the average P/N ratio for high-performance teams was 5.6 (nearly six positive comments for every one negative comment). The P/N ratio for medium-performance teams was 1.9 (nearly two positive comments for every one negative comment) and .36 for low-performance teams (almost three negative comments for every positive comment).[14] Heapy characterized the interactions of the teams this way:

> High performance teams were characterized by an atmosphere of buoyancy that lasted during the whole meeting. By showing appreciation and encouragement to other members in the team, they created emotional spaces that were expansive and opened possibilities for action and creativity. They were also fun to watch and there was rarely a dull moment during their meetings. In addition, they accomplished their tasks with ease and grace. In stark

contrast, low performance teams struggled with their tasks, operated in very restrictive emotional spaces created by lack of mutual support and enthusiasm, often in an atmosphere charged with distrust and cynicism.

Clearly a little negativity goes a long way. So it seems the rule for successful feedback should look more like (++++++/−) than (+/−/+). Not only do these findings contradict the feedback sandwich rule, they also seem to defy the conventional wisdom of seasoned line managers and HR practitioners. While I can't be definitive about what conventional wisdom is, it probably doesn't say we should be overly positive with employees. If anything, conventional wisdom probably favors a more critical approach to dealing with employees: "iron sharpens iron," "no pressure, no diamonds," "hold their feet to the fire." The archetype conjured up for conventional wisdom in feedback is more like Donald Trump or Simon Cowell, than Mr. Rogers.

But these results should not come as a surprise. There is ample research that suggests being positive is better than being negative. For example, researchers Barbara Fredrickson and Marcial Losada find that a higher ratio of positivity to negativity is more typical of the human experience in general and is associated with optimal mental health and human functioning.[15] Research from positive psychology reaches similar conclusions showing positive interventions increase satisfaction, fulfillment, motivation, well-being, and performance, and can provide a reservoir of energy to draw on under more difficult circumstances.[16] Research on marriages from counseling psychology also supports a positive offset for feedback, and marriage isn't a bad metaphor for the relationship between an employee and a workgroup or organization. Psychologist and marriage guru Jon Gottman has done extensive research on marriages and what explains their success or failure. His research puts the magic ratio of positive to negative interactions at five to one. Marriages that hit this ratio are more successful over the long term, and those that don't are more likely to end in divorce.[17]

The impact of positive or negative feedback can also depend on the goal. Is your goal to achieve something good or to prevent something bad from happening? Research by psychologists Dina Van-Dijk and Avi Kluger showed that negative feedback is more effective where prevention is the goal (e.g., safety, compliance) and in cases where accuracy and adherence to rules, policies, and procedures are important. When the goal is to avoid punishment negative feedback increases motivation and performance, while positive feedback can actually hurt performance. This may explain the success of radar speed signs; they mostly provide negative feedback preventing us from becoming lighter in our wallets. In contrast, for more traditional tasks and goals where individuals hope to achieve something good and are looking for rewards, positive feedback helps motivation and performance and negative feedback hurts motivation and performance.[18]

Other researchers like Richard Boyatzis and Daniel Goleman are combining research from positive psychology, leadership, and neuroscience to study not just the impact of positive and negative feedback on productivity and well-being, but the impact of positive and negative leaders.[19] Their research shows that more positive leaders (he calls them "resonant") activate areas of the brain associated with being open to new ideas and other people, and more negative leaders (he calls them "dissonant") deactivate these areas and activate areas associated with narrowed attention, decreased compassion, and negative emotion.[20] What is fascinating about this research is these effects happen very quickly and occur at the emotional level first, mostly below the level of conscious awareness. This means employees begin to react emotionally to the actions of their positive or negative leader before they have had an opportunity to think through and understand the implications or impact of those actions. [21]

The benefit of this positive feedback offset can also be explained by research on the potency of negative versus positive feedback. Responses to negative feedback, experiences, and emotions are far stronger than their positive counterparts. We know intuitively that leaders who approach employees critically ignite stronger neural responses from them, and as we discussed previously activate areas of the brain that impair thinking and perceiving, and inhibit learning.[22] Research by Roy Baumeister and his colleagues confirmed this asymmetry across many different events: life events, relationship outcomes, social network patterns, interpersonal interactions (including feedback), and learning processes. In nearly every case, Baumeister's research showed bad events were more potent than good events.[23] Teresa Amabile reached similar conclusions in her research. She found negative experiences (setbacks) were two to three times more potent than positive experiences in affecting engagement and the quality of inner work life.[24] The loss-aversion bias we discussed in Chapter 3 also reinforces this point: the pain of losing is more than twice the pleasure of winning.

I realize this discussion about positive feedback can feel very idealistic—almost "utopian"—especially to "old-school" business leaders who were taught to "kick ass and take names." I don't mean to imply that feedback should never be negative. The important point of this discussion is the evidence favors a more positive, compassionate, and encouraging approach for improving well-being, satisfaction, and performance, and that a predominantly negative approach to feedback will likely have costs and unintended consequences. Negative feedback should be used sparingly. It should be used when the circumstances (and consequences) are more serious or urgent and/or when prevention is the goal.

The last point I will make on this topic is that feedback isn't necessarily something you do to someone else or that someone else does to you. People get their own feedback. Most people know how their work is going or can get there very quickly with a few good questions and a little coaching. The best advice I received with respect to giving feedback was "turn the volume up just loud enough for them to hear it." If they already know the meeting with the customer went badly, you don't need to tell them again. You may be irritated that you lost a good customer, but unloading on your employee again is meeting your own needs not the needs of your employee. If they know it already no need to say it again. Focus on why it went badly and how to improve the next time.

Who Is Doing It Differently?

There are several companies moving to a more continuous model of PM, focusing on employee-supervisor conversations, feedback, and coaching instead of discrete PM events. Many of these companies are moving in this direction in conjunction with a move away from performance ratings.

Gap, Inc.: Twelve Performance Conversations

Gap moved from a traditional PM process focused on ratings and annual reviews to a process with more regular, ongoing conversations.[25] Supervisor feedback and coaching were critical elements to their process. They had already made a significant investment in educating their leaders about Carol Dweck's research on fixed versus growth mindset, so providing feedback and coaching from a growth mindset became an important part of their approach.[26] Their process included 12 performance conversations throughout the year, initiated primarily by employees as they needed input, advice, and help with their work. They also trained supervisors and created guides to help supervisors facilitate these conversations with employees.

Cargill: Everyday Performance Management

Cargill made a fundamental shift in their thinking about PM from what they describe as an over-engineered formal system with cyclical, intermittent activities to an ongoing process with a set of day-to-day behaviors to be developed and maximized (e.g., ongoing communication, feedback and coaching, ongoing development). At Cargill they called this an "everyday PM mindset," defined by the several principles consistent with PM 2.0.

- Effective PM is an ongoing process not an annual meeting and a form to fill out.
- Day-to-day activities and practices predict PM quality rather than forms and ratings.
- Employee-manager relationships are at the heart of effective PM.
- PM needs to be flexible to address different business needs.

To reinforce this new mindset, they focused PM around the daily work not as a separate process marked as semiannual or annual events and requirements. Accordingly, their new approach emphasized employees and supervisors having ongoing, effective conversations, and de-emphasized and simplified administrative requirements. Ongoing employee-manager discussions was the mechanism to define and align expectations, build trust, seek and provide feedback and coaching, and develop and engage employees. They developed innovative PM training to help employees and supervisors learn and practice the new behaviors, and packaged the training in an innovative, automated tool. While it is still early, this everyday PM approach has shown promising results in improving the quality and frequency of feedback and the perceptions of the value of the PM process.[27]

Other companies are making similar moves. Medtronic abandoned performance ratings in 2011 and moved to a system providing more real-time feedback, coaching, and development for employees. Under their old system, employees spent far too much time making their self-appraisals stand out by documenting everything they did. In their new process, managers become coaches who support employees in achieving their objectives and pursing their individual career goals and development. Performance coaching sessions were no longer about managers giving a rating on past behaviors; they were about improving on future behaviors and results. Motorola also moved away from traditional PM ratings in 2012 toward a more continuous feedback model. They made the change because supervisors and employees were too focused on the year-end rating and not focused enough on giving people helpful feedback, especially to millennials who wanted more feedback.

Adobe has made similar changes that focus heavily on feedback, coaching, and development discussions. They have formal quarterly reviews but expect informal "check-ins" during the year and they provide flexibility as to how frequently employees and supervisors need to check in. Netflix also eliminated performance reviews several years ago and instead expects

supervisors to have conversations about performance as an orga
their work. They also instituted informal 360-degree feedback a
employees should stop, start, and continue. Finally, Atlassian a
performance reviews and evaluations in 2010. They replaced PM with continuous feedback and coaching and a focus on strengths. Employees and
supervisors have weekly one-on-one conversations, and once a month they
focus on different coaching topics. They created conversation guides and
training for supervisors to help them with these monthly conversations.[28]

PM 2.0: New Paradigms and New Practices

Just like with goals, PM 2.0 represents a paradigm shift in the way organizations think about feedback. PM 1.0 relies on monitoring and surveillance, and catching people doing something wrong. It also relies on keeping score during the year in order to evaluate performance and deliver
rewards and other consequences. PM 2.0 focuses on progress, connecting
with employees, and giving them what they need to make progress on their
most important objectives. It focuses less on feedback and more on support
by providing whatever is necessary to ensure goals are achieved. Table 8.1
shows the shift in paradigms from PM 1.0 to PM 2.0.

TABLE 8.1 The Paradigm Shift From PM 1.0 to PM 2.0	
From PM 1.0 . . .	**. . . to PM 2.0**
• Monitoring and surveillance is necessary to hold employees accountable and ensure they are fulfilling the terms of the contract	• Feedback is focused on helping employees achieve their goals
• Keeping score is important and employees need to know the score and where they stand	• Feedback is in the service of progress, helping employees make progress against their goals
• Feedback is primarily negative, correcting employees when they get off track	• Feedback is primarily positive and work/ task-related; negative feedback is used sparingly

Key Messages

- While feedback can be powerful for changing behavior, it doesn't always improve performance.
- Feedback is important because it tells employees about the progress they are making against their goals. Feedback should not be disconnected from goals.
- Feedback should be focused on the day-to-day work employees are doing.
- Feedback is not enough. Employees are motivated by progress against their goals.
- Positive feedback is more powerful in motivating high performance than negative feedback.

$$9$$

We Versus Me

No man is an island.

—John Donne

*To be nobody but yourself in a world which is doing its best, night and day,
to make you everybody else, means to fight the hardest battle that any
human being can fight, and never stop fighting.*

—e. e. Cummings[1]

Look at the illustration in Figure 9.1. What do you see? What would you say is happening?

Researchers Michael Morris from Stanford University and Kaiping Peng from the University of Michigan did a series of studies with high school students showing them pictures and videos like this, asking them similar questions. They were studying how people's theories affected their judgments and attributions about behavior. It turned out what students said about Figure 9.1 depended a lot on the country where they lived. Students from the United States said the lone fish to the right was leading the others.

Next Generation Performance Management, pages 127–146
Copyright © 2017 by Information Age Publishing
127

Figure 9.1   A group of fish with one separated from the rest.

Students from China said the lone fish to the right was being expelled from the group and chased away.[2]

Stanford University researchers Heejung Kim and Hazel Rose Markus were interested in a similar question. They asked students to complete a short questionnaire and offered them a gift of a pen in exchange for their participation. Students got to choose from five pens that were two different colors. In all conditions one color was less common, representing a minority of the pens available to the student, and the other color was more common, representing the majority of the pens. Which color did the students choose? Again the answer depended on the country in which the students lived. Students from the United States or Europe overwhelmingly chose a pen that was the more unique color. Students from Asia chose the pen that was the more common color.[3]

Studies like these illustrate something very important about our behavior, our judgments, and even our worldview: they are heavily influenced by cultural context. People from different cultures tend to view the cause of behavior differently, something researchers call "agency." Western cultures like the United States are very individualistic, seeing individuals themselves as the causal agent with their behaviors based on their own thoughts, feelings, and actions.[4] Asian cultures on the other hand tend to be more interdependent and collectivistic, seeing individual actions as heavily influenced by others and contextual or situational factors and in many cases even directed by the larger group itself.

This difference even affects how individuals view themselves. Americans tend to see the self as distinct from the group and preservation of individual integrity as essential to the self. Americans want to "stand out." In the words of e. e. Cummings, "to be nobody but yourself in a world which is doing its best, night and day, to make you everybody else." In the West "the squeaky wheel gets the grease." In contrast, Asians and people from more collectivistic cultures view the self as much more interconnected to the larger collective. People from these cultures recognize the self is less distinct from the collective, that their own actions are determined by and contingent on the thoughts, feelings, and actions of others. For these individuals conformity with the group may be seen as personally rewarding as well as socially sanctioned. Asians want to "fit in." In the East, "the nail that sticks out gets pounded down."[5]

These studies require us to step back and take a critical look at our HR practices, especially performance management (PM). Our practices are a projection of the culture we come from and of the worldviews of the leaders running our organizations. Our PM practices are bound up in our worldview, and our worldview affects how we think about topics like motivation and control. And, although we are not conscious of it, this research shows us our own worldview has no greater claim to the truth than other worldviews.

Organizations Are Meritocracies

In the context of this discussion it should come as no surprise to you that PM 1.0 is a western creation. Performance is an individual sport, organizations are meritocracies, and talented individuals are rewarded and celebrated. The individual employee takes center stage in PM 1.0, individuals set objectives, individuals receive feedback, individual performance is evaluated, and individuals are differentially rewarded. Individual success is celebrated, individual failure is punished, and organizational success is determined by the success of talented individuals. In a meritocracy we celebrate the initiative of the lone fish in Figure 9.1; we give that fish the highest rating and the biggest rewards, and that fish is first in line for promotion. With PM 1.0 the message to employees is clear: Do your best to stand out and to separate yourself from your fellow employees. The message to leaders is clear as well: Do all you can to differentiate, celebrate, recognize, and reward those who stand out because they hold the key to your success.

Benchmarking statistics reinforce this individualistic picture of current PM practices.[6]

■ 95% of organizations set individual objectives while only 41% set team-based objectives.

- ▪ 82% of companies link individual compensation decisions to performance ratings, while few companies connect rewards to team or organizational performance (only 20% use team-based incentives, 32% link pay increases to business unit performance, and 53% link rewards to corporate performance).

Meritocracy like any ideology reflects our most closely held beliefs and values. It acts as the filter through which we see everything and everybody. It is so close to us and so deep in the background of our thinking we usually aren't aware it is operating. When we design HR practices meritocracy is a given; we unconsciously design it in.

Meritocracy wasn't originally something to be emulated. The idea of meritocracy comes from British Sociologist Michael Young's 1958 novel *The Rise of the Meritocracy*.[7] This book is actually a satirical essay that describes a dystopian society in a future United Kingdom in which intelligence and merit have become the central tenet of society replacing previous divisions of aristocracy and social class. The result is a society stratified between a merited, elite, power-holding class and a disenfranchised underclass of the "less-merited." The irony of Young's story is that a society based on merit turns out to be more elitist, classist, and divisive than the structure it replaced. It is interesting that none of the negative connotations Young intended carried forward to the popular view of meritocracy today.

As I said in Chapter 3, our worldview has a lot to do with the problems of PM and with our inability to solve them in any lasting way. I think Michael Young had it right; I think meritocracy (and meritocratic thinking) is why PM 1.0 fails us today. This ideology and the principles represented in it are increasingly out of step with the nature of organizations and employees today.

Meritocracy Is Outdated

Meritocracy has its roots mostly in the experiences of the early days of the United States and in the historical experience of the United States, as a nation of immigrants. It reflects a number of influences (historical, cultural, economic, religious, and political) embodied in ideals like the American dream, rugged individualism, the Protestant work ethic, and the self-made man. For example, meritocracy embodies both the political and economic blueprints foundational to the United States. The political blueprint emphasizes the central role of individual rights and freedom, especially religious and political rights, all of which are reflected in the Declaration of Independence. The economic blueprint came directly from Adam Smith's *An Inquiry into the Nature and Wealth of Nations* published in 1776.[8] This was quickly adopted as the informal bible of American free-market capitalism. It emphasized rational self-interest, individual competition, private ownership, and laissez-faire principles.

All of these influences put a premium on individualism and view individual ability and hard work as the recipe for success. I hope you are having flashbacks to Chapter 3. The theories and paradigms I discussed in that chapter reflect these same influences; they put the individual at the center and focus on financial rewards as a central motivating force.

The problem with this thinking is the circumstances that gave rise to meritocracy are very different than circumstances today. Organizations are different, jobs are different, and people are different. In an agrarian and artisan economy, Adam Smith's principles made sense. In an industrial economy Edward Thorndike and Fredrick Taylor's principles made sense. These principles don't fit the realities in which today's organizations find themselves. This is why, scientific evidence reviewed in this book doesn't support them very well. The problems organizations face today are infinitely more complex and we cannot simply ride on the backs of a few smart individuals who are handsomely rewarded to solve them.

The Case Against Individuals (and for Teams)

Work Is Increasingly Being Done in Teams

The idea of a meritocracy, where you give credit and reward to the few to the exclusion of the many, is increasingly out of step with the way work is being done and the way value is created in organizations today. The use of teams in organizations has increased dramatically in the past two decades. The vast majority of organizations today report they use teams to get work done, and the ability to work with others and collaborate is a critical survival skill for much of today's workforce.[9] Work in today's organizations is also increasingly knowledge-based, and this knowledge is being produced by narrow, splintered subfields that require more cross-disciplinary collaboration both inside and outside of the company. The world is becoming so complex that organizations can't know and do everything on their own any longer.

Despite this trend, organizations stubbornly cling to meritocracy and individualism, and employ PM 1.0 practices that glorify the contributions of talented individuals. This culture of "star worship" began with the publication of McKinsey and Company's now famous report *The War for Talent* and it accelerated with the introduction of the concept of "A players" by Bradford Smart in his book *Topgrading*.[10] This culture has been carried to new heights by today's tech industry. Facebook's Mark Zuckerberg famously said in a *New York Times* interview that, "Someone who is exceptional in their role is not just a little better than someone who is pretty good, they are 100 times better."[11] Marc Andreessen the cofounder of Netscape made similar claims saying, "Five great programmers can completely outperform 1,000 mediocre programmers."[12] These statements help explain the "hero worship" and the outrageous salaries and bonuses paid by tech companies.

Individual Talent Is Overrated

Taken literally, the statements by Zuckerberg and Andreessen suggest that stars are at least 100 times better than the average employee and maybe 200 times better. While these statements make interesting reading, most experts and most scientific evidence would dispute them.[13] The overzealous worship of individual talent has come to be known as the "talent myth" and many writers and researchers have been critical of its assumptions. Writers Jeffrey Pfeffer and Robert Sutton took aim at the talent myth in their classic evidence-based management book *Hard Facts, Dangerous Half-Truths, and Total Nonsense*.[14] They highlight a number of problems with the talent myth, attacking the assumptions on which it is based using rigorous scientific research: Talent is hard to identify and spot in advance, talent isn't fixed and immutable, and good systems are more important than good people.

Popular writer Malcom Gladwell also took on the talent myth in a *New York Times* article where he profiled the poster child of star worship: Enron.[15] Enron put superstars at the center of its organization and employed many classic PM 1.0 practices like ruthless evaluations and rankings and extreme differentiation of rewards. By now most of you know their story didn't end well. Bill Taylor recently took on the talent myth in the tech world in a two-part essay in *Harvard Business Review*. "*Great People Are Overrated*."[16] In making their case against the talent myth, Taylor and other writers referenced the work of management researcher Boris Groysberg that illustrated many of the problems with individualism and meritocratic thinking. Groysberg and his colleagues looked at the performance of superstar stock analysts from 1988 through 1996. They found that when stars left their current company to join a new company, their performance declined. Nearly half of the stars did worse in the year after they left their current company and performance fell overall by an average of 20%. Groysberg found that hiring stars even had negative effects on the performance of the firms that hired them: their valuations and stock prices declined after hiring stars.[17]

One of the key takeaways from Grosberg's study is that the performance of stars and the firms that employed them declined because performance was a function of more than individual talent. The success of any company (and any company's strategy) requires that a company possess a number of capabilities: bundles of people, processes, and technology. Star worship implies the people part of this recipe is far more important than the other parts. Groysberg's research suggests that success has as much (or more) to do with other organizational factors (e.g., processes and technology) in addition to the availability of resources, the quality of leadership and the quality of the team working with the star.

Worship Teams Instead of Individuals

If you are intent on worshiping something, the science says you are better off worshiping teams than you are smart individuals.[18] While there is certainly research that argues for caution when relying on groups (e.g., groupthink, the Abilene paradox, social loafing, free riding), the overwhelming sentiment based on decades of research is that groups tend to outperform individuals especially doing what many people do every day in organizations, which is deal with complex tasks without a right answer where quality of the solution is important.[19] Despite the fact that organizations are relying more on teams and collaboration, and despite evidence supporting the effectiveness of teams, most organizations continue to employ PM practices that manage, evaluate, and reward individuals.

Even an organization as progressive as Google, which has received a lot of press for their research studying what makes teams effective at Google, still seems to be mired in PM 1.0 thinking.[20] I recently attended a conference where representatives from Google were discussing their research. I asked them about star worship, and the aforementioned statements made by Zuckerberg and Andreessen. I wanted to know how they felt about the tech industry's worship of individual talent in light of their professed commitment to teams. They said they believed in individual creativity and genius, but acknowledged it took teams to bring innovation to market. In an effort to "reassure me" however, they added they still believed in the importance of pay-for-performance (P4P) and meritocracy, evaluating individuals and differentiating rewards, but completely missing my point. Evidently they wanted to reassure me they had not become socialists at Google. I told them this did not reassure me.[21] Organizational success is a team game at Google, but motivation and rewards is apparently still an individual game. I single out Google not to be critical of them, but to illustrate how deep and pervasive the ideology of meritocracy is that even one of the most progressive and admired organizations on the planet, which has made a substantial investment in teams, cannot or will not see past it. Even Google sees the lone fish in Figure 9.1 as leading the others. So it is not at all clear that building a PM system in the image of meritocracy focused on evaluating, differentiating, and rewarding individuals is effective. The science doesn't support it, and an individualistic view of motivation and control is insufficient to deal with the complexity faced by most organizations today. We need a different ideology and different paradigms to fit the complexity and collaborative nature of work in today's organizations, and we need look no further than today's news headlines to find it.

People Are Social

Friday, November 13, 2015, gunmen and suicide bombers killed 130 people and injured hundreds in attacks at a stadium, a concert hall, and restaurants and bars in Paris. The following day the Islamic State claimed responsibility for the attack. On June 12, 2016, a 29-year-old security guard killed 49 people and wounded 53 others in an attack inside Pulse, a gay nightclub in Orlando, Florida. In a 911 call shortly after the shooting, the shooter pledged allegiance to the Islamic State, protesting American-led interventions in Iraq and Syria. In explaining why people commit such acts, terrorist expert and anthropologist Scott Atran from the University of Michigan reflects on a call he received from a medical school in Khartoum where a professor told him that her best students had just left the school to found a medical unit for the Islamic State. The professor was dumbfounded and the families of the students were at a complete loss to explain their decisions. Why would very bright students from well-to-do families with promising careers ahead of them seemingly throw it all away to support a terrorist organization that makes a living killing people?[22]

It turns out that people who commit terrorist acts aren't sick or mentally ill, and in the case of Islamic terrorists most of them aren't even religious fanatics. Atran maintains that most foreign volunteers and supporters are fairly normal in terms of psychological attributes like empathy, compassion, idealism, and wanting mostly to help rather than hurt other people. More important than their background or their psychological state is the fact that these people are socially motivated. They are drawn to like-minded people and are keen to adopt their causes. Three-quarters of those who become foreign fighters travel in a group, often with people they know such as friends and family.[23] These young people are looking for something to believe in and something to belong to and these groups give it to them. Terrorist organizations and other organizations that do harm aren't the only ones who understand the pull of a compelling purpose along with a group of committed believers. Even "legitimate" organizations get people to do things "normal" people don't do. People involved in Greenpeace, for example, routinely drive small boats into the path of large commercial fishing vessels putting their lives and the lives of others at risk. What makes people do these things? In short, other people do.

People Need to Belong

The need to form and maintain social bonds—to belong— is among the most powerful of human motives.[24] Our thoughts, feelings, and behaviors are profoundly influenced by our need to maintain quality relationships and to avoid rejection by others. In fact, the relationships and commonalities we have with others are a big part of the way we define ourselves (e.g., I am a psychologist, I am a Hoosier). The lessons we learn from terrorist and other groups is these relationships can exert a tremendous force on us. They motivate us to act in ways that further the aims of these groups.

When Dan Pink wrote about motivation in his best-selling book *Drive*, he emphasized the importance of purpose, autonomy, and mastery citing the research done by psychologist Edward Deci. Recall I discussed Deci's research in Chapter 6. According to Deci, human beings have inherent growth tendencies and psychological needs for competence (Pink called this mastery), autonomy, and relatedness, and the fulfillment of these needs is critical for optimal health, well-being, and growth.[25] Pink talked about competence and autonomy but he didn't talk about relatedness. Relatedness is the forgotten need in much of contemporary talk about motivation, and the scientific evidence shows this need is important for optimal functioning in many different domains. People with stronger social ties tend to be healthier and happier; they also tend to work harder and will be more productive. Conversely, people who are socially isolated experience more anxiety, jealousy, depression, stress, mental illness, and criminal tendencies. Feeling lonely predicts early death as much as major health risk behaviors like smoking.[26] Threats to belonging have similar effects. For example, people who are told they will spend their lives alone perform worse on intellectual tests.[27] Research on ostracism has shown that threats to belonging cause people to experience hurt feelings, sadness, anxiety, loneliness, and shame, and they exhibit lower levels of motivation and effort.[28] These same effects happen at work. People who are more socially isolated at work are less satisfied, more likely to quit, and have poorer job performance and overall well-being.[29]

What is even more surprising is these same kinds of positive and negative effects are observed even for relationships that are more superficial. Returning to the terrorist example, we have all heard the stories of people committing these acts only to discover they were radicalized on the Internet without ever setting foot in the Middle East or meeting a real terrorist face-to-face. Research shows people are influenced by the goals and motivations of others, even unfamiliar others relatively automatically as a consequence of seemingly innocuous things (e.g., they share the same birthday, have the same taste in bands, or their last names begin with the same letter). Researchers call this "mere belonging." Small commonalities with others can have dramatic effects on motivation and performance.[30] An example of the power of mere belonging comes from research in education focused on closing the achievement gap between minority and White students. In one study by Harvard University researcher Hunter Gelbach and his colleagues, the researchers asked students and teachers to complete a "get-to-know-you" questionnaire asking about learning preferences, personal characteristics, and values. They then shared this information with students and teachers, illustrating areas of commonality. Black and Latino students who found they had things in common with their teacher improved their performance in the class by nearly half a letter grade. This simple intervention closed the achievement gap between the Black and Latino students and the White students by 60%.[31]

So our connections with others at work and in our personal lives can be very powerful motivators. Employees will work hard to support the goals of their team and to maintain the respect and support of their teammates. We don't do enough within our organizations to facilitate connections between people and what's worse, HR practices like those embodied in PM 1.0 have exactly the opposite effects: alienating employees and turning them against one another. This puts socially motivated employees in a terrible bind. PM 2.0 solves this problem by focusing more energy on teams and less on individuals, unleashing the power of teams to motivate, control, and achieve.

Applying PM 2.0 to Teams

Teams Need Goals Too

PM 2.0 emphasizes direction for teams as well as for individuals. Team objectives are important because employees need to feel their work makes a contribution to something bigger than themselves. Team goals don't just make employees feel good, teams with clear goals are also more effective. The research support for the benefits of team goals is very strong, and the recipe is much the same as it is for individuals; specific, difficult team goals have a positive impact on team performance particularly when members have a say in them.[32] Setting goals for teams has the same positive benefits regardless of the complexity of the work and the level of interdependence of the work. So this practice can be used with all types of teams. Despite this research, benchmarking statistics from Chapter 7 show that only 41% of organizations set team-based objectives.

When you give a group of people something meaningful to accomplish together, it changes how they behave and interact. It creates "motivational magic." Team members bring more enthusiasm to the work and they communicate better, cooperate more, and work harder. They develop a shared vision of their work and they become more cohesive and confident, something researchers call "potency." The research on potency is clear, teams feel more potent when they have clear goals and clear processes to accomplish them, and teams that feel more potent are more effective.[33]

Frame Individual Goals in the Context of Team Goals

As organizations rely more on teams, it will be common for employees to have both personal goals and team goals. For example, sales people may have individual sales goals and departmental goals, and employees working on cross-functional product teams may have functional goals and product team goals. Researchers Ad Kleingeld, Heleen van Mierlo, and Lidia Arends from the Netherlands saw the potential for confusion, conflict, and lack of coordination inherent in this situation. They distinguished between two different types of individual goals: egocentric, which focused employees on their own individual work, and group-centered, which focused employees on how their individual work contributes to achieving group goals. Their research showed that when individuals had egocentric goals they developed strategies that were competitive with other individuals in the group and the performance of the group suffered. When individuals had group-centric goals they developed strategies that were more cooperative, which lead to better performance for the group.

Research from social interdependence theory reaches similar conclusions. Collaborative goal structures lead to many more positive outcomes for teams than competitive goal structures. Employees work harder, they have more positive relationships, they support one another better, and they are more productive.[34] Research on ostracism also shows that the wrong goal structures for teams can have damaging effects on workplace relationships and team dynamics. Cooperative goals that are more team-friendly reduce ostracism while competitive goals increase ostracism.[35]

This research has important implications for organizations with team-based work systems and individually focused PM systems. Many elements of PM 1.0—individually-focused objectives, forced distribution, and pay-for-performance—create incentives for individuals to work against each other in ways that can actually undermine the success of the teams they support. Companies won't get the productivity-enhancing benefits of teams without team-friendly goal structures.

Coach Individuals on How They Can Better Support the Team

Teams need feedback, coaching, and support just like individuals do. In fact, they probably need more. Employees working together on common goals encounter plenty of issues that need to be sorted out by the team and the leader. They will struggle with direction, roles and responsibilities, team processes, and interpersonal relationships. Team structures require a different way of managing individuals.[36] Supervisors will still need to have one-on-one meetings with individuals, but these meetings will focus on more than individual contributions. They will also focus on how employees can work better with, and better support, the team.

Implement Team-Friendly Reward Practices

Applying PM 2.0 principles to teams will fail unless we move away from traditional, individualistic reward practices like differentiation and pay-for-performance toward more team-friendly reward practices. Unfortunately, what many companies do is apply the same principles at the team level: rating team performance, making team rewards contingent on team performance ratings (or other measures), and differentiating individual rewards based on relative contributions to team goals. This is PM 1.0 dressed up for teams, and these practices aren't likely to work any better at the team level than they do at the individual level.

The most effective programs for teams are so called "shared capitalism" or "participatory capitalism" programs that base worker rewards on the performance at the level of the workgroup, organization, or firm. These programs are less popular in organizations than traditional individual P4P programs, and PM 1.0 thinking is the reason. The economic rationale is simple: Individuals are self-interested and will maximize their own utility at every turn. If you dilute the ability of employees to affect their own outcomes, they will reduce their effort and "free ride" on the efforts of the others in the group. The psychological rationale is similar. Psychologists who study social loafing and expectancy theory argue that individuals will exert less effort when their outputs are combined with others, and individual motivation will decline when rewards become disconnected from individual effort.

Reward systems, more than any other topic I discuss in this book, is where I encounter the most resistance in moving to PM 2.0. Business leaders and HR professionals are fine with clearer goals and more feedback, and they can even get comfortable giving up performance ratings. However they fight to the death when you suggest they abandon individual P4P programs fearing their employees will literally stop working and head for the exits. Shared capitalism programs violate all the PM 1.0 principles they hold dear. They couldn't possibly work. But they do. Despite dire predictions of free riding by "experts" and despite the fears of business leaders and HR professionals that such programs steer us toward socialism and mediocrity, these programs work.

Douglas Kruse, Richard Freeman, and Joseph Blasi reviewed the effectiveness of a number of these programs in their 2010 NBER report: *Shared Capitalism at Work*.[37] Their research focused on employee ownership, employee stock ownership, profit-sharing, gain-sharing, and stock-option programs. Their review showed that while these programs are much less popular in organizations they were broadly related to workplace performance.[38] These programs were generally associated with higher levels of company performance and productivity, lower turnover and greater loyalty, and the willingness to work hard, particularly when combined with other high-performance policies (e.g., involvement and participation, low levels of intrusive supervision, and fixed pay at or above market levels).

Companies that implement profit-sharing programs, for example, are more productive than companies that don't and the gains can be substantial. Gain-sharing plans show similar positive benefits especially when employees participate in the development of the program. Employee ownership, employee stock ownership, and stock-option programs show positive benefits as well.[39] It is clear that companies can get the benefits of individual P4P programs without the expense, effort, and side effects that typically accompany them. Shared capitalism programs can also be used for jobs and in circumstances where individual programs don't work well (e.g., high complexity, collaborative environments). Economist Christopher Adams captured the difficulty economists have with the effectiveness of these programs in writing specifically about profit sharing in a manufacturing context.

> The use of profit sharing amongst production line workers in large manufacturing firms seems to defy economic logic. The idea that joint ownership can do much for incentives when the number of workers is large seems wrong on the face of it. After all, each worker bears the full cost of his own effort, but reaps at most $1/N$ of the benefit in an N-worker firm. Despite the general incredulousness of economists, these types of incentives schemes

are used in large firms and moreover such schemes have been found to improve firm performance.[40]

The effectiveness of these kinds of programs suggests free riding isn't a significant problem and there is now a substantial research literature on the topic of free riding. Much of the research on free riding uses what's called a "public goods" game. In the typical game individuals are given tokens and they can keep them or put them in a public pot, the proceeds of which are evenly divided among all players. The public pot is typically set up to return to players a percentage of the total contributions, divided equally among all players whether an individual contributes to it or not. The payoff to the group is always maximized if everyone puts all their tokens in the public pot. University of Wisconsin economists Gerald Marwell and Ruth Ames did an extensive series of public-good experiments that highlighted the failure of traditional economic thinking surrounding free riding. Their experiments were designed to maximize free riding by minimizing normative and social effects among individuals. Economic thinking says it would be irrational for a self-interested individual to contribute to the group pot when they could keep their tokens and collect their share of the group pot at the same level as everyone else. In fact, Marwell and Ames polled five economists and asked them what percentage of their tokens they predicted subjects would contribute to the group pot. Their findings were fascinating (especially if you like to surprise economists).

- The economists predicted subjects would contribute 20% to the public pot. This is interesting because it suggests economists don't really fully believe their own assumptions since rational economists should predict rational subjects would contribute 0% to the group exchange.
- Subjects across their experiments contributed substantially to the group pot, despite the fact that conditions were designed to maximize free riding. Actual contributions were two to three times what economists predicted (40% to 60% of their tokens).
- Graduate students in economics contributed the least to the group pot of all subjects tested (20% of their tokens). Free riding seems to be mostly a problem among economists, although the fact that they contributed anything suggests they are not 100% committed to their own principles.

The findings by Marwell and Ames are typical of free riding research. There have been several reviews of this research concluding free riding is not a significant problem.[41] These effects are much less of a problem in normal work settings with more stable, permanent groups and interdependent work activities and where individual efforts are publicly visible and peers can influence behavior. Most economists now talk about free riding more as a "tendency" and are focused on explaining why people don't free ride as much as they should and how to minimize these tendencies. [42] Research in psychology shows that group and social effects can actually increase productivity. If members of the group work harder, this can "spill over" on other individuals and they will increase their efforts.[43]

The subject of free riding is another of many examples where the rhetoric and hysterics we hear from business leaders and HR professionals is not supported by the science. This topic is also an example of what happens when people generalize broadly from research done in one narrow setting. The original research on free riding was done by economists Eugene Kandel and Edward Lazear with medical and legal partnerships where individuals worked independently of one another.[44] In these arrangements they found that as the partnerships grew in size (and income was dependent on the profitability of the partnership) individual efforts decreased. These findings have been overgeneralized. These partnerships are not typical of work arrangements in organizations, and we now know these effects are much reduced or disappear altogether in more traditional work contexts.

Abandoning traditional, individual P4P programs and moving to team- and organization-based reward programs is one of many changes to compensation programs PM 2.0 requires. Organizations still need competitive compensation programs to attract talent and keep talented employees from being attracted away. We will talk more about options for redesigning compensation programs in Chapter 10.

Who Is Doing It Differently?

Google: Building a Better Team

There are several reasons why I highlight Google's practices. First, few organization have made as big a commitment to work teams and their effectiveness as Google.[45] Google invested 5 years in measuring their teams and studying what made them effective. Second, they have a disciplined planning process, which they call OKRs—objectives and key results. This is how Google employees establish priorities, plan their work, and measure their progress.[46] This is how Google executes its strategy and how they get alignment throughout the organization. They use it at all levels, for individuals, teams, organizations, and the company. All the OKRs at the higher levels are public so team members understand the context for their work.

At the team level, OKRs emphasize how individual objectives complement team objectives.

Their process is also very participative with managers and employees brainstorming ideas for attacking team objectives. In addition, their process is very flexible; OKRs are not etched in stone, they intend them to be directional assuming things will change. They also don't have rigid rules about how they are set and how frequently they are reviewed. What they have created is a more "light-weight" process that can be tailored to meet local needs.

To be sure, there are things I don't like about what Google does. They grade and weigh their OKRs and have more sophisticated scoring processes than I would want. They also use these scores to evaluate and differentiate rewards for people. By now you know I think this is a mistake. However, they are doing a lot that I like that you can emulate.

Cisco: Team Management System

Cisco is one of the world's most successful and enduring technology companies. Cisco sees a team-based organizational model as fundamental to its strategy, and they have approached maximizing the productivity of their teams in an integrated way.[47] They set up a new leadership and team intelligence organization focused entirely on leadership and team development, team leader selection, performance management, and intelligence gathering for Cisco teams and leaders around the world. One of its early priorities was to redesign PM to better fit a team-based work system. Prior to their redesign, Cisco was the poster-child for PM 1.0 with a rigid cycle, sophisticated ratings, forced distributions, and a complex rater calibration process. In 2012 they began to challenge the assumptions behind performance ratings and made a commitment to do something different.[48] Like Google, Cisco studied its best teams to understand what set them apart. One of the differentiating factors was that members of the best teams got to play to their strengths, and Cisco began to assess the strengths of each team member, using this information to staff teams and coach team members in their work.

Cisco also made a commitment to technology that enabled team leaders to assess and manage the performance of each team member, and that helped team members communicate with and make requests for support from their team leaders.[49] It created dashboards for team leaders, team members, and higher level leaders. The team leader dashboard allowed the leader to see the strengths and priorities of each team member, and there was also space to document their check-in meetings with team members.

Any team member could request a check-in with their leader and research showed that team members and leaders who made better use of these regular discussions were more effective. The team leader dashboard also provided information on the collective strengths and priorities of team members so they could make more informed decisions about collaboration opportunities. Future releases of this tool will allow team members to see each other's priorities and strengths to facilitate collaboration opportunities without the intervention of the team leader.

Cisco designed its solution to be very flexible with few mandatory elements; team leaders and members decide the best way to use the tools and the process. The company also has a "minimalist" approach to technology with simple ways for team members to alert their leaders to what they need to discuss during their check-in meetings. Also incorporated were simple assessments for teams to measure their progress and determine the priorities for their team development efforts. These "bite-sized" technology pieces are a far cry from the massive technology applications typical of most PM systems. As was the case with Google, I don't like everything Cisco has done. It still measures the performance of its team members quantitatively, and these measures are still subject to many of the problems I described in Chapter 4. In addition, it still differentiates performance and rewards and makes other HR decisions based on this information. These decisions certainly factor into the thinking of the team leaders who make the assessments and can affect their motives for their ratings.

Netflix: Market-Based Pay and Company Bonuses

Netflix is one of the premier online providers of video content. On a normal weeknight Netflix accounts for more than a third of all Internet traffic entering North American homes.[50] Netflix completely abandoned individual merit increases and bonuses.[51] It realized the value of their top people and it did its best to attract the best talent by paying people at the top of the market. The company applied three tests to determine the market value of their employees:

- What could the person get elsewhere?
- What would we pay for a replacement?
- What would we pay to keep the person if they had a better offer elsewhere?

Successful people earn more because Netflix pays more to keep them. One key difference in its approach is it pays the person not the job. Netflix has an annual compensation review and answers these three questions for every employee each year. Each supervisor aligns his or her people to the market every year. There is no central pool of money for base pay increases each year. People's pay can move up and potentially down as the demand for their skills in the marketplace changes. There are no bonuses based on individual performance or company performance, and individuals can decide for themselves if they want to trade salary for stock or stock options. Individuals decide how much they want to link their rewards to the success of the company. One of the biggest benefits of what Netflix does is efficiency and simplicity. It avoids the costs and the complexity of administering multiple pay plan elements; it puts maximum money in the hands of employees and gives them the freedom to decide how they want to spend it.

Atlassian: Out With the Individual, in With the Group

Some of you may recall this company from Dan Pink's book *Drive*. Atlassian is an Australian software firm that helps developers track, collaborate, code, and ship their products. It had a traditional performance management process and like other companies found it wasn't working for them. It didn't inspire discussions about improving performance, it disrupted, demotivated, and caused unnecessary anxiety. It also took a lot of time. The company did its own internal analysis and talked with other technology companies about their experiences. Atlassian found nothing out there to copy so they started from scratch. Among the many things it did was eliminate performance ratings and the merit increases and bonuses that were connected to them.[52] People were paid at the top of the market. The company also maintained a profit sharing plan to allow people to share in the company success and started giving every staff member stock options so all employees had an opportunity to benefit from the company's success.

Fog Creek Software: Out With Sales Commissions

I mentioned Fog Creek Software in Chapter 6. After Fog Creek found its sales reps were spending 20% of their time tracking how much money was owed them, and after much hand wringing, it finally decided to get rid of sales commissions. What happened? As Dan Ostlund blogged: "Nothing. No catastrophes struck us. No earthquakes. No plagues. No one quit." Fog Creek's sales actually went up. Salespeople started thinking about service and started taking a more long-term view of sales prospects. People started sharing information, pitching in, and helping others.[53]

Other companies are also abandoning PM 1.0 reward practices and focusing on other ways to motivate their employees. SAS Institute, the venerable software firm, has abandoned most of its focus on financial incentives, and firms like Fog Creek Software and others have eliminated sales commissions with seemingly no ill effects.[54] Southwest Airlines also depends more on its mission, its culture, the work, and the supportive community it creates to motivate employees.[55]

PM 2.0: New Paradigms and New Practices

PM 2.0 represents a shift in the approach organizations take to drive individual and organizational performance (see Table 9.1 for a summary). PM 1.0 assumes that individual success is the path to organizational success, and it relies on individualistic strategies to motivate and control behavior: individual goals, individual feedback and monitoring, individual evaluation, and individual rewards. It relies on tactics like competitive goals, transparent evaluation, forced distributions, and differentiation of rewards to create competition among employees. PM 1.0 practices pay disproportionate attention to top performers, celebrating and rewarding their accomplishments.

PM 2.0 focuses less on individuals and more on teams, reflecting the trend in organizations toward team-based work and the growing body of research showing the superiority of teaming and collaboration in driving organizational success. PM 2.0 relies on relationships and shared purpose to motivate high performance instead of carrots and sticks. It relies on cooperative and team-centered goals and team-friendly reward systems to direct, align, motivate, and control behavior in organizations.

So despite our deepest fears we don't lose anything by abandoning meritocracy. Adopting a more collectivistic approach to managing people and

TABLE 9.1 Paradigm Shifts Required for PM 2.0	
From PM 1.0...	...to PM 2.0
• Meritocracy and individualism	• Collectivism
• Competition	• Collaboration
• Economic and instrumental motives (money and P4P)	• Relationship and belonging motives
• Individual, competitive goals	• Cooperative team goals; individual goals framed in the context of team goals
• Individual reward programs	• Team and organizational reward programs

managing their behavior and performance can pay dividends in the form of greater well-being, happiness, engagement, alignment, and productivity.

Key Messages

- PM 1.0 is a western creation, with the individual at the center.
- Organizations are meritocracies where individual talent is seen as the key to success.
- Meritocracy is an outdated ideology based on historical circumstances that no longer apply today.
- A PM process rooted in meritocracy and individualism is increasingly at odds with the increased use of teams in organizations.
- The environments in which organizations compete today are far too complex to rely on smart individuals to ensure organizational success.
- Individual talent is overrated. Organizations tend to overvalue individual talent as a source of competitive advantage and undervalue the other factors including the efforts of teams and groups.
- People are social and have a strong need to belong to groups, organizations, and other collectives. Organizations that tap into this need can achieve stronger alignment and higher productivity than organizations relying on other forms of motivation (e.g., financial incentives).
- PM 2.0 designs PM practices with teams in mind, setting team goals, developing individual goals in the context of team goals, and implementing team-friendly reward structures.

10

Next Generation Performance Management: PM 2.0

I cannot help fearing that men may reach a point where they look on every new theory as a danger, every innovation as a toilsome trouble, every social advance as a first step toward revolution, and that they may absolutely refuse to move at all.
—Alexis de Tocqueville

Don't be too timid and squeamish about your actions. All life is an experiment. The more experiments you make the better.
—Ralph Waldo Emerson

After nine chapters I hope you are left with three thoughts : (a) Performance management (PM) 1.0 isn't working; (b) The paradigms behind it are antiquated; and (c) We need to abandon PM 1.0 practices and replace them with more effective practices based on paradigms better supported by science. This chapter integrates the glimpses of PM 2.0 that I have given you throughout this book. Most of the ideas behind PM 2.0 are grounded in the science reviewed here, peppered with my own personal experiences.

TABLE 10.1 Paradigm Shift From PM 1.0 to PM 2.0	
From PM 1.0 . . .	**. . . to PM 2.0**
• Contracts	• Goals and direction
• Surveillance	• Alignment, dialogue and discussion
• Feedback	• Progress
• Negative	• Positive
• Weakness	• Strength
• Judging	• Supporting
• Competition ("Me")	• Collaboration ("We")
• Money, differentiation, pay-for-performance	• Purpose, meaning, and belonging

But first a disclaimer: PM 2.0 isn't a set of specific practices, it is a blueprint, a set of objectives, principles, and general recommendations. Use this blueprint to create your own process that fits your circumstances.

At the core of PM 2.0 is a shift in paradigms about motivating and controlling employee behavior and performance in organizations (see Table 10.1).

The essence of PM 2.0 can be summed up in a few key ideas.

- Design PM to be a key part of the organization's management process.
- Focus PM on direction and connection making goal setting, alignment, and progress the backbone and central motivating force.
- Stop the formal evaluation of performance.
- Stop differentiating individual rewards based on individual performance.
- Implement other practices to fill the void left by abandoning ratings, differentiation, and pay-for-performance (P4P).
- Leverage direction and connection with teams as well as individuals, tapping into the power of employees' social needs to motivate and align.

Clear Purpose

As I shared in Chapter 1, PM 2.0 is a part of an organization's management and governance processes. Its purpose should be to translate strategy and organizational priorities into team and individual priorities, identifying and controlling what gets worked on and by whom. It provides direction for employee efforts aligning their efforts with important team and organizational goals. It acts as a control system ensuring employees stay focused on the right activities and as a support system helping employees make progress toward their goals every day. PM 2.0 is about direction, alignment, control, and progress in the service of important organizational goals.

Sound Principles

PM 2.0 reflects a number of important principles that are based on sound theory and research as well as practical experience. Use these principles to guide your design efforts.

- Context heavy. Emphasize ongoing discussions between supervisors and employees about organization and team priorities and how employee efforts align with these priorities. This context gives meaning and purpose to employees' work. Alignment and commitment are achieved over time through ongoing discussions not through contracts and reward contingencies.
- Performance focus. Focus on enabling employee achievement and performance instead of measuring and evaluating it.
- Progress mindset. Help employees make day-to-day progress against their team and individual goals. This requires more than feedback and coaching. It involves problem solving and providing resources, information, and other support.
- High touch. Regular, ongoing dialogue between supervisors and employees should be a central element of your process. They should talk regularly about the work, how it aligns with important priorities, how it is going, where employees are getting stuck, and how supervisors can help.
- Fit the work. Your process should be designed around the cadence of the work, not around an arbitrary calendar of programmed events.
- Positive. Your process should have a positive, encouraging, and supportive tone to it. Criticism, negative feedback, and punishment should be used sparingly.
- Collaborative. Focus more on the efforts and contributions of the team and less on the individual. Avoid practices that pit individuals against one another and suboptimize the team.
- Purpose oriented. Use the power of the work and the larger purpose the work serves as a key motivating force for employees, instead of money, individual differentiation, and P4P.

- Simple. Formal documentation and other requirements should be kept to a minimum. Design for the 99% of employees not the 1%.
- Flexible. Your process needs to be flexible enough to handle the diversity of roles and circumstances in your company while staying consistent with these principles.
- Supervisor driven. Supervisors should be responsible for this process not employees. PM is a management process; it is management's responsibility.

Effective Practices

There are two simple practices central to PM 2.0: direct and connect with four simple steps. Supervisors direct employees and their work toward important team and organizational priorities, and then connect with them regularly to provide feedback and coaching to facilitate progress in their work. Employees perform the work and execute against their objectives, and adjust as the work evolves and as priorities change. These activities are carried out in the service of progress against important goals for individuals and teams, leveraging the power of team members to facilitate progress, commitment, and performance. These four steps represent an ongoing, fluid set of activities cycling back and forth as employees perform their work, encounter setbacks, and make adjustments as the context changes. It is through this ongoing cycle of discussing direction, shaping the work, and connecting to facilitate progress that goals are ultimately achieved.

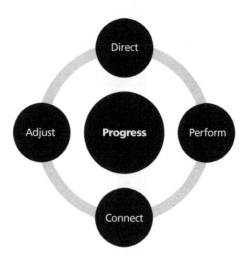

Figure 10.1 Key elements of PM 2.0.

Direct

PM 2.0 is based on a foundation of clear direction and alignment. This doesn't mean supervisors tell employees what to do. Directing is less like a drill sergeant barking orders and more like a conductor working with an orchestra. There are several important elements to providing direction for employees.

Regular Discussions

Employees need to have ongoing discussions about the context for their work; a once-a-year planning meeting is not enough to sustain employee motivation, engagement, and performance. If employees have a deep understanding of the goals of the team and organization and the larger impact achieving these goals will have, they will feel a part of something bigger than themselves. They will also be in a better position to make the right decisions on their own during their day-to-day work.

Write Goals Down

Writing goals down creates a sense of public commitment. Although they should be written, employees shouldn't necessarily be expected to do the writing. PM 2.0 is a management responsibility. Managers own the process of creating goals and objectives for the team and for assigning responsibilities and allocating the work to employees. This doesn't mean supervisors write them and hand them to employees. A list of goals should be the outcome of a dialogue between employees and supervisors. The documentation becomes a formality with the supervisor playing the role of scribe, not dictator. Employee goals should also be framed positively (e.g., retaining customers instead of not losing customers). This focuses employees on the desired results. In dieting, your goal should be to eat healthy not avoid chocolate.

Incorporate Stretch

Your business objectives probably have stretch in them so employees need to understand this means they will have stretch in their objectives. Objectives that are meaningful, important, and challenging activate all the motivational magic. Break complex objectives into smaller, more-achievable pieces and give employees the chance to experience early success, building their confidence to persist with the rest of the work.

Be Flexible

Objectives should not be etched in stone or documented in agonizing detail. Things will change and employees will need to adjust, revise, or even abandon what they are doing. Employees need to be clear on what they are striving for in order for them to commit. Objectives need to be specific enough to provide direction and they should clarify the standard of success without going overboard. In Stephen Covey's book *The Seven Habits of Highly Effective People*, he tells the story of working with his son to take care of the lawn. He tells his son "green and clean."[1] Discussing goals should also be an ongoing, organic process that happens when it is needed according to the unique cadence of the job and the work. When something new needs to be done, planning and goal-setting should happen. When projects are completed and employees have the capacity for additional work, planning and goal-setting should happen. For employees in jobs where the work is routine and standardized (e.g., production work), adjust your process. It makes no sense to force employees in these roles through regular performance planning and objective-setting discussions to satisfy a bureaucratic requirement.

Whats and Hows

While PM 2.0 focuses on performance, employee objectives should focus on more than just getting results. Organizations that endure for the long-term, fight the battles of today and the battles of tomorrow. You can't win the battles of tomorrow without a steady focus on improving yourself and improving and maintaining the quality of the relationships with those around you. Many organizations call these the *hows* (how results are achieved) in contrast to the *whats* (the results achieved). Researchers call these "organizational citizenship behaviors" (OCBs); they don't show up in a job description but they still promote the effective functioning of the group and organization.[2] Employee objectives need some balance between getting results today and developing the capability to get results tomorrow. This applies to the employee's own knowledge and skills as well. Employees should have development objectives that reflect important knowledge or skills they need to acquire to accomplish the work. These should be included in the PM plan, not in a separate development plan or section. Longer term development and career-oriented objectives should be addressed in a separate career planning process.

Simple Documentation

Whatever form you create or application you use should have a place to document shared team objectives and individual objectives. That's it. There is no need to weight or rate objectives on their difficulty or importance, nor is there a need for elaborate metrics, measures, or targets. If they are working on it, it should be important. You should not require any additional formal documentation for most employees. Other documentation will happen in regular one-on-one check-in meetings. If you have employees who are not meeting expectations where some negative action is likely, then more documentation should be required for those employees. Create a separate "performance improvement process" for those employees with more stringent documentation requirements.

Connect

After employees have the direction they need, it is time for them to "perform." Getting clarity on context, direction, and objectives is just the beginning of supervisor-employee discussions. There are several important elements for connecting with employees to support them in achieving their goals.

Have Regular Discussions

Supervisors should connect regularly with employees about their work discussing what's going well, where they are getting stuck, and how they can get unstuck. This cycle should fit the role, the work, and the employee's needs. For employees whose work is more project-focused, employees and supervisors should meet during the project as well as more formally at the end of projects to discuss lessons learned that can be applied to new projects. Some companies call these "after-action reviews." The purpose of these reviews is not to judge and evaluate performance but to capture what was learned so they can be incorporated into new projects.[3]

Frame the Supervisor's Role in Terms of Progress

The day-to-day focus of PM 2.0 is progress: supporting employees so they can make progress toward their goals and so the team and organization can make progress toward their goals. In this sense PM 2.0 is really "progress management." Employees need more than feedback to make progress. They need resources, information, problem solving, and help overcoming barriers they encounter in their work. David Rock describes a useful framework for supervisors to help employees make progress.[4] He uses two dimensions to describe how supervisors approach feedback with their employees: "ask versus tell" and "problem versus solution" (Figure 10.2). The typical PM 1.0 feedback approach is for supervisors to tell employees what they are doing wrong (lower left quadrant). Rock suggests 75% of the time employees know what they did wrong and they know what the problem is. Supervisors focus too much on the problem. Effective feedback and coaching

Figure 10.2 TAP model (Rock, 2006).

involves asking employees questions, helping them think through what the issue is, and focusing on solutions (upper right quadrant).

Keep Goals and the Work Front and Center

For goals to work their magic, employees need feedback on their progress. Goal-oriented feedback does not focus on what happened in the past and what employees did wrong, but it focuses on the future and the impact adjustments will have on future goal achievement. This orientation can also make supervisor-employee interactions more positive, more focused on progress, and more productive in general. Feedback should also focus on the task at hand. The more feedback gets away from the task and the goals employees are trying to accomplish, the less effective it is in improving employee performance.

Make It Easy for Employees to Get Their Own Feedback

Employees get feedback on their work in many ways including their own direct experience. Organizations should take advantage of more impersonal channels for providing feedback using email exchanges or other new software applications and social media tools to ensure employees get the feedback they need in ways that are less emotionally charged.[5] Many PM applications have these capabilities already incorporated in their systems.

Be Positive

Supervisors should encourage employees and reinforce performance through positive feedback and coaching. Supervisors should express confidence in their employees' ability to accomplish their objectives and reassure employees they will provide the support needed. This comes naturally when supervisors help employees leverage their strengths instead of fixing their weaknesses. Researcher Avi Kluger and his colleagues have integrated many of these principles into an alternative to traditional performance appraisals that incorporates several effective elements of positive psychology.[6]

- The "feed-forward" interview. The supervisor talks with the employee about the positive experiences they've had at work and where they were happy and energized. Next they discuss the conditions that made these experiences possible and the extent to which these conditions are present in the employees' current work situation.
- Reflected best self-feedback. This process identifies strengths by focusing on when employees are at their best and by developing critical weaknesses, not so they become strengths but so they don't become liabilities.
- Developing strengths. Employees participate in regular exercises where they document the positive things that happen daily, why they happen, and how they can use their signature strengths.
- 3–1 positive to negative ratio. The goal is to focus more energy on positive feedback creating positive energy and to use negative feedback sparingly, primarily for prevention-oriented goals.
- Win-win approach. Employees focus on goals that help both the team/organization and the individual.

The authors applied these principles in redesigning PM at Soda Stream with encouraging results and positive reactions from employees and supervisors. Richard Boyatzis and his colleagues outlined a similar approach to helping leaders develop effective relationships. This approach could be incorporated into PM training for supervisors to improve their feedback and coaching skills. Boyatzis and his colleagues effectively implemented these ideas with FifthThird bank.[7]

Team PM

Focusing on direction and connection will take us a long way toward improving PM as will stopping destructive PM 1.0 practices like evaluation, differentiation, and P4P. However, we won't harness the full power of PM 2.0 if we focus all our energy on individuals, ignoring the role of the team in motivating high performance and driving organizational success. Direction and connection apply to teams, but they need to sit within a broader framework. To optimize PM 2.0 for teams we need a team management system. One simple model I have used focuses on four elements teams need for success that are oriented around four simple questions team members

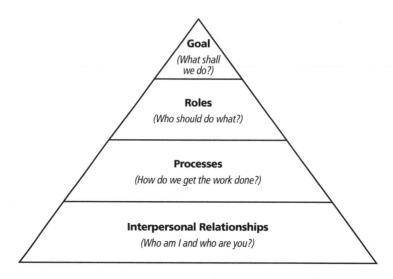

Figure 10.3 The GRPI model of team effectiveness (Rubin, Plovnick, & Fry, 1977).

need to answer for themselves (Figure 10.3).[8] Managing team performance means addressing these four elements, and not surprisingly direction and connection are central to all four.

Set Team Goals

Teams need goals for the same reasons individuals need goals. And just like with individuals, team goals are a product of ongoing conversations between the leader and team members about the larger organizational context how the team's work fits within this context.

Set Individual Goals in the Context of Team Goals

Break team goals up into individual goals in order to resolve ambiguity among team members. What part of this am I responsible for? How does my work align with the work of the team? Where do I play a lead role in accomplishing the work, and where do I play a support role helping others get their work done? Individual goals need to be written in the context of the team's goals so they reinforce that we are all working toward the same goals. Individual goals need to be coordinated so they create a spirit of cooperation instead of competition.

Facilitate Progress for Teams

Conversations should happen in regular meetings with the team and with individuals, applying the principles of direction and connection to answer questions about roles, processes, and relationships. Much of the day-to-day planning, feedback, and coaching work in teams can be enabled with technology in the form of social media or crowdsourced planning and feedback tools or other technology incorporated into existing PM software applications. These tools make it easy for team members to share goals and provide each other with feedback and coaching. Many team management systems that are technology-enabled will already have these planning and feedback capabilities incorporated in them.

Depending on their maturity, teams may take on some of the work related to direction and connection themselves (without the involvement of the leader). All the principles discussed so far related to direction and connection still apply to the case where team members are working with each other.

Create a Supportive Environment

Creating effective teams requires more than focusing on the work, it requires creating an environment where everyone can do their best. Here are suggestions based on sound research evidence.

- Self-management. Teams that handle more of their own governance will be more cohesive and effective.
- Clear and transparent communication and information sharing. These behaviors are effective for creating and maintaining the trust needed for strong relationships.
- Share the load. Strong relationships and cohesive teams are built by people who help each other.
- Cooperation. Relationships are stronger on teams where there is more emphasis on cooperative versus competitive behaviors.
- Conflict management. Poorly managed conflict can destroy a team. Team cohesion will be stronger when there is a clear process for managing the inevitable conflicts that arise.
- Team composition. Teams are more cohesive when members feel they have the people with the right background, experiences, styles, skills, and abilities that complement each other and are relevant for the work to be done.
- Psychological safety. Teams need an environment where their unique talents and differences can be expressed and leveraged.[9] This was the most important factor emerging from Google's study of their successful teams.
- Work on the team. Effective teams not only do the work but they spend time discussing and working on their own functioning. They can spend time on this in their team meetings or in

dedicated training or team development sessions to improve how they work together.

When supervisors get goals, roles, and processes right and create the right kind of environment, their teams develop strong bonds between members driven by the commitment they have to the goals of the team and the trust and respect they have for one another. Researchers call this cohesion, and more cohesive teams are more productive teams.[10]

Provide Team Rewards

It is hard to create a supportive and collaborative environment where teams can thrive without team-friendly rewards practices. PM 2.0 makes individual rewards contingent on team, organization, and company success using programs like profit sharing, gain-sharing, stock options, and employee ownership. These programs emphasize organizational success and they create an identification with organizational goals: When the organization wins, we all win. Gain-sharing programs can be implemented in organizations focused on a variety of different productivity improvement and cost savings objectives that are relevant to that organization. Importantly, a move to team-based rewards does not mean that organizations don't manage performance. If an individual is not pulling his/her weight on the team and if teams cannot manage this situation themselves, then the leader needs to deal with this situation accordingly. Organizations still need a disciplinary process and a performance improvement process to deal with poor performance. Poor performance needs to be managed aggressively in PM 2.0 in order to maintain the trust and support of team members.

Fill the Void

There is no question PM 2.0 will feel a lot different to you—it won't feel right. It will feel like you have been dragging around a ball and chain and now it's not there anymore. It will feel like something is missing. It won't feel right because everything you have ever associated with PM and motivation and control will be gone. Evaluation, a heavy focus on financial rewards, P4P, and extreme differentiation of rewards will all be gone. It won't feel right because information you relied on in the past to make decisions won't be available anymore. It won't feel right because your primary levers for driving and reinforcing organizational change are gone. You must believe you don't need these practices anymore that they weren't benefiting you in the first place. You must abandon them.

PM 2.0 can't work unless you eliminate ratings and rankings. Employees don't need a rating to align their efforts with organizational goals and to motivate them to achieve their goals. Supervisors know if employees are making progress against their goals, and they don't need to rate employees to communicate that performance must improve or rate employees to show they appreciate the progress being made. Not having to "keep score" and differentiate performance frees supervisors to recognize and leverage strong performance, and to coach and improve weak performance. You need to trust you can find other ways to make the downstream decisions that depended on performance ratings, and you need to acknowledge that the quality of these ratings was so bad you won't be losing useful information anyway.

PM 2.0 can't work unless you stop relying on money, P4P, and differentiation of rewards to motivate employees and drive organizational change. I am not asking you to abandon all focus on money and rewards. Money attracts—you need competitive compensation to get people in the door. Rewards and compensation are big parts of a company's employment value proposition, and candidates are attracted by competitive salaries and a P4P philosophy, so you need a good story to tell. Your compensation philosophy should focus on paying competitive salaries, you should consider paying top talent and employees with critical skills more toward the top of the market. You should also implement team- and organization-based reward programs to attract, reward, and motivate employees.

I am not asking you to abandon your P4P philosophy. The problem with this philosophy is it is solely defined by one element: annual differentiation of rewards based on individual performance ratings. There are other important elements in a P4P philosophy. The most important element is that poor performance is not tolerated. Supervisors know if an employee isn't cutting it, and performance for these employees needs to be aggressively managed. It needs to improve or employees should be moved or separated. There is nothing that irritates strong performers more than lack of discipline in dealing with poor performers. Pay for performance also means that when "we" win (as teams, organizations, or the company) I share in the rewards. Start paying for the performance of the collective. P4P also means employees who perform are rewarded over time. As employees succeed they should have opportunities to be promoted and take on more responsibility with higher salaries. As employees develop critical skills that are valued in the marketplace, their salaries should be adjusted accordingly. Finally, P4P is really "reward for performance" where reward is broader than just money. Employees are inspired and motivated by lots of things that have nothing to do with money such as a meaningful purpose, challenging work that makes an impact, and simple acknowledgment and recognition for a job well-done.

PM 2.0 requires that you trust the science. You need to trust that PM 2.0 doesn't lose any motivational power by abandoning PM 1.0 practices; in fact it gains motivational power. Yes PM 2.0 will feel different, but you need to trust that goals, direction, meaning, progress, and belonging can do the motivational heavy lifting.

Supporting PM 2.0

Making PM 2.0 a success will require other supportive changes not the least of which is a significant investment in leadership capability. PM 2.0 will put a lot of pressure on supervisors. You will need to invest time in redefining the role of supervisors in your company and setting new expectations for them. It will be more important than ever to put the right people into supervisor jobs, train them well, and give them the resources to be successful.

Supervisor Selection and Promotion

Implementing PM 2.0 requires strong supervisors. Organizations don't invest enough energy and resources making sure they put the right people in supervisory jobs.

The leadership ranks in most organizations are full of supervisors who were promoted based on their strong performance or their technical/functional skills, but don't have the people skills to excel in supervisor roles. These supervisors will struggle with PM 2.0. When companies do invest in supervisor capability it is usually through investments in training and development, not selection and promotion.

If you don't have the right people with the right "wiring" in these jobs, training won't help. As the saying goes, "You can't make a silk purse out of a sow's ear." If you invest heavily in identifying the right supervisors with the right skills to begin with, PM 2.0 will come more naturally to them and your training will be more effective.

Supervisor Expectations

Companies will need to review the expectations they have for their supervisors. Can supervisors "get ahead" by simply doing their own individual contributor work and not investing the necessary time and attention supporting their staff? A supervisor's success needs to depend on the success of their employees in order for PM 2.0 to be effective.

Supervisor Training

Supervisors will need to learn new skills and display new behaviors. You will likely need to strengthen and re-align your supervisor training efforts, focusing heavily on topics like those covered in this book. Supervisors will also need new tools and job aids. For example, Peter Heslin developed a useful checklist for building self-efficacy and Fred Nickols developed a tool called The Goals Grid that describes the different types of goals employees should have.[11]

Employee Communications and Orientation

PM 2.0 doesn't require employees to be trained, at least not in the way supervisors need to be trained. Employees need communication about PM 2.0 and orientation to the role they will play. In many cases this will be done as part of your change management activities sharing things like the business case for change, the solution, the value for them, etc. You will also need to manage employees' expectations and help them understand how interactions with their supervisor will change under PM 2.0.

Work Unit Planning Process

PM 2.0 stands on the shoulders of this process. If you have one already, leverage it. If you don't have one, develop one. Local work units should spend time thinking about their goals and objectives and how they align with the goals and objectives of the organization and company. Leaders need to discuss with employees the goals for their work groups and organizations. This should not be a long, bureaucratic process. It should happen at least annually and it should provide important context for team and employee goals.

IT Application to Support Your PM Process

This topic may be one of the most important considerations for those of you contemplating changes to PM in your organization. If you are not careful and thoughtful this technology will cause you great pain and suffering (it may cause you great pain and suffering even if you are careful!). About half of global companies have technology-based solutions in place for PM, and another 35% plan to implement them in the future.[12] Most companies are at best marginally satisfied with their PM application, and satisfaction with PM applications tends to lag satisfaction with other technology applications (e.g., learning management system).[13]

Companies marketing these applications advertise a number of benefits and advantages, many of which don't materialize or are not fully realized. While a full discussion of the advantages and disadvantages of these technology solutions is beyond the scope of this book, suffice to say you need to do your homework in this area. Having recently been through one of these projects I would strongly encourage you to talk with other companies and find out what you are in for. Talk to people on the ground in companies that have been through these software implementations and are managing PM processes enabled by these solutions. There are also good benchmarking and research reports available from HR consultants and think tanks. These firms provide comprehensive reviews of these applications and the key players involved.[14]

My opinion is that companies who have invested heavily in technology to support their HR and talent management systems may need to rethink their technology needs for PM. PM 2.0 requires much "lighter" technology to support it. These applications generally come with lots of overhead and cost and consume lots of resources; they end up being the "tail that wags the dog" in PM projects. In the end you need to ask yourself if this technology will help your PM process improve the performance of employees and the organization. I have found it hard to answer "yes" to this question. If you eliminate ratings, differentiation, and P4P I would argue you don't need a big, complicated software application for PM.

Conclusion: Hard Work Ahead, Eyes Wide Open

At the time of this writing few companies had gone very far down the road toward PM 2.0. Companies like Kelly Services, Netflix, Atlassian, and Fog Creek Software have been the most aggressive, while others are conducting more limited experiments with certain elements (e.g., getting rid of ratings). Time will tell how effective these experiments will be and how many other companies follow their lead. It also remains to be seen how effective it will be to go only partway down this path (e.g., eliminate ratings but keep individual differentiation of rewards).

Although it may not feel like it, I think we are in the very early days of rethinking PM. My own experience tells me it will be a painful journey. I have been on the front lines of this effort and I have plenty of scars to show for it. The current state is held in place by a complex system of entrenched beliefs and assumptions reinforced by widely available information from dominant external players validating those beliefs. Leaders will react violently to these recommendations, accusing you of being a socialist, of being soft on performance, and letting poorer performers get away with murder. The PM 2.0 antibodies will mobilize very quickly and there will be plenty of doomsday talk: "All of our best performers will leave," "We won't be able to compete for talent." Believe me it will be easier to stay with PM 1.0 and continue to throw money at people and endure the noise that comes from the workforce.

That's why I'm not asking you to change your PM practices right now. I'm asking you to talk about it. I'm asking you to have an open dialogue and debate, to surface your assumptions and beliefs and suspend them for the time being. I'm asking you and your leaders to consider the possibility that the assumptions you take for granted are wrong. I'm asking you to conduct the exercise. Creativity expert Edward DeBono asks people to engage in lateral thinking to find creative solutions to their problems. This requires provocation. You should assume what you know and take for granted is wrong, and write provocations to move your thinking outside the typical, well-worn paths. You mentally burn the ships in the harbor.[15] We see the topics of motivation and rewards through a lens that has been narrowed by our paradigms (economics and behavioristic psychology), our culture (individualistic), and our business models (dog-eat-dog capitalism fueled by the demands of shareholders and capital markets). There are other ways of looking at the world that reveal new ideas for motivating employees and ensuring employees and organizations enjoy the rewards they deserve. It won't be easy, but I think it *can* be done. Companies who emerge on the other side of this transition will find it much easier to focus on organizational performance without all the distractions caused by frequent and expensive tinkering with a PM process that is flawed at the core.

Key Messages

- Performance management 2.0 abandons the outdated paradigms of PM 1.0 and puts in place new paradigms, principles, and practices that are better supported by scientific research.
- At the foundation of PM 2.0 is a clear purpose: direction, alignment, control, and progress in the service of important organizational goals.

- ▪ This purpose is achieved not by contracts, surveillance, evaluation, and differentiation of rewards, but by directing employee efforts, connecting with them to facilitate progress, and finding other ways to motivate them.

End Notes

Preface and Introduction

1. Suddath, C. (2013, November 7). Performance reviews: Why bother. *Business-week*. Retrieved from http://www.businessweek.com/articles/2013-11-07/the-annual-performance-review-worthless-corporate ritual
2. Knowledge@Wharton (2011). *Should performance reviews be fired?* Retrieved from http://knowledge.wharton.upenn.edu/article.cfm?articleid=2760)
3. McGregor, J. (2013, February 14). The corporate kabuki of performance reviews. *The Washington Post*. Retrieved from http://www.washingtonpost.com/national/on-leadership/the-corporate-kabuki-of-performancereviews

   Kabuki is a classical Japanese dance-drama, but American political pundits use the term in a derogatory manner as a synonym for political posturing. Either way it fits.
4. This topic was the third most popular topic in the *Journal of Applied Psychology* from 2003 to 2007, and second most popular topic in *Personnel Psychology*, both top-tier journals in the field of industrial and organizational psychology.
5. Corporate Executive Board. (2016). *The real impact of eliminating performance ratings: Insights from employees and managers*. Research report. Retrieved from https://www.cebglobal.com/content/dam/cebglobal/us/EN/best-practices-decision-support/human-resources/pdfs/eliminate-performance-ratings.pdf
6. Bersin by Deloitte. (2014, April). *Global human capital trends 2014: Engaging the 21st-century workforce*. Deloitte University Press. Retrieved from Re-

Next Generation Performance Management, pages 165–211
Copyright © 2017 by Information Age Publishing

trieved from http://www2.deloitte.com/global/en/pages/human
-capital/articles/human-capital-trends-2014.html

7. McGregor, D. (1957, May/June). An uneasy look at performance appraisal. *Harvard Business Review*, 89–94.

8. Lawler, E. E., Benson, G. S., & McDermott, M. (2012, fourth quarter). Performance management and reward systems. *WorldAtWork Journal*, 19–28.

9. Based on an i4cp study of 1,427 organizations by Armitage and Parrey. (2012). Cited in Ledford, J. (2013). Review of center for effective organization's performance management research. Presentation to i4cp's PM exchange group.

10. Ultimate Software (2014). *A manager's guide to perfecting performance management: How to transform your employee review process.* Retrieved from http://freebizmag.tradepub.com/free-offer/a-managers-guide-toperfecting-performance-management-how-to-transform-your-employee-review-process/w_ulti09?sr=hicat&_t=hicat:688#sthash.5KZQ3wkS.dpuf

Chapter 1: Last Generation Performance Management: PM 1.0

1. Ryan, L. (2010, February). Ten management practices to axe. *BusinessWeek.* Retrieved from http://www.businessweek.com/managing/content/feb2010/ca2010024_442061.htm

2. For a good overview of typical PM activities see Aguinis, H. (2013). *Performance management.* Upper Saddle River, NJ: Pearson.

   Benchmarking statistics related to current practices can be found in the following reports: Mercer (2012). Current trends in performance management. Mercer briefing, August 23.

   Gorman, C. A., Ray, J., Nugent, C., Thibodeaux, C. N., List, S., Lonkar, S., Bradley, S., Mason, M., Pittington, L., & Pokhrel-Willet, S. (2012). *A preliminary survey of performance management practices in the United States.* Paper presented at the 2012 annual conference of the Society for Industrial and Organizational Psychologists, San Diego, CA.

   Mercer (2012, March). *Compensation planning in 2012: Today's landscape.*

3. See the following:

   Mercer, 2012, performance management *op. cit.*

   Lee, R., Rose, J., & O'Neil, C. (2013). Redefining performance management at the top. *People & Strategy*, 36, 46–49.

4. For additional details see:

   Conference Board (2013). *Performance management 3.0 survey report.*

   Conference Board (2014). *Job satisfaction: Progress at a snail's pace.* Research Report.

5. For additional details see:

   Mercer, 2012, *Performance management op. cit.*

Cornerstone on Demand. (2012). *The cornerstone on demand.* 2013 U.S. Employee Report.

Mercer (2011, May). *Next generation of pay for performance.* Survey report.

Globoforce (2013, Summer). *Empowering employees to improve employee performance.* Workforce Mood Tracker report.

6. Bersin by Deloitte (2014, April). *Global human capital trends 2014: Engaging the 21st-century workforce.* Seattle, WA: Deloitte University Press.

7. Conference Board (2013). *Performance management 3.0.* Survey report.

8. If you want to read more about the variety of PM changes made over the years, see:

Lawler, E. E. (2010). *Performance management: Creating an effective appraisal system.* Center for Effective Organizations. CEO Publication G 10-16 (584).

Pulakos, E. D., & O'Leary, R. S. (2011). Why is performance management broken? *Industrial and Organizational Psychology, 4,* 146–164.

Oberoi, M., & Rajgarhia, P. (2013). What your performance management system needs most. *Gallup Business Journal,* Retrieved from http://www.gallup.com/business-journal/161546/performance-managementsystem-needs.aspx

Pulakos, E. D. (2005). *Performance management: A roadmap for developing, implementing and evaluating performance management systems.* Society for Human Resources Management.

i4cp. (2011). Performance management playbook: Tools and techniques for managing performance. Institute for Corporate Productivity.

Landy, F., & Farr, J. L. (1980). Performance rating. *Psychological Bulletin, 87*(1), 72–107.

Gerhart, B., Rynes, S. L., & Fulmer, I. S. (2009). Pay and performance: Individuals, groups, and executives. *The Academy of Management Annals, 3,* 251–315.

Dominick, P. G. (2013). Forced rankings: Pros, cons, and practices. In J. W. Smither & M. London (2009) *Performance management: Putting research into practice* (pp. 411–443). San Francisco, CA: Jossey-Bass.

9. Aguinis, H. (2013). *Performance management.* Upper Saddle River, NJ: Pearson.

10. Those interested in a richer treatment of this history can consult the following sources:

Murphy, K. R., & Cleveland, J. N. (1995). *Understanding performance appraisal.* Thousand Oaks, CA: SAGE.

Koontz, H. (1971). *Appraising managers as managers.* New York, NY: McGraw-Hill.

11. For a review of MBO, see:

Drucker, P. F. (1954). *The practice of management.* New York, NY: Harper Business. (reissued 2006).

Carroll, S. J., & Tosi, H.L. (1973) *Management by objectives.* New York, NY: Macmillan.

McGregor, D. (1957). An uneasy look at performance appraisal. *Harvard Business Review,* (May–June), 89–94.

12. For more information on the history of PM and a comparison of PM with PA and MBO, see:

Armstrong, M. (2009). *Armstrong's handbook of performance management: An evidence-based guide to delivering high performance* (4th edition). London, England: Kogan Page.

13. The following are models I like and suggest you consult:

Nadler, D. A., & Tushman, M. L. (1988). *Strategic organization design.* Glenview, IL: Scott, Foresman.

Hanna, D. (1988). *Designing organizations for high performance.* Upper Saddle River, NJ: Prentice Hall.

Hanna, D. (2013). *The organizational systems model: A tool for developing high performance.* The RBL Group, Inc.

Galbraith, J. R. (1995). *Designing organizations.* San Francisco, CA: Jossey Bass.

14. For example, see

Judson, A. (1990). *Making strategy happen.* Cambridge, MA: Blackwell.

15. If you want to read more about the legal aspects of PM, see:

Coens, T., & Jenkins, M. (2002). *Abolishing performance appraisals: Why they backfire and what to do instead.* San Francisco, CA: Berrett-Kohler.

Malos, S. B. (1998). Current legal issues in performance appraisal. In J. W. Smithers (Ed.) *Performance appraisal: State of the art in practice* (pp. 49–95). San Francisco, CA: Jossey-Bass.

Smither, J. W., & London, M. (2009). *Performance management: Putting research into practice.* San Francisco, CA: Jossey-Bass.

Pulakos, E. D. (2009). *Performance management: A new approach to driving business results.* New York, NY: Wiley.

Kahn, S. C., Brown, B. B., & Lanzarone, M. (1996). *Legal guide to human resources.* Boston, MA: Warrant, Gorman, & Lamont.

Chapter 2. Paradigms: The Natural Laws of PM 1.0

1. Satell, G. (2014, September 5). A look back at why Blockbuster really failed and why it didn't have to. *Forbes Online.* Retrieved from http://www.forbes.com/sites/gregsatell/2014/09/05/a-look-back-at-why-blockbuster-really-failed-and-why-it-didnt-have-to/

2. Black, J. S., & Gregersen, H. B. (2002). *Leading strategic change: Breaking through the brain barrier.* New York, NY: Prentice Hall.

3. Mintzberg H. (1994). *The rise and fall of strategic planning.* New York, NY: Simon & Schuster.

4. Bly, R. (1990). *Iron John: A book about men.* San Francisco, CA: Addison-Wesley.

5. For a nice account of the history of this time period from a psychological perspective, see Miller, G. A. (2003). The cognitive revolution: A historical perspective. *Trends in Cognitive Science, 7,* 141–144.

6. For more details on these early pioneers in behaviorism, see:

   Thorndike, E. L. (1898). Animal intelligence: An experimental study of the associative processes in animals. *Psychological Monographs: General and Applied, 2,* 1–109.

   Skinner, B. F. (1974). *About behaviorism.* New York, NY: Random House.

7. Taylor, F. W. (1967). *The principles of scientific management.* New York, NY: W. W. Norton. Originally published in 1911.

8. Ryan, T. A. (1958). Drives, tasks, and the initiation of behavior. *American Journal of Psychology, 71,* 74– 93.

9. Locke, E. A. (1968). Toward a theory of task motivation and incentives. *Organizational Behavior and Human Performance, 3,* 157–189.

10. Simon, H. A. (1957). *Models of man, social and rational: Mathematical essays on rational human behavior in a social setting.* New York, NY: Wiley.

11. For an overview of all of their work, see Kahneman, D. (2012). *Thinking, fast and slow.* New York, NY: Farrar, Strauss and Giroux.

12. Ariely, D. (2009, July/August). The end of rational economics. *Harvard Business Review,* 78–84.

13. Bloomberg Business Week. (2013). *Michael Lewis on the next crisis.* Retrieved from http://www.businessweek.com/articles/2013-09-12/michael-lewis-on-the-next-crisis

14. Argyris, C., & Schon, D. A. (1974). *Theory in practice: Increasing professional effectiveness.* San Francisco, CA: Jossey-Bass.

15. Argyris, C. (1990). *Overcoming organizational defenses: Facilitating organizational learning.* Boston, MA: Allyn & Bacon.

16. For an overview of classical economics, see Hollander, S. (1987). *Classical economics.* Oxford, England: Blackwell.

17. For an overview of agency theory as it applies to organizations, see Eisenhardt, K. M. (1989). Agency theory: An assessment and review. *Academy of Management Review, 14,* 57–74.

18. For an overview of tournament theory, see Connelly, B. L., Tihanyi, L., Crook, T. R., & Gangloff, K. A. (2014). Tournament theory: Thirty years of contests and competition. *Journal of Management, 40*(1), 16–47.

19. For additional details on how these theories have influenced PM see the following:

    Gerhart, B., & Rynes, S. L. (2003). *Compensation: Theory, evidence, and strategic implications.* Thousand Oaks, CA: Sage.

    Rynes, S. L., Gerhart, B., & Parks, L. (2005). Performance evaluation and pay for performance. *Annual Review of Psychology, 56,* 571–600.

20. For a good review of reinforcement theory and the approach and philosophy, see Luthans, F., & Kreitner, R. (1975). *Organizational behavior modification.* Glenview, IL: Scott Foresman.

21. For an overview of expectancy theory, see Vroom, V. H. (1964). *Work and motivation.* New York, NY: McGraw-Hill.

22. Several weeks later I learned one of the organizers of the conference was ease-dropping on our conversation and wrote a blog post about our ex-

change. In it he wonders if some great truth had just been revealed. I would argue it had, but I'm not certain he and I would agree on what that truth was. Here is the reference to that blog post: Stevenson, C. (2012, June 20). *Paying people to show up.* American Management Association. Retrieved from http://www.amanet.org/training/articles/Paying-People-to- Show-Up.aspx

Chapter 3. The Forces Against Change

1. Rigby, D. K., & Bilodeau, B. (2013). *Management tools and trends.* Retrieved from http://www.bain.com/publications/articles/management-tools-and-trends-2013.aspx

2. For an overview of formal benchmarking, see Camp, R. C. (1989). *Benchmarking. The search for industry best practices that lead to superior performance.* Milwaukee, WI: ASQ Quality Press.

   Jeffry Pfeffer and Robert Sutton distinguish between formal benchmarking and casual benchmarking. See Pfeffer, J., & Sutton, R. I. (2006, January). Evidence-based management. *Harvard Business Review,* 63–74.

3. These statistics come from the websites and the marketing materials for these firms.

4. McGraw, M. (2012). *Running lean.* Retrieved from http://www.hreonline.com/HRE/print.jhtml?id=533343295

5. For more information on institutional theory, see Scott, W. R. (1995). *Institutions and organizations.* Thousand Oaks, CA: Sage.

6. Pfeffer, J. (2007). Human resources from an organizational behavior perspective: Some paradoxes explained. *Journal of Economic Perspectives, 21,* 115–134.

7. The subject of adopting management and organizational practices based on evidence of their effectiveness is called "evidence-based management." For more on this subject, see Pfeffer, J., & Sutton, R. I. (2006). *Hard facts, dangerous half-truths and total nonsense: Profiting from evidence-based management.* Boston, MA: Harvard Business School Press.

   For more on this as it relates to PM, see Colquitt, A. L. (2013, October). Reflections on the state of I/O research and practice: Lessons learned from performance management. *The Industrial Organizational Psychologist.*

8. Sackett, D. L., Rosenberg, W. M. C., Gray, J. A., Haynes, R. B., & Richardson, W. S. (1996). Evidence based medicine: What it is and what it isn't. *British Medical Journal, 312,* 71–72.

9. Among the strongest advocates are Denise Rousseau, Jeffrey Pfeffer, and Robert Sutton. For more information, see the following:

   Rousseau, D. M. (2005). Is there such a thing as "evidence based management." *Academy of Management Review, 31,* 256–269.

   Rousseau, D. M., Manning, J., & Denyer, D. (2008). Evidence in management and organizational science: Assembling the field's full weight of scientific knowledge through reflective reviews. *Annals of the Academy of Management, 2,* 475–515.

Pfeffer & Sutton, *op cit.*

10. Rynes, S. L., Brown, K. G., & Colbert, A. E. 2002. Seven common misconceptions about human resource practices: Research findings versus practitioner beliefs. *Academy of Management Executive, 18,* 92–103.

11. Pfeffer & Sutton, *op cit.*

Chapter 4. Evaluating Performance: A Fool's Errand

1. Sherif, M. (1935). A study of some social factors in perception. *Archives of Psychology, 27,* 187.

2. Tsay, C. J. (2013). Sight over sound in the judgment of music performance. *Proceedings from the National Academy of Sciences, 110,* 14580–14585.

3. See the following for example:

   Benjamin, D. J., & Shapiro, J. M. (2006, November). *Thin-slice forecasts of gubernatorial elections.* Working paper 12660. National Bureau of Economic Research, Cambridge, MA.

   Todorov, A., Mandisodza, A. N., Goren A., & Hall, C. C. (2005). Inferences of competence from faces predict election outcomes. *Science, 308,* 1623–1626.

   Ballew, C. C., & Todorov, A. (2007). Predicting political elections from rapid and unreflective face judgments. *Proceedings from the National Academy of Sciences, 104,* 17948–17953.

   Ambady, N., & Rosenthal , R. (1993). Half a minute: Predicting teacher evaluations from thin slices of nonverbal behavior and physical attractiveness. *Journal of Personality and Social Psychology, 64,* 431–441.

   Rule, N. O., & Ambady, N. (2008). The face of success: Inferences from chief executive officers' appearance predict company profits. *Psychological Science, 19,* 109–111.

4. David Rock has written about this movement and for a couple of high-profile recent examples, look at what GE and Deloitte are doing:

   Rock, D., & Jones, B. (2015, November 6). What really happens when companies nix performance ratings. *Harvard Business Review.* Retrieved from https://hbr.org/2015/11/what-really-happens-when-companies-nix-performance-ratings

   Buckingham, M., & Goodall, A. (2015, April). Reinventing performance management. *Harvard Business Review,* 40–50.

   Nisen, M. (2015). *Why GE had to kill its annual performance review after more than 3 decades.* Retrieved from http://qz.com/428813/ge-performance-review-strategy-shift/

5. These and other statistics related to current practices can be found in the following reports:

Mercer (2012). *Current trends in performance management.*

Lawler, E. E., Benson, G. S., & McDermott, M. (2012, October/December). Performance management and reward systems. *WorldAtWork Journal,* 19–28.

Towers Watson (2011, September 22). The talent management and rewards imperative for 2012: Leading through uncertain times. *Talent management and Rewards Survey Report, North America.*

I4cp (2012). *Performance management playbook: Managing critical performance challenges.* Research report.

Buck Consultants. (2011, September). *Compensation planning for 2012.* Cited in S. Rothier, & E. Lodwick (2012, January 13). Research report: Pay-for-performance. WRG Information Research Center, Mercer Consulting.

Sibson Consulting. (2010, Fall). *Results from the real pay-for-performance study.* Cited in Rothier, S., & Lodwick, E. (2012, January 13). Research report: Pay-for-performance. WRG Information Research Center, Mercer Consulting.

McKinsey & Company. (2009, November). Motivating people: Getting beyond money. *McKinsey Quarterly.*

Center for Effective Organizations (2013). Summary of performance management research, presentation to i4cp PM Exchange Group.

Stevenson, C. (2013). *Performance management: Sticking with what doesn't work.* Retrieved from http://www.i4cp.com/trendwatchers/2013/10/31/performance-management-sticking-with-what-doesn-t-work

6. For example, see:

Festinger, L. (1954). A theory of social comparison processes. *Human Relations, 7,* 117–140.

Adams, J. S. (1965). Inequity in social exchange. In L. Berkowitz (Ed.), *Advances in social psychology* (pp. 267–299). New York, NY: Academic Press.

7. Bryson, B., & Read, J. L. (2009). *Total engagement: Using games and virtual worlds to change the way people work and businesses compete.* Boston, MA: Harvard Business Press.

8. Svenson, O. (1981). Are we all less risky and more skillful than our fellow drivers? *Acta Psychologica, 2,* 143–148.

9. Meyer, H. H. (1980). Self-appraisal of job performance. *Personnel Psychology, 33,* 291–295.

For similar arguments, see:

Brown, J. D. (1986). Evaluations of self and others: Self-enhancement biases in social judgments. *Social Cognition, 4,* 353–376.

Miller, D. T., & Ross, M. (1975). Self-serving biases in the attribution of causality: Fact or fiction? *Psychological Bulletin, 82,* 213–225.

Kruger, J., & Dunning, D. (1999). Unskilled and unaware of it: How difficulties in recognizing one's own incompetence lead to inflated self-assessments. *Journal of Personality and Social Psychology, 77*, 1121–1134.

10. See the following for more details:

Barankay, I. (2011). *Rankings and social tournaments: Evidence from a crowdsourcing experiment.* Working paper, University of Pennsylvania, Philadelphia.

Mercer, 2012, *op. cit.*

Towers Watson (2013, March). *Performance management briefing.*

Towers Watson (2012). *Talent management and rewards survey report.*

11. See the following articles:

Eriksson, T., Poulsen, A., & Villeval, M. C. (2009). Feedback and incentives: Experimental evidence. *Labour Economics, 16*, 679–688.

Barankay, *op. cit.*

Fehr, E., & Gachter, S. (2000). Fairness and retaliation: The economics of reciprocity. *Journal of Economic Perspectives, 14*, 159–181.

12. Casas-Arce, P., & Martinez-Jerez, F. A. (2009). Relative performance compensation, contests, and dynamic incentives. *Management Science, 55*, 1306–1320.

13. See the following articles:

Bandiera, O., Barankay, I., & Rasul, I. (2005). Social preferences and the response to incentives: Evidence from personnel data. *Quarterly Journal of Economics, 120*, 917–962.

Fehr & Gachter, *op. cit.*

14. For an example of where relative feedback helped performance, see Blanes, I., Vidal, J., & Nossol, M. (2009). *Tournaments without prizes: Evidence from personnel records.* Working paper. Social Science Research Network. Retrieved from http://personal.lse.ac.uk/blanesiv/tournaments.pdf

15. If we were to get technical here, not all of this is error. Some things we call luck may actually be related to a person's talent. For example, we only give big projects to our best people. For a more detailed explanation of these effects, see: Murphy, K. R. (2008). Explaining the weak relationship between job performance and ratings of job performance. *Industrial and Organizational Psychology, 1*, 148–160.

16. See the following references for more details:

Deming, W. E. (1994). *The new economics* (2nd ed.). Cambridge, MA: MIT Center for Advanced Engineering Study.

Coens, T., & Jenkins, M. (2002). *Abolishing performance appraisals: Why they backfire and what to do instead.* San Francisco, CA: Berrett-Kohler.

17. The upper left is the Hering Illusion, named for Ewald Hering, a physiologist in 1861. Top middle is the Ebbinghaus illusion, also called Titchner circles. Ebbinghaus was a German psychologist living in the late 1800s. Titchener popularized the illusion in the English speaking world.

18. Upper right is the Kanizsa Triangle Illusion. This illusion was described by Italian psychologist Gaetano Kanizsa in 1955. According to the Gestalt law of closure, we tend to see objects that are close together as a related group. In the case of the Kanizsa Triangle, we even see contour lines that don't exist and ignore gaps in order to form a cohesive image.

19. For more information on the invisible gorilla, see: Chabris, C., & Simons, D. (2011). *The invisible gorilla: How our intuitions deceive us.* New York, NY: Harmony. Retrieved from http://www.theinvisiblegorilla.com/gorilla_experiment.html

20. Lower right is the old woman/young woman illusion. This illusion shows that figure and ground are interchangeable. The origin is thought to be an anonymous German postcard dating from 1888. The faces-chalice illusion at the lower-middle is similar, sometimes called Rubin's vase for Danish psychologist Edgar Rubin, developed around 1915. This is also a classic figure-ground illusion.

21. Nickerson, R. S., & Adams, M. J. (1979). Long-term memory for a common object. *Cognitive Psychology, 11,* 287–307.

22. Rink, M. (1999). Memory for everyday objects: Where are the digits on numerical keypads? *Applied Cognitive Psychology, 13,* 329–350.

23. Those of you who watched the popular Netflix documentary "Making a Murderer" got a strong dose of this. For a good review of this research, consult Wells, G. L., & Olson, E. A. (2003). Eyewitness testimony. *Annual Review of Psychology, 54,* 277–295.

24. Shaw, J., & Porter, S. (2015). Constructing rich false memories of committing a crime. *Psychological Science, 26,* 291–301.

25. Bridge, D. J., & Paller, K. A. (2012). Neural correlates of reactivation and retrieval-induced distortion. *The Journal of Neuroscience, 29,* 12144–12151.

26. Kahneman, D. (2012). *Thinking, fast and slow.* New York, NY: Farrar, Strauss and Giroux.

    For a popular review of some of this work as it relates to decision making, see Hammond, J. S., Keeney, R. L., & Raiffa, H. (1999, September/October). The hidden traps in decision making. *Harvard Business Review,* 3–9.

27. Authors of many PM books describe these errors and rating tendencies. The following resources provide more detail:

    Aguinis, H. (2013). *Performance management.* Upper Saddle River, NJ: Pearson.

    Pulakos, E. D. (2009). *Performance management: A new approach to driving business results.* New York, NY: John Wiley.

    Smither, J. W., & London, M. (2009). *Performance management: Putting research into practice.* San Francisco, CA: Jossey-Bass.

    For more detail on how to address these errors see London, M., Mone, E. M., & Scott, J. C. (2004). Performance management and assessment: Methods for improving rater accuracy and employee goal setting. *Human Resources Management, 43,* 319–336. As you will see, my recommendation will be to give up on performance ratings altogether, not trying to improve them. Research shows most of these methods improve things very little.

28. Selected references for studies of bias in sports contests:

Myers, T., Nevill, A. M., & Al-Nakeeb, Y. (2010). An examination of judging consistency in a combat sport. *Journal of Quantitative Analysis in Sports, 6,* 1–16.

Madden, J. M. (1975, May). A note on Olympic judging. *Professional Psychology,* 111–113.

For examples of the impact of position effects, see:

Greenless, I., Dicks, M., Holder, T., & Thelwell (2007). Order effects in sport: Examining the impact of order of information presentation on attributions of ability. *Psychology of Sport and Exercise, 8,* 477–489.

Bruin, W. B. (2006). Save the last dance II: Unwanted serial position effects in figure skating judgments. *Acta Psychologica, 123,* 299–311.

Carney, D. R., & Banaji, M. M. (2012). First is best. *PLoS ONE, 7,* 1–5.

Morgan, H. N., & Rotthoff, K. W. (2014). The harder the task, the higher the score: Findings of a difficulty bias. *Economic Inquiry, 52,* 1014–1026.

29. Selected references for studies of bias in nonsports contests:

Swift, S. A., Moore, D. A., Sharek, Z. S., & Gino, F. (2013). Inflated applicants: Attribution errors in performance evaluation by professionals. *PLoS ONE 8,* 1–15.

Plucker, J. A., Kaufman, J. C., Temple, J. S., & Qian, M. (2009). Do experts and novices evaluate movies the same way? *Psychology & Marketing, 26,* 470–478.

30. Hodgson, R. T. (2008). An examination of judge reliability at a major U.S. wine competition. *Journal of Wine Economics, 3,* 105–113.

Other research shows similar problems:

The Guardian (2013). *Wine-tasting: It's junk science.* Retrieved from https://www.theguardian.com/lifeandstyle/2013/jun/23/wine-tasting-junk-science-analysis

The Wall Street Journal (2009). *A hint of hype, a taste of illusion.* Retrieved from https://www.wsj.com/articles/SB10001424052748703683804574533840282653628

Hodgson, R. T. (2009). An analysis of the concordance among 13 U.S. wine competitions. *Journal of Wine Economics, 4,* 105–113.

Cao, J., & Stokes, L. (2013). *Evaluation of wine judge performance based on a simple t-test.* Working paper. Retrieved from http://www.wine-economics.org/aawe/wp-content/uploads/2013/07/Cao_Stokes.pdf

31. Mantonakis, A., Rodero, P., Lesschaeve, I., & Hastie, R. (2009). Effects of serial position on preferences. *Psychological Science, 20,* 1309–1312.

32. Bernardin, H. J., & Villanova, P. (1986). Performance appraisal. In E. A. Locke (Ed.), *Generalizing from laboratory to field settings* (pp. 43–62). Lexington, MA: Lexington Books.

33. Kozlowski, S. W. J., Chao, G. T., & Morrison, R. F. (1998). Games raters play: Politics, strategies, and impression management in performance apprais-

al. In J. W. Smither (Ed.), *Performance appraisal: State of the art methods for performance appraisal* (pp. 163–205). San Francisco, CA: Jossey-Bass.

For a good review of this literature, see: Spence, J. R., & Keeping, L. (2011). Conscious rating distortion in performance appraisal: A review, commentary, and proposed framework for research. *Human Resource Management Review, 21*, 85–95.

34. For examples, see the following:

Zitzewitz, E. (2006). Nationalism in winter sports judging and its lessons for organizational decision making. *Journal of Economics and Management, 15*, 67–99.

Zitzewitz, E. (2003). *Lessons for business from Olympics judging.* Retrieved from https://www.stanford.edu/group/knowledgebase/cgi-bin/2003/02/15/lessons-for-business-from-olympics-judging/

Forbes (2012, June 10). *Boxing's integrity suffers another black eye after Bradley-Pacquiao split decision.* Retrieved from https://www.forbes.com/sites/kurtbadenhausen/2012/06/10/controversial-pacquiao-loss-delivers-blow-to-potential-mayweather-mega-bout/#2820a8225d41

Bialik, C. (2012, July 27). Removing judges' bias is Olympic-size challenge. *Wall Street Journal.* Retrieved from http://online.wsj.com/news/articles/SB10000872396390044347710457755125352159721 4

35. Callahan, B. P., Mulholland, S. E., & Rotthoff, K. W. (2012). *Cultural bias: Gymnasts, judges, and bilateral trade agreements.* Unpublished paper. Seton Hall, South Orange, NJ.

36. O'Neill, T. A., Carswell, J. J., & McLarnon, M. J. W. (2012) *Performance ratings have larger rater and small ratee components, usually.* Paper presented at the annual meeting of the Society for Industrial and Organizational Psychology, San Diego, CA.

For a scathing critique of ratings, see:

Adler, S. A., Campion, M., Colquitt, A. L., Grubb, A., Murphy, K., Ollander-Krane, R., & Pulakos, E. (2016). Getting rid of performance ratings: Genius or folly?—A debate. *Industrial and Organizational Psychology, 9*, 219–253.

The interested reader should also consult Murphy, K. R. (2008). Explaining the weak relationship between job performance and ratings of job performance. *Industrial and Organizational Psychology, 1*, 148–160.

This research area is not for the "faint of heart." This is a very technical area and the analyses conducted involve very complex measurement and statistical techniques. There are also many different approaches and techniques to answer this question that can make it a difficult area for practitioners to digest.

37. Landy, F., & Farr, J. L. (1980). Performance rating. *Psychological Bulletin, 87*, 72–107.

38. See the following articles for a good review of this research:

Woehr, D. J., & Huffcutt, A. I. (1994). Rater training for performance appraisal: A quantitative review. *Journal of Occupational Psychology, 67,* 189–205.

Hauenstein, N. M. A. (1999). Training raters to increase the accuracy of appraisals and the usefulness of feedback. In J. W. Smithers (1998) *Performance management: Putting research into practice.* San Francisco, CA: Jossey-Bass.

39. See for example:

Conway, J., & Huffcutt, A. (1997). Psychometric properties of multi-source performance ratings: A meta-analysis of subordinate, supervisor, peer, and self-ratings. *Human Performance, 10,* 331–360.

Harris, M., & Schaubroeck, J. (1988). A meta-analysis of self-supervisor, self-peer, and peer-supervisor ratings. *Personnel Psychology, 41,* 43–62.

40. Palmer, J. K., & Loveland, J. M. (2008). The influence of group discussion on performance judgments: Rating accuracy, contrast effects and halo. *The Journal of Psychology, 142,* 117–130.

41. For an overview of this practice, see:

Dominick, P. G. (2013). Forced rankings: Pros, cons, and practices. In J. W. Smither & M. London (2009). *Performance management: Putting research into practice* (pp. 411–443). San Francisco, CA: Jossey-Bass.

Stewart, S. M., Gruys, M. L., & Storm, M. (2010). Forced distribution performance evaluation systems: Advantages, disadvantages and keys to implementation. *Journal of Management and Organization, 16,* 168–179.

42. See the following for more details:

Mercer, 2012 *op. cit.*

Towers Watson, 2013, *op. cit.*

Towers Watson, 2012, *op. cit.*

43. For examples of what critics of forced rankings have to say, see:

Pfeffer, J., & Sutton, R. I. (2006). *Hard facts, dangerous half-truths and total nonsense: Profiting from evidence-based management.* Boston, MA: Harvard Business School Press.

Boyle, M. (2001, May 28). Performance reviews: Perilous curves ahead. *Fortune.*

Rock, D. (2013, May 8). Performance management and forced ranking should be ditched. *The Australian Financial Review.*

For examples of what proponents of forced rankings have to say, see:

Welch, J. F. (2001). *Jack: Straight from the gut.* New York, NY: Warner Books.

Grote, D. (2005). *Forced ranking: Making performance management work.* Boston, MA: Harvard Business School.

See the following for examples of other research critical of this practice:

Baumann, H. M., Schleicher, D. J., Green, S. G., & Bull-Schaefer, R. A. (2012). *The role of rater personality in forced distribution rating systems.* Paper presented at the 27th Annual Conference of the Society for Industrial and Organizational Psychology, San Diego, CA.

Wu, L., Ferris, L., Kwan, H. K., Chiang, F., & Snape, E. (2013). *You compete me: Competition and cooperation goals predict workplace ostracism.* Presentation at Society for Industrial and Organizational Psychology meeting, Houston, TX.

Schleicher, D., Bull, R., & Green, S. (2009). Rater reactions to forced distribution systems. *Journal of Management, 35,* 899–927.

44. O'Boyle, E., & Aguinis, H. (2012). The best and the rest: Revisiting the norm of normality of individual performance. *Personnel Psychology,* 65, 79–119.

45. The Microsoft story played out over a 2-year period. The first act was reported by Eichenwald, K. (2012, July 3). *Microsoft's downfall: Inside the executive mails and cannibalistic culture that felled a tech giant. Vanity Fair.* The second act, along with the demise of Steve Ballmer was reported in late 2013: Yarrow, J. (2013, November 12). *Microsoft just killed the controversial "stack ranking" review system that killed employee morale.* Retrieved from http://www.businessinsider. com/microsoft-just-killed-its-controversial-stackranking-employee-review -system-2013-11. In the final act, they announced their new process: See Ritchie, J., Dodge, L., & Rettenmyer, N. (2014, March). *The Microsoft story: A new approach to performance and development.* WorldatWork webinar.

46. For other accounts of the experiences of both Microsoft and Yahoo see:

The Economist. (2013, November 16). *Ranked and yanked..* Retrieved from http://www.economist.com/news/business/21589866-firms-keep -grading-their-staff-ruthlessly-may-not-get-best-them-ranked-and-yanked

Brustein, J. (2013, November 12). Yahoo's latest HR disaster: Ranking workers on a curve. *Bloomberg Businessweek Technology.* Retrieved from http:// www.businessweek.com/articles/2013-11-12/yahoos-latest-hr-disaster- ranking-workers-on-a-curve

47. Examples include: Netflix; ConAgra; Kelly Services; Adobe; Motorola; Medtronic; REI; Expedia; and Juniper Networks. See the following sources for additional details about what these companies are doing in this area:

McCord, P. (2014, January/February). How Netflix reinvented HR. *Harvard Business Review,* 71–76.

This report is about Cargill. Pulakos, E. D., Hanson, R. M., Arad, S., & Moye, N. (2014). *Performance management can be fixed: An on-the-job experiential learning approach for complex behavioral change.* PDRI/CEB Report. Retrieved from https://www.pdri.com/images/uploads/PM%20Reform%20 -%20Driving%20Behavior%20Change.pdf

This case study is about Kelly Services. Garr, S. G. (2012). *Abandoning performance scores.* Bersin & Associates Case Study. Retrieved from http://blog. bersin.com/abolishing-performance-scores-kelly-services-style/

Bersin & Associates (2013, September 26). *Adobe case study.* Webinar.

Pietz, J. (2013, November 4). The end of "valued performers" at Motorola. *Chicago Business News.*

McGregor, J. (2013, February 14). The corporate kabuki of performance reviews. *The Washington Post.*

7Geese (2013, October 7). *Eliminating performance ratings: Learn how Medtronic did it.* Retrieved from http://blog.7geese.com/2013/10/07/eliminating -performance-ratings-learn-how-medtronic-inc-did-it/

Stevenson, 2013, *op. cit.*

Mercer Consulting (2011, June 22). *Innovation in action: Juniper Network's creative new approach to talent management.* Innovation conversations: People at the heart of performance webcast.

48. Rock & Jones, 2015, *op. cit.*
49. Nisen, M. (2015). *Why GE had to kill its annual performance review after more than three decades.* Retrieved from http://qz.com/428813/ge-performance-review-strategy-shift/
50. Mercer (2011). *Next generation of pay for performance.* Survey report, May.
51. Buckingham & Goodall, 2015, op. cit.

Chapter 5. Money: It's a Crime

1. Thanks to John Boudreau for bringing this example to my attention. See Khatib, F. et al (2011). Crystal structure of a monomeric retroviral protease solved by protein folding game players. *Nature Structural & Molecular Biology 18,* 1175–1177.

   This example is also highlighted in the Netflix documentary about the Internet *Lo and Behold.*

2. Incentive Federation, Inc. (2015, January). *Incentive market study.* Prepared for The Incentive Federation by Intellective Group.

3. These and other statistics related to current practices can be found in the following reports:

   Rothier, S., & Lodwick, E. (2012, January 13). *Research report: Pay-for-performance.* WRG Information Research Center, Mercer Consulting.

   Mercer (2012, March). *Compensation planning in 2012: Today's landscape.*

   Mercer (2012). *Current trends in performance management.*

   Institute for Corporate Productivity. (2011). *Tying pay to performance.* Research brief.

   Pascarella, P. (1997). Compensating teams. *Across the board, 34,* 16–22.

   Hewitt (2004, May). *Paying for performance, 2003–04 WorldAtWork survey brief.*

   Mercer (2011, May). *Next generation of pay for performance. Survey report.*

   Hewitt Associates. (2010). *Companies around the world focus on rewarding high performance through variable pay programs.* Hewitt News Release Archive. Retrieved from http://aon.mediaroom.com/index.php?s=25825&item=607.

Buck Consultants. (2011, September). Compensation planning for 2012. Cited in S. Rothier, & E. Lodwick (2012, January 13). *Research report: Pay-for-performance.* WRG Information Research Center, Mercer Consulting.

Towers Watson (2011, September 22). *The talent management and rewards imperative for 2012: Leading through uncertain times. Talent management and rewards survey report, North America.*

Sibson Consulting (2010, Fall). Results from the real pay-for-performance study. Cited in Rothier, S., & Lodwick, E. (2012, January 13). *Research report: Pay-for-performance.* WRG Information Research Center, Mercer Consulting.

McKinsey & Company. (2009, November). Motivating people: Getting beyond money. *McKinsey Quarterly.*

4. Several authors have made this point as well:

Manzoni, J. F. (2008). On the folly of hoping for A, simply because you are trying to pay for A. *Studies in Managerial and Financial Accounting, 18,* 19–41.

Pfeffer, J., & Sutton, R. I. (2006). *Hard facts, dangerous half-truths and total nonsense: Profiting from evidence-based management.* Boston, MA: Harvard Business School Press.

Pfeffer, J. (1998, May/June). Six dangerous myths about pay. *Harvard Business Review,* 109–119.

Grant, A., & Singh, J. (2011, March 30). The problem with financial incentives—and what to do about it. *Knowledge@Wharton.* Retrieved from http://knowledge.wharton.upenn.edu/article/the-problem-with-financial -incentives-and-what-to-do-about-it/

5. Dan Pink for example highlights some of these in his book. See Pink, D. H. (2009). *Drive: The surprising truth about what motivates us.* New York, NY: Riverhead Books.

6. Bureau of Labor Statistics (2014). *Volunteering in the United States, 2013.* Retrieved from http://www.bls.gov/news.release/volun.nr0.htm

7. See the following sources for more details on these efforts.

CNN. (2014, March 12). *Crowdsourcing volunteers comb satellite photos of Malaysia Airlines jet.* Retrieved from http://www.cnn.com/2014/03/11/us/ malaysiaairlines-plane-crowdsourcing-search/

Jastrzebski, S. (2014, March 11). *Evolved science: Crowds can catalog bugs faster.* Retrieved from http://wabe.org/post/evolved-science-crowdsourcing- makes-cataloging-bugs-faster

8. Van Herpen, M., Van Praag, M., & Cools, K. (2005). The effects of performance measurement and compensation on motivation: An empirical study. *De Economist, 153,* 303–329.

9. Books by Daniel Kahneman and Dan Ariely provide numerous examples of where traditional economic principles are questioned. Ariely's book is a fun and interesting look at the field of behavioral economics, a field which is beginning to rewrite the rules of classical economics.

Kahneman, D. (2012). *Thinking, fast and slow*. New York, NY: Farrar, Strauss and Giroux.

Ariely, D. (2010). *Predictably irrational: The hidden forces that shape our decisions*. New York, NY: Harper Collins.

10. See the following:

Malone, K. (2014, March 4). *"Lexus lanes" and the price of saving time*. National Public Radio. Retrieved from https://www.marketplace.org/2014/03/04/business/lexus-lanes-and-price-saving-time

Janson, M., & Levinson, D. (2014). *Hot or not: Driver elasticity to price on the MnPASS hot lanes*. Working paper. University of Minnesota, Minneapolis.

11. See the following studies for more details:

Cable, D. M., & Judge, T. A. (1994). Pay preferences and job search decisions: A person-organization fit perspective. *Personnel Psychology, 47*, 317–348.

Trank, C. Q., Rynes, S. L., & Bretz, R. D. (2002). Attracting applicants in the war for talent: Differences in work preferences among high achievers. *Journal of Business and Psychology, 16*, 331–345.

12. For more on their research, see the following references:

McCabe, D. L., & Trevino, L. K. (1995). Cheating among business students: A challenge for business leaders and educators. *Journal of Management Education, 19*, 205–218.

McCabe, D. L., & Trevino, L. K. (1996). What we know about cheating in college, *Change, 28*, 29–33.

13. Niemiec, C. P., Ryan, R. M., & Deci, E. L. (2008). The path taken: Consequences of attaining intrinsic and extrinsic aspirations in post-college life. *Journal of Research in Personality, 43*, 291–306.

14. Easterlin, R. (1974). Does economic growth improve the human lot? Some empirical evidence. In P. David & M. Reder (Eds.), *Nations and households in economic growth: Essays in honor of Moses Abramovitz*. New York, NY: Academic Press.

15. Easterlin, R. A., McVey, L. A., Switek, M., Sawangfa, O., & Zweig, J. S. (2010). *The happiness-income paradox revisited*. Proceedings from the National Academy of Sciences, 107, 22463–222468.

16. Brickman, P., Coates, D., & Janoff-Bulman, R. (1978). Lottery winners and accident victims: Is happiness relative? *Journal of Personality and Social Psychology, 36*, 917–27.

Admittedly this study was very small, with only 22 participants. While Lottery winners were more satisfied than nonlottery winners, the difference was not statistically significant.

17. Results of individual studies depend on several factors including how they studied this subject, how they measured income and how they defined happiness. While there is not much support for the assumption that money can buy happiness, the reasons behind it are complex and important.

Studies done in single countries or multiple countries typically find curvilinear relationships when they look at raw income. People with low and high income levels are *less* satisfied; people with middle income levels are *more* satisfied. Many researchers argue, however, that income should be transformed using a log transformation, since a difference of $10K is larger at lower income levels than it is at a higher income level. When income is transformed we see a modest positive relationship, people with higher incomes are more satisfied.

Studies done in a single country, looking at income changes and happiness changes over time typically find no relationship between income and happiness. Incomes increase over time but happiness stays flat. This is the Easterlin Paradox.

Other research suggests the nature of this relationship depends on how you define happiness or well-being. Researchers Daniel Kahneman and Angus Deaton suggest there are two components to well-being: emotional well-being—the emotional quality of an individual's everyday experience (e.g., Positive affect, stress, feeling blue); and evaluation of life—the thoughts people have about their life. It turns out life evaluation is strongly related to income, increasing steadily with Income. Emotional well-being is not as strongly related to income; it increases modestly with income at lower income levels (although not as sharply as life evaluation does), begins to flatten at middle income levels and flattens completely after about $75,000. Many people may have heard happiness peaks at $75,000 and does not increase after that. Kahneman & Deaton's work is the origin of this finding. For more details on this research, see Kahneman, D., & Deaton, A. (2010). High income improves evaluation of life but not emotional well-being. *PNAS, Psychological and Cognitive Sciences, 107,* 16489–16493.

18. Campbell, A., Converse, P. E., & Rodgers, W. L. (1976). *The quality of American life: Perceptions, evaluations, and satisfactions.* New York, NY: Russell Sage Foundation.

19. Tellegen, A., Lykken, D. T., Bouchard, T. J., Wilcox, K. J., Segal, N. L., & Rich. S. (1988). Personality similarity in twins reared apart and together. *Journal of Personality and Social Psychology, 54,* 1031–1039.

20. Brickman, P., & Campbell, D. T. (1971). Hedonic relativism and planning the good society. In M. H. Appley (Ed.), *Adaptation-level theory: A symposium.* New York, NY: Academic Press, 287–302.

21. Diener, E. (2000). Subjective well-being. *American Psychologist, 55,* 34–43.

22. Helson, H. (1948). Adaptation-level as a basis for a quantitative theory of frames of reference. *Psychological Review, 55,* 297–313.

23. De Waal, F. (2013). *Moral behavior in animals.* TEDx Peachtree talk. Retrieved from http://www.ted.com/talks/frans_de_waal_do_animals_have_morals.html

24. For an overview of this research, consult Clark, A. E., Frijters, P., & Shields, M. A. (2008). Relative income, happiness, and utility: An explanation for the Easterlin paradox and other puzzles. *Journal of Economic Literature, 46,* 95–144.

25. Judge, T. A., Piccolo, R., Podsakoff, N. P., Shaw, J. C., & Rich, B. L. (2010). The relationship between pay and job satisfaction: A meta-analysis of the literature. *Journal of Vocational Behavior, 77,* 157–167.

26. Heath, C. (1999). On the social psychology of agency relationships: Lay theories of motivation overemphasize extrinsic incentives. *Organizational Behavior and Human Decision Processes, 78,* 25–62.

27. Beer, M., & Katz, N. (2003). Do incentives work? The perceptions of a world-wide sample of senior executives. *Human Resource Planning, 26,* 30–44.

28. For more details of the work of Voh's and her colleagues, see:

    Vohs, K. D., Mead, N. L., & Goode, M. R. (2006). The psychological conse-quences of money. *Science.* 314, 1154–1156.

    Gasiorowska, A., Chaplin, L., Zaleskiewicz, T., Wygrab, S., & Vohs, K. (2016). Money cues increase agency and decrease prosociality among children: Early signs of market mode behavior. *Psychological Science, 27,* 331–344.

    Vohs, K. D. (2015). Money priming can change people's thoughts, feelings, motivations and behaviors: An update on 10 years of experiments. *Journal of Experimental Psychology, 144,* 73–85.

29. Devoe, S. E., Pfeffer, J., & Lee, B. Y. (2013). Why does money make money more important? Survey and experimental evidence. *Industrial Labor Rela-tions Review, 66,* 1078–1096.

30. Griffeth, R. W., Hom, P. W., & Gaertner, S. (2000). A meta-analysis of ante-cedents and correlates of employee turnover: Update, moderator tests, and research implications for the next millennium. *Journal of Manage-ment, 26,* 463–488.

31. WorldAtWork. (2014). *Bonus programs and practices.* Survey report.

32. Meyer, J. P., Stanley, D. J., Herscovitch, L., & Topolnytsky, L. (2002). Affective, continuance, and normative commitment to the organization: A meta-analysis of antecedents, correlates and consequences. *Journal of Vocational Behavior, 61,* 20–52.

Chapter 6. A Pleasant Death of Performance-Based Pay

1. Ludwick, J. (2004, January 30). How to collect overtime in under 8 hours. *Albuquerque Journal.* Retrieved from http://www.abqjournal.com/news/metro/139316metro01-30-04.htm

2. Meyer, H. (1975). The pay-for-performance dilemma. *Organizational Dynam-ics, 3,* 39–50.

3. Hall, B. J., & Murphy, K. J. (2003). The trouble with stock options, *Journal of Economic Perspectives, 17,* 3, 49–70. Cited in Grant, A., & Singh, J. (2011). The problem with financial incentives—and what to do about it. *Knowl-edge@Wharton,* March 30, 2011.

4. Sources for the statistics to follow can be found in the following reports:

Rothier, S., & Lodwick, E. (2012, January 13). *Research report: Pay-for-performance.* WRG Information Research Center, Mercer Consulting.

Mercer. (2012a, March). *Compensation planning in 2012: Today's landscape.*

Mercer. (2012b). *Current trends in performance management.*

Institute for Corporate Productivity. (i4cp) (2011). Tying pay to performance. Research report.

Pascarella, P. (1997). Compensating teams. *Across the Board, 34,* 16–22.

Hewitt (2004, May). *Paying for performance.* 2003–04 WorldAtWork survey brief.

Mercer (2011, May). *Next generation of pay-for-performance.* Survey report.

Hewitt Associates. (2010). *Hewitt survey shows slight rebound in global corporate spending on salary increases this year.* Retrieved from http://aon.mediaroom.com/index.php?s=25825&item=607

Buck Consultants. (2011, September). Compensation planning for 2012. Cited in S. Rothier, & E. Lodwick (2012, January 13). *Research report: Pay-for-performance.* WRG Information Research Center, Mercer Consulting.

Towers Watson. (2011). *The talent management and rewards imperative for 2012: Leading through uncertain times.* Talent management and rewards survey report, North America.

Sibson Consulting. (2010). Results from the real pay-for-performance study, Fall. Cited in Rothier, S., & Lodwick, E. (2012). *Research report: Pay-for-performance.* WRG Information Research Center, Mercer Consulting.

Dewhurst, M., Guthridge, M., & Mohr, E. (2009, November). Motivating people: Getting beyond money. *McKinsey Quarterly.*

Hudner, J., & Oliver, K. (2013). *Current trends and new directions in variable pay.* Working Report, Pearl Meyer & Partners, 2013.

PayScale.com (2014). *Compensation best practices.* 2014 Report. Retrieved from https://www.slideshare.net/Payscale/2014-compensation-best-practices-report-31489209

5. For example, see:
Meyer, 1975, *op. cit.*

Lowrey, C. M., Petty, M. M., & Thompson, J. W. (1996). Assessing the merit of merit pay: Employee reactions to performance-based pay. *Human Resource Planning, 19,* 1, 26–37.

Other sources in this area were cited in Chapter 5 in the section of the role of money in attraction.

6. Here are the citations for the eight meta-analysis studies. The first five are the most frequently mentioned in the literature on incentives and P4P:
Camerer, C. F., & Hogarth, R. M. (1999). The effects of financial incentives in experiments: A review and capital-labor-production framework. *Social Science Working Paper #1059,* California Institute of Technology.

Guzzo, R. A., Jette, R. D., & Katzell, R. A. (1985). The effects of psychological-ly-based intervention programs on worker productivity: A meta-analysis. *Personnel Psychology, 38,* 275–291.

Incentive Research Foundation. (2002). *Incentives, motivation and workplace performance: Research & best practices.* Final Report. Available at http://theirf.org/research/

Jenkins, D. G. Jr., Mitra, A., Gupta, N., & Shaw, J. D. (1998). Are financial incentives related to performance? A meta-analytic review of empirical research. *Journal of Applied Psychology, 83,* 777–787.

Judiesch, M. K. (1994). *The effects of incentive compensation systems on productivity, individual differences in output variability and selection utility.* Doctoral dissertation. University of Iowa, Iowa City.

Locke, E. A., Feren, D. B., McCaleb, V. M., Shaw, K. N., & Denny, A. T. (1980). The relative effectiveness of four ways of motivating employee performance. In K. D. Duncan, M. M. Gruenberg, & D. Wallis, *Changes in working life* (pp. 363–388). New York, NY: Wiley.

Stajkovic, A. D., & Luthans, F. (1997). A meta-analysis of the effects of organizational behavior modification on task performance, 1975–1995. *Academy of Management Journal, 40,* 1122–1149.

Weibel, A., Rost, K., & Osterloh, M. (2010). Pay-for-performance in the public sector: Benefits and (hidden) costs. *Journal of Public Administration Research and Theory, 20,* 387–412.

It is worth noting these meta-analysis studies are not without their critics. There is always subjectivity involved in deciding which studies to include and which to exclude. Meta-analysis studies always exclude far more studies than they include. There is also subjectivity in how to classify studies in terms of the specific boundary conditions being tested.

7. Some of these studies are very sloppy. They typically use archival data from large-scale national surveys, databases, or panel studies. In many cases, they know little or nothing about the programs in place in organizations or what other types of changes may have accompanied the introduction of the P4P programs. The researchers may only know the organization has an incentive system in place; they may not know who is eligible for it or even if the incentive is linked to individual performance, group performance or even firm performance. Finally, in some of these studies, the performance measures are self-reported judgments of organizational performance. Here are selected citations for some more recent studies:

Bryson, A., Freeman, R., Lucifora, C., Pellizzari, M., & Perotin, V. (2012). *Paying For performance: Incentive pay schemes and employees' financial participation.* Centre for Economic Performance. Discussion paper # 1112.

Gielen, A. C., Kerkhofs, M. J. M., & van Ours, J. C. (2010). How performance-related pay affects productivity and employment. *Journal of Population Economics, 23,* 291–301.

8. Listed below are key studies reviewing this research:

   Springer, M., Hamilton, L., McCaffrey, D. F., Ballou, D., Le, V., Pepper, M., Lockwood, J. F., & Stecher, B. M. (2010). Teacher pay for performance: Experimental evidence from the project on incentives in teaching. *Vanderbilt University, National Center on Performance Incentives report.*

   Mathematica (2009). *Summary: Pay-for-performance.* Mathematica, Inc. Working Brief.

   Perry, J. L., Mesch, D., & Paarlberg, L. (2006). Motivating employees in a new governance era: The performance paradigm revisited. *Public Administration Review,* July/August, 505–514.

9. Lazear, E. (2000). Performance pay and productivity. *American Economic Review, 90,* 1346–1361.

10. Pfeffer, J., & Sutton, R. I. (2006). *Hard facts, dangerous half-truths and total nonsense: Profiting from evidence-based management.* Boston, MA: Harvard Business School Press.

11. Lemieux, T., MacLeod, W. B., & Parent, D. (2009). Performance pay and wage inequality. *The Quarterly Journal of Economics, 124,* 1–50.

12. This assumption can be tricky to test. Most research in this area looks at the relationship between variation in total pay and performance. Variation in pay happens for nonperformance-related reasons (e.g., starting pay and job structure) as well as for performance-related reasons (performance-based pay increases, bonuses and variable pay). Some of these reasons are more "legitimate" (e.g., based on differences in experience or credentials) while others are less legitimate (e.g., performance-based pay based on biased supervisor performance ratings). We know from Chapter 4 that a significant portion of the pay differentiation based on performance ratings will be due to illegitimate reasons. There is also lots of variability in how researchers have attempted to answer this question that makes it difficult to compare studies and draw firm conclusions. This "messiness" is typical in behavior science research and this is how research typically proceeds over time. The answer that is most appealing to me both empirically and theoretically (and not examined in most of the early research) is a "hump-shaped" relationship. Some dispersion in pay is legitimate, so everyone being paid the same amount (no or low dispersion) might seem unfair and lead to lower performance. It also makes sense to me that higher-levels of dispersion would be difficult to justify given the problems with bias in performance measurement and would create problems with the workforce. It makes sense that the "sweet-spot" for pay dispersion in terms of productivity and performance is somewhere in the middle, driven by legitimate factors like differences in experience and credentials.

13. Mahy, B., Rycx, F., & Volral, M. (2011). Does wage dispersion make all firms productive? *Scottish Journal of Political Economy, 58,* 455–489.

14. Shaw, J. D. (2014). Pay dispersion. *Annual Review of Organizational Psychology and Organizational Behavior, 1,* 521–544.

15. For example, see:

Wageman, R., & Baker, G. (1997). Incentives and cooperation: The joint effects of task and reward interdependence on group performance. *Journal of Organizational Behavior, 18*, 139–158.

Pfeffer, J., & Langton, N. (1993). The effect of wage dispersion on satisfaction, productivity, and working collaboratively: Evidence from college and university faculty. *Administrative Science Quarterly, 38*, 382–407.

16. Trevor, C. O., Reilly, G., & Gerhart, B. (2012). Reconsidering pay dispersion's effect on the performance of interdependent work: Reconciling sorting and pay inequality. *Academy of Management Journal, 55*, 585–610.

17. Bloom, M. (1999). The performance effects of pay dispersion on individuals and organizations. *Academy of Management Journal, 42*, 25–40.

18. Sommers, P. M. (1998). Work incentives and salary distributions in the National Hockey League. *Atlantic Economic Journal, 26*(1), 119–119.

19. For more on the Google story see:

Hardy, Q. (2007). *Close to the vest*. Retrieved from http://www.forbes.com/global/2007/0702/028.html

Greg Linden, *Google cuts founders awards*. Geeking with Greg, Thursday, July 05, 2007. Retrieved from http://glinden.blogspot.com/2007/07/google-cuts-founders-awards.html

20. Several meta-analysis studies have looked at this question. See the following for example:

Griffeth, R. W., Hom, P. W., & Gaertner, S. (2000). A meta-analysis of antecedents and correlates of employee turnover: Update, moderator tests, and research implications for the next millennium. *Journal of Management, 26*, 463–488.

Hom, P. W., & Griffeth, R. W. (1995). *Employee turnover*. Cincinnati, OH: Southwestern.

Williams, C. R., & Livingstone, L. P. (1994). Another look at the relationship between performance and voluntary turnover. *Academy of Management Journal, 37*, 269–298.

21. The individual studies and meta-analyses in this area have significant problems in terms of their ability to answer our specific question. Testing this hypothesis rigorously requires research with multiple companies, some of which have P4P systems and some of which don't. It is hard to test this within one company because most companies have a single set of reward practices. Answering this question also requires a way to control for other factors that affect the type of reward practices used and the level of turnover observed. For example, different reward systems tend to be favored by different industries and occupational groups which may have different turnover profiles.

Contingent rewards are more likely to be used for some positions than others and in bigger companies versus smaller companies. Also, turnover tends to be higher in certain occupations than others. Finally, certain demographic factors are strongly related to turnover (e.g., tenure). Rigorous research needs to account for these factors. The 3 studies listed below account for many of these factors:

O'Halloran, P. L. (2009). *Do performance-pay workers experience less job turnover and longer tenures?* Paper presented at Ninth Global Conference on Business and Economics, Cambridge, England. ISBN: 978-0-9742114-2-7.

Haines, V. Y., Jalette, P., & Larose, K. (2006). The influence of human resources management practices on employee voluntary turnover rates in the Canadian non-governmental sector. *Industrial and Labor Relations Review, 63*, 228–246.

Batt, R., Colvin, A. J. S., & Keefe, J. (2002). Employee voice, human resource practices and quit rates: Evidence from the telecommunications industry. *Industrial and Labor Relations Review, 55*, 573–594.

22. See the following studies for example:

Pfeffer, J., & Davis-Blake, A. (1992). Salary dispersion, location in the salary distribution, and turnover among college administrators. *Industrial and Labor Relations Review, 45*, 753–763.

Bloom, M., & Michel, J. G. (2002). The relationships among organizational context, pay dispersion, and managerial turnover. *Academy of Management Journal, 45*, 33–42.

Pfeffer & Langton, 1993 *op. cit.*

Shaw, J. D., & Gupta, N. (2007). Pay system characteristics and quit patterns of good, average, and poor performers. *Personnel Psychology, 60*, 903–923.

23. Holmstrom, B. (1989). Agency costs and innovation. *Journal of Economic Behavior and Organization 12*, 305–327.

24. Amabile, T. M., Conti, R., Coon, H., Lazenby, J., & Herron, M. (1996). Assessing the work environment for creativity. *The Academy of Management Journal, 39*, 1154–1184.

25. Azoulay, P., Graff Zivin, J. S., & Manso, G. (2011). Incentives and creativity: Evidence from the academic life sciences. *Journal of Economics, 42*, 527–554.

26. Cui, V., & Yanadori, Y. (2013). Creating incentives for innovation? The relationship between pay dispersion in R&D groups and firm innovation performance. *Strategic Management Journal, 34*, 1502–1511.

27. Kerr, S. (1975). On the folly of rewarding A, while hoping for B. *Academy of Management Journal, 18*, 769–783.

28. See the following references for more details about these examples:

Larkin, I. (2009). *The cost of high-powered incentives: Employee gaming in enterprise software sales.* Working Paper. Harvard Business School, Boston, MA.

Adams, S. J., Heywood, J. S., & Rothstein, R. (2009). Teachers, performance pay, and accountability: What education should learn from other sectors. *Education Policy Institute Series on Alternative Teacher Compensation Systems.* Retrieved from http://epi.3cdn.net/1452343613a3e41b03_o1m6bwlvt.pdf

Schemo, D. J. (2004, January 18). As testing rises, ninth grade becomes pivotal. *The New York Times.*

Shen Y. (2003). Selection incentives in a performance-based contracting system. *Health Services Research, 38,* 535–552.

Grant, A., & Singh, J. (2011, March 30). The problem with financial incentives—and what to do about it. *Knowledge@Wharton.*

29. See the following:

Denis, D. J., Hanouna, P., & Sarin, A. (2006). Is there a dark side to incentive compensation? *Journal of Corporate Finance, 12,* 467–488.

Agarwal, S., & Wang, F. H. (2009). Perverse incentives at the banks? Evidence from a natural experiment. *Working paper.*

30. See the following references for more details about these examples:

Paarsch, H., & Shearer, B. (2000). Piece rates, fixed wages, and incentive effects: Statistical evidence from payroll records. *International Economic Review, 41,* 59–92.

Mathematica, 2009, *op. cit.*

Adams et al., 2009, *op. cit.*

31. See the following for example:

Podsakoff, P. M., & MacKenzie, S. B. (1997). Impact of organizational citizenship behavior on organizational performance: A review and suggestions for future research. *Human Performance, 10,* 133–152.

Wright, P. M., George, J. M., Farnsworth, R., & McMahan, G. C. (1993). Productivity and extra-role behavior: The effects of goals and incentives on spontaneous helping. *Journal of Applied Psychology, 78,* 374–381.

Dekop, J. R., Mangel, R., & Cirka, C. C. (1999). Getting more than you pay for: Organizational citizenship behavior and pay-for-performance plans. *Academy of Management Journal, 42,* 420–428.

32. Beer, M., & Cannon, M. D. (2004). Promise and peril in implementing pay-for-performance. *Human Resource Management, 43,* 3–48.

33. Burks, S., Carpenter, J., & Goette, L. (2006). *Performance pay and the erosion of worker cooperation: Field experimental evidence.* Institute of Labor Economics Discussion Paper # 2013.

34. Bloomberg Business Week. (2013). *Michael Lewis on the next crisis.* Retrieved from http://www.businessweek.com/articles/2013-09-12/michael-lewis-on-the-next-crisis

35. Manzoni, J. F. (2008). On the folly of hoping for A, simply because you are trying to pay for A. *Studies in Managerial and Financial Accounting, 18,* 19–41.

36. Gneezy, U., Meier, S., & Rey-Biel, P. (2011). When and why incentives (don't) work to modify behavior. *Journal of Economic Perspectives, 25,* 1–21.

Dan Ariely also discusses similar research in his book *Predictably Irrational.* For example, offering to pay a friend to help you move makes it less likely that you will get help. See Ariely, D. (2010). *Predictably irrational: The hidden forces that shape our decisions.* New York, NY: Harper Collins.

37. Gneezy, U., & Rustichini, A. (2000). A fine is a price. *The Journal of Legal Studies, 29*, 1–17.

38. Ferraro, F., Pfeffer, J., & Sutton, R. I. (2005). Economics language and assumptions: How theories can become self-fulfilling. *Academy of Management Review, 30*, 8–24.

39. Many authors write about this issue in the context of P4P systems. For example see:

    Pink, D. H. (2009). *Drive: The surprising truth about what motivates us.* New York, NY: Riverhead Books.

    Pfeffer & Sutton, 2006, *op. cit.*

40. There has been considerable controversy surrounding this finding since Deci's initial research in the early 1970s. Some of the controversy relates to whether the undermining effect exists at all. Other discussions don't dispute the undermining effects but instead focus on the boundary conditions and limits of when it occurs and the underlying processes that explain it.

    Deci's original research can be found in Deci, E. L. (1971). Effects of externally-mediated rewards on intrinsic motivation. *Journal of Personality and Social Psychology, 18*, 105–115. It is not only the reward that is important but the entire system related to the rewards, e.g., the measurement system for gathering information on performance, the monitoring of that performance, the context in which this takes place. All of these factors can affect the needs for competency and autonomy.

41. There have been many different types of studies done in this area but most are laboratory experiments. There have been 8 meta-analysis studies reviewing research on this question:

    Deci, E. L., Ryan, R. M., & Koestner, R. (1999). A meta-analytic review of experiments examining the effects of extrinsic rewards on intrinsic motivation. *Psychological Bulletin, 125*, 627–668.

    Rummel, A., & Feinberg, R. (1988). Cognitive evaluation theory: A meta-analytic review of the literature. *Social Behavior and Personality, 16*, 147–164.

    Wiersma, U. J. (1992). The effects of extrinsic rewards on intrinsic motivation: A meta-analysis. *Journal of Occupational and Organizational Psychology, 65*, 101–114.

    Tang, S. H., & Hall, V. C. (1995). The over-justification effect: A meta-analysis. *Applied Cognitive Psychology, 9*, 365–404.

    Cameron, J., & Pierce, W. D. (1994). Reinforcement, reward, and intrinsic motivation: A meta- analysis. *Review of Educational Research, 64*, 363–423.

    Wiebel, A., Rost, K., & Osterloh, M. (2009). Pay for performance in the public sector: Benefits and (hidden) costs. *Journal of Public Administration Research and Theory, 20*, 387–412.

    Cameron, J., Banko, K. M., & Pierce, W. D. (2001). Pervasive negative effects of rewards on intrinsic motivation: The myth continues. *The Behavior Analyst, 24*, 1–44.

Bowles, S., & Polanía-Reyes, S. (2012). Economic incentives and social preferences: Substitutes or complements? *Journal of Economic Literature, 50,* 368–425.

42. Shirom, A., Westman, M., & Melamed, S. (1999). The effects of pay systems on blue-collar employees' emotional distress: The mediating effects of objective and subjective work monotony. *Human Relations, 52,* 1077–1097.

43. Ostlund, D. (2012). *Why do we pay sales commissions?* [Blog].Retrieved from http://blog.fogcreek.com/why-do-we-pay-sales-commissions/

44. See Hackman, J. R., & Oldham, G. R. (1980). *Work redesign.* Reading, MA: Addison-Wesley.

45. Wrzesniewski, A., & Dutton, J. E. (2001). Crafting a job: Revisioning employees as active crafters of their work. *Academy of Management Review, 26,* 179–201.

Chapter 7. Purpose, Direction, and Meaning

1. Hopkins, M. S. (2011, Winter). Steve Jobs, the way John Sculley tells it. *MIT Sloan Management Review.* Retrieved from http://sloanreview.mit.edu/article/steve-jobs-the-way-john-sculley-tells-it/

2. Sheff, D. (1985, February). Interview with Steve Jobs. *Playboy Magazine.* Retrieved from http://allaboutstevejobs.com/sayings/stevejobsinterviews/playboy85.php

3. Allen, B. (2013). *NASA Langley Research Center's contributions to the Apollo program.* Langley Research Center. *NASA.* Retrieved from http://www.nasa.gov/centers/langley/news/factsheets/Apollo.html

4. Some estimates putting the success rate as low as 10%. See Judson, A. S. (1990). *Making strategy happen.* Cambridge, MA: Blackwell.

5. For a good critique of cascading of goals, see Pulakos, E. D., & O'Leary, R. S. (2011). Why is performance management broken? *Industrial and Organizational Psychology, 4,* 146–164.

6. These and other statistics related to current practices can be found in the following reports:

   Mercer (2012). *Current trends in performance management.*

   Lawler, E. E., Benson, G. S., & McDermott, M. (2012, October/December). Performance management and reward systems. *WorldAtWork Journal,* 19–28.

   Towers Watson. (2011, September 22). *The talent management and rewards imperative for 2012: Leading through uncertain times.* Talent management and rewards survey report, North America.

   i4cp. (2012). *Performance management playbook: Managing critical performance challenges.* Retrieved from https://www.i4cp.com/playbooks/performance-management-playbook-managing-critical-performance-challenges

Buck Consultants. (2011, January 13). Compensation planning for 2012, September. Cited in S. Rothier, & E. Lodwick (2012), *Research report: Pay-for-performance.* WRG Information Research Center, Mercer Consulting.

Sibson Consulting (2010, January 13). Results from the real pay-for-performance study, Fall. Cited in Rothier, S., & Lodwick, E. (2012). *Research report: Pay-for-performance.* WRG Information Research Center, Mercer Consulting.

McKinsey & Company (2009, November). Motivating people: Getting beyond money. *McKinsey Quarterly.*

Center for Effective Organizations. (2013). *Summary of performance management research.* Presentation to i4cp PM Exchange group.

Stevenson, C. (2013, October 31). *Performance management: Sticking with what doesn't work.* Institute for Corporate Productivity (i4cp). Retrieved from http://www.i4cp.com/trendwatchers/2013/10/31/performance-man-agement-sticking-with- what-doesn-t-work

Gorman, C. A., Ray, J., Nugent, C., Thibodeaux, C. N., List, S., Lonkar, S., Bradley, S., Mason, M., Pittington, L., Pokhrel-Willet, S. (2012). *A preliminary survey of performance management practices in the United States.* Paper presented at the 2012 annual conference of the Society for Industrial and Organizational Psychologists, San Diego, CA.

7. Oracle. (2012, June). *Goal setting: A fresh perspective.* White paper. Retrieved from http://www.oracle.com/us/media1/goal-setting-fresh-perspective -ee-1679275.pdf

8. For a short review of the goal-setting literature, see Locke, E. A., & Latham, G. P. (2002). Building a practically useful theory of goal setting and task motivation: A 35-year odyssey. *American Psychologist,* 57, 705–715. For a more detailed review, see Locke, E. A., & Latham, G. P. (2013). *New developments in goal setting and task performance.* East Sussex, England: Routledge.

Other narrative reviews on the effectiveness of goal setting:

Latham, G. P., & Yukl, G. A. (1975). A review of research on the application of goal setting in organizations. *The Academy of Management Journal,* 18, 824–845.

Locke, E. A., Shaw, K. N., Saari, L. M., & Latham, G. P. (1981). Goal setting and task performance: 1969–1980. *Psychological Bulletin,* 90, 125–152.

Locke, E. A., & Latham, G. P. (1990). *A theory of goal setting and task performance.* Englewood Cliffs, NJ: Prentice Hall.

O'Leary-Kelley, A. M., Martocchio, J. J., & Frink, D. D. (1994). A review of the influence of group goals on group performance. *Academy of Management Journal,* 37, 1285–1301.

Meta-analysis studies are the "gold standard" of research. These studies aggregate the results of many individual studies together to estimate overall effectiveness of some treatment or intervention of interest. They also help identify the boundary conditions under which that intervention is more or less effective. Meta-analysis studies are preferable to more "narrative" or descriptive reviews of research because they statistically combine data across studies and test conditions under which results are stronger or weaker.

Meta-analysis studies on the effectiveness of goal setting:

Chidester, T. R., & Grigsby, W. C. (1984). A meta-analysis of the goal setting performance literature. *Academy of Management Proceedings*, 202–206.

Tubbs, M. E. (1986). Goal setting: A meta-analytic examination of the empirical evidence. *Journal of Applied Psychology*, 71, 474–483.

Kleingeld, A., van Mierlo, H., & Arends, L. (2011). The effect of goal setting on group performance: A meta-analysis. *Journal of Applied Psychology*, 96, 1289–1304.

9. Locke, E. A., & Latham, G. P. (1990). *A theory of goal setting and task performance.* Englewood Cliffs, NJ: Prentice Hall.

10. For additional background on the space race see Murray, C., & Cox, C. B. (1989). *Apollo: The race to the moon.* New York, NY: Simon & Schuster.

11. Klein, H. J., Wesson, M. J., Hollenbeck, J. R., & Alge, B. J. (1999). Goal commitment and the goal-setting process: Conceptual clarification and empirical synthesis. *Journal of Applied Psychology*, 84, 885–896.

12. Rogers, B. (2013, May 21). *Culture of purpose is key to success according to new research from Deloitte: Interview with Deloitte chairman Punit Renjen.* Retrieved from http://www.forbes.com/sites/brucerogers/2013/05/21/culture-of-purpose-is-key-to-success- according-to-new-research-from-deloitte/

13. See the following for example:

Seligman, M. E. P., & Csikszentmihalyi, M. (2000). Positive psychology: An introduction. *American Psychologist*, 55, 5–14.

Dutton, J. E., & Sonenshein, S. (2009). Positive organizational scholarship. In S. Lopez (Ed.), *Encyclopedia of positive psychology.* New York, NY: Wiley-Blackwell.

Hurst, A. (2016). *The purpose economy.* Boise, ID: Elevate.

14. Pink, D. H. (2009). *Drive: The surprising truth about what motivates us.* New York, NY: Riverhead Books.

15. Amabile, T., & Kramer, S. (2009). *The progress principle: Using small wins to ignite joy, engagement and creativity at work.* Boston, MA: Harvard Business School Press.

16. See the following for example:

Rosso, B. D., Dekas, K. H., & Wrzesniewski, A. (2010). On the meaning of work: A theoretical integration and review. *Research in Organizational Behavior*, 30, 91–127.

Leider, R. J. (1997). *The power of purpose: Creating meaning in your life and work.* San Francisco, CA: Berrett-Koehler.

Dik, B. J., Byrne, Z. S., & Steger, M. F. (2013). *Purpose and meaning in the workplace.* New York, NY: American Psychological Association.

17. For example, see Arnold, K. A., Turner, N., Barling, J., Kelloway, E. K., & McKee, M. C. (2007). Transformational leadership and psychological well-

being: The mediating role of meaningful work. *Journal of Occupational Psychology, 12,* 193–203.

18. For example, see the following articles:

Shanafelt, T. D., West, C. P., Sloan, J. A., Novotny, P. J., Poland, G. A., Menaker, R., Rummans, T. A., & Dyrbye, L. N. (2009). Career fit and burnout among academic faculty. *Archives of Internal Medicine, 169,* 990–995.

Niemiec, C. P., Ryan, R. M., & Deci, E. L. (2009). The path taken: Consequences of attaining intrinsic and extrinsic aspirations in post-college life. *Journal of Research in Personality, 43,* 291–306.

Rodell, J. B. (2013). Finding meaning through volunteering: Why do employees volunteer and what does it mean for their jobs? *Academy of Management Journal, 56,* 1274–1294.

19. Bureau of Labor Statistics. (2015). *Volunteering in the United States—2015.* Retrieved from http://www.bls.gov/news.release/volun.nr0.htm

20. Hackman, J. R., & Oldham, G. R. (1980). *Work redesign.* Reading, MA: Addison-Wesley. Others who have argued similarly include Chris Argyris, Ed Lawler and Fredrick Hertzberg

Argryis, C. (1964). *Integrating the individual and the organization.* New York, NY: Wiley.

Lawler, E. E. (1969). Job design and employee motivation. *Personnel Psychology,* 22, 426–435.

Herzberg, F., Mausner, B., & Snyderman, B. (1959). *The motivation to work.* New York, NY: Wiley.

21. For additional information about the TOMS story, see:

Mendez, A., Gomez-Gurrola, D., Khan, S., & Hunter, A. (2011). *TOMS Shoes: A case study examining a company at the forefront of social entrepreneurship and CSR.* Working Paper, International University, Geneva. Retrieved from http://www.scribd.com/doc/65279961/TOMS-Shoes-Integrated-CSR-Strategy#scribd

Chu, J. (2013). *TOMS sets out to sell a lifestyle, not just shoes.* Fast Company. Retrieved from http://www.fastcompany.com/3012568/blake-mycoskie-toms

Groden, C. (2013). TOMS hits 10 million mark on donated shoes. *Time Magazine,* June 26. Retrieved from http://style.time.com/2013/06/26/toms-hits-10-million-mark-on-donated-shoes/

22. For more information about Patagonia, see:

Rowledge, L. R., Barton, R. S., & Brady, K. S. (1999). *Case studies in strategy and action toward sustainable development.* Case 4: Patagonia: First ascents: Finding a way toward quality of life and work (pp. 95–122). Oxford, England: Greenleaf.

Patagonia. (2015). *Patagonia (clothing).* Retrieved from https://en.wikipedia.org/w/index.php?title=Patagonia(clothing)&oldid=687745700

Stevenson, S. (2012, April 26). Patagonia's founder is America's most unlikely business guru. *The Wall Street Journal Magazine.* Retrieved from http://www.wsj.com/articles/SB10001424052702303513404577352221465986612

Henneman, T. (2011, November). Patagonia fills payroll with people who are passionate. *Workforce Management.*

23. Karl Weick provides an overview of this problem in dealing with large-scale social problems and is critical of the way social science research attacks these problems. He advocates social scientists redefine large-scale social problems into smaller problems and go after small wins. See Weick, K. E. (1984). Small wins: Redefining the scale of social problems. *American Psychologist, 39,* 40–49.

24. For more information on Sony's efforts in this area see, Sony (2010, April 7). *Sony launches "road to zero" environmental plan and sets 2015 mid-term targets.* Sony press release. For an overview of Sony's efforts, see the following site: http://www.sony.net/SonyInfo/csr/eco/RoadToZero/

25. See the following for the matrix of targets by sub-goal and product lifecycle stage: http://www.sony.net/SonyInfo/csr_report/environment/management/gm2015/index4.html

26. See the following:

Ordonez, L. D., Schweitzer, M. E., Galinsky, A. D., & Bazerman, M. H. (2009). *Goals gone wild: The systematic side effects of over-prescribing goal setting.* Harvard Business School working paper 09-083.

Schweitzer, M. E., Ordonez, L. D., & Douma, B. (2002). *The dark side of goal setting: The role of goals in motivating unethical decision making.* Academy of Management Proceedings.

27. This has primarily been a criticism leveled at MBO systems. See Latham, G. P., & Wexley, K. N. (1981). *Increasing productivity through performance appraisal.* Reading, MA: Addison-Wesley.

28. Hurst, 2016, *op. cit.*

Aaron Hurst has partnered with Fast Company to profile a number of companies, including Steelcase and REI. See the following:

Hurst, A. (2016, December 8). *How Steelcase rearranged its workplace to create a purposeful office.* Fast Company.

Hurst, A. (2016, November 23). *How REI's CEO's quest for purpose inspired him to take back black Friday.* Fast Company.

29. Personal conversation, December 4, 2014. See also Ollander-Krane, R. (2015, April). Gap Inc. presentation at annual Bersin IMPACT conference.

30. Pulakos, E. D., Hanson, R. M., Arad, S., & Moye, N. (2014). *Performance management can be fixed: An on-the-job experiential learning approach for complex behavioral change.* Corporate Executive Board research report.

Chapter 8. Feedback and Progress

1. Insurance Institute for Highway Safety. (2013). *General statistics.* Retrieved from http://www.iihs.org/iihs/topics/t/general-statistics/fatalityfacts/overview-of-fatality- facts#Speeding

2. Trafficalm. (2014). *Traffic impact study: Are radar speed signs effective?* Retrieved from http://trafficalm.com/donec-at-mauris-enim-duis-nisi-tellus/

3. Pew Research Center. (2014). *Mobile technology fact sheet.* Retrieved from http://www.pewinternet.org/fact-sheets/mobile-technology-fact-sheet/

4. Kluger, A. N., & DeNisi, A. (1996). The effects of feedback interventions on performance: A historical review, a meta-analysis, and a preliminary feedback intervention theory. *Psychological Bulletin, 119,* 254–284.

5. See the following report for detailed statistics:

   Conerstone on Demand. (2013). *U.S. employees have spoken.* U.S. employee report conducted by Kelton. Retrieved from https://www.cornerstoneondemand.com/resources/brief/u-s-employees-have-spoken-managers-and-employers-take-note/2625

   Deloitte Consulting (2014). *Global human capital trends 2014: Engaging the 21st century workforce.* Survey report by Deloitte Conslting LLP and Bersin by Deloitte.

   Gorman, C. A., Ray, J., Nugent, C., Thibodeaux, C. N., List, S., Lonkar, S., Bradley, S., Mason, M., Pittington, L., & Pokhrel-Willet, S. (2012). *A preliminary survey of performance management practices in the United States.* Presentation at the annual meeting of the Society for Industrial and Organizational Psychologists, San Diego, CA.

   Mercer (2012). *Current trends in performance management.*

6. For examples of books that take this perspective, see:

   Culbert, S. A., & Rout, L. (2010). *Get rid of the performance review: How companies can stop intimidating, start managing, and focus on what really matters.* New York, NY: Hachette Book Group.

   Lee, C. D. (2006). *Performance conversations: An alternative to appraisals.* Tucson, AZ: Fenestra Books.

   Markle, G. L. (2000). *Catalytic coaching: The end of the performance review.* Westport: Quorum.

   Rock, D. (2009). *Your brain at work.* New York, NY: HarperCollins.

7. The following articles review the literature on the effectiveness of feedback:

   Alvero, A. M., Bucklin, B. R., & Austin, J. (2001). An objective review of the effectiveness and essential characteristics of performance feedback in organizational settings (1985–1998). *Journal of Organizational Behavior Management, 21,* 3–29.

   Balcazar, F., Hopkins, B. L., & Suarez, Y. (1985). A critical, objective review of performance feedback. *Journal of Organizational Behavior Management, 7,* 65–89.

Hattie, J., & Timperley, H. (2007). The power of feedback. *Review of Educational Research, 77,* 81–112.

Kluger & DeNisi, *op.cit.*

8. Oettingen, G. (2014). *Rethinking positive thinking: Inside the new science of motivation.* New York, NY: Penguin

9. Barsade, S. G., & Gibson, D. (2007). Why does affect matter in organizations? *The Academy of Management Perspectives, 21,* 36–59.

10. Lyubomirsky, S., King, L., & Diener, E. (2005). The benefits of frequent positive affect: Does happiness lead to success? *Psychological Bulletin, 131,* 803–855.

11. Pychyl, T. A. (2008, June 7). Goal progress and happiness. *Psychology Today.* Retrieved from https://www.psychologytoday.com/blog/dont-delay/200806/goal-progress-and-happiness

12. Amabile, T., & Kramer, S. (2009). *The progress principle.* Boston, MA: Harvard Business Review press.

13. Several authors discuss this research. For example, see Rock, 2009, *op. cit.*

14. Losada, M., & Heaphy, E. (2004). The role of positivity and connectivity in the performance of business teams: A nonlinear dynamics model. *American Behavioral Scientist, 47,* 740–765.

15. Fredrickson, B. L., & Losada, M. F. (2005). Positive affect and complex dynamics of human flourishing. *American Psychologist, 60,* 678–686.

Full disclosure is in order here; parts of this paper have been discredited and partially withdrawn. The authors ground their findings in some very complex mathematical modeling using differential equations drawn from fluid dynamics, a subfield of physics. Researchers Nick Brown and Alan Sokal criticize the application and relevance of these equations and point out numerous fundamental conceptual and mathematical errors. The paper's authors retracted the modeling elements but other elements of the article remain valid and are unaffected by this correction notice, notably (a) the supporting theoretical and empirical literature, (b) the data drawn from two independent samples, and (c) the finding that positivity ratios were significantly higher for individuals identified as flourishing relative to those identified as nonflourishing. The critique can be seen here:

Brown, N., Sokal, A. D., & Friedman, H. L. (2013). The complex dynamics of wishful thinking: The critical positivity ratio. *American Psychologist, 68,* 801–813.

16. Seligman, M. E. P., Steen, T. A., Park, N., & Peterson, C. (2005). Positive psychology progress: Empirical validation of interventions. *American Psychologist, 60,* 410–421.

17. See the following references for more details on this research:

Gottman, J. M. (1994). *Why marriages succeed or fail.* New York, NY: Simon and Schuster.

Gottman, J. M., Markman, H., & Notarius, C. (1977). The topography of marital conflict: A sequential analysis of verbal and nonverbal behavior. *Marriage and the Family, 39,* 461–477.

Gottman, J. M., Rose, F., & Mettetal, G. (1982). Time-series analysis of social interaction data. In T. Field & A. Fogel (Eds.), *Emotion and early Interaction* (pp. 261–289). San Francisco, CA: Erlbaum.

18. See the following articles for more details:

Van Dijk, D., & Kluger, A. N. (2004). Feedback sign's effect on motivation: Is it moderated by regulatory focus? *Applied Psychology: An International Review, 53*, 113–135.

Van Dijk, D., & Kluger, A. N. (2011). Task type as a moderator of positive/negative feedback effects on motivation and performance: A regulatory focus perspective. *Journal of Organizational Behavior, 32*, 1084–1105.

19. For more detail, see the following books:

Boyatzis, R., & McKee, A. (2005). *Resonant leadership: Renewing yourself and connecting with others through mindfulness, hope, and compassion.* Boston, MA: Harvard Business School Press.

Goleman, D., Boyatzis, R., & McKee, A. (2002). *Primal leadership: Realizing the power of emotional intelligence.* Boston, MA: Harvard Business School Press.

20. For a brief overview of their research on resonant and dissonant leaders, see Boyatzis, R. (2012). Neuroscience and the link between inspirational leadership and resonant relationships. *Ivey Business Journal,* January-February. For a more detailed overview, see Boyatzis & McKee, *op. cit.*

21. They refer to this as a "contagion" effect. The neurobiology of this contagion affect is fascinating, although still highly controversial. It is also very technical. I will not go into detail about the neurological systems involved in contagion and mimicry. Suffice to say that employees respond and react quickly and unconsciously to their leaders. The behavior and emotions of the leader are contagious to their employees. An employee's interpretation and reaction to an interaction with their boss is understood and interpreted first at the emotional level. In the context of our earlier discussion of David Rock's research on the brain, the more primitive threat center of the brain (the limbic system) picks up signals before the rational and cognitive center of the brain does (pre-frontal cortex). The following references explain these effects in more depth:

Boyatzis, R. (2011, January/February). Neuroscience and leadership: The promise of insights. *Ivey Business Journal.*

Boyatzis, R. E., Smith, M., & Beveridge, A. J. (2012). Coaching with compassion: Inspiring health, well-being, and development in organizations. *The Journal of Applied Behavioral Science, 49*, 153–178.

22. Researchers Barbara Fredrickson and Marcial Losada also conduct a thorough review of this research in Fredrickson & Losada, *op. cit.*

23. Baumeister, R. F., Bratslavsky, E., Finkenauer, C., & Vohs, K. D. (2001). Bad is stronger than good. *Review of General Psychology, 5*, 323–370.

24. Amabile & Kramer, *op. cit.*

25. This information came from a teleconference facilitated by David Rock's firm the NeuroLeadership group in March of 2014. Several companies including

Gap, Inc. participated on the call, describing what they were doing on performance management.

26. Dweck, C. S. (2006). *Mindset: The new psychology of success.* New York, NY: Random House.

27. Pulakos, E. D., Hanson, R. M., Arad, S., & Moye, N. (2014). *Performance management can be fixed: An on-the-job experiential learning approach for complex behavior change.* White paper. Corporate Executive Board.

28. For more detail on how these companies are approaching PM see:

7Geese Blog. (2012, October 7). *Eliminating performance ratings: Learn how Medtronic did it.* Retrieved from http://blog.7geese.com/2013/10/07/eliminating-performance-ratings-learn-how- medtronic-inc-did-it/

Bersin & Associates. (2013). *Adobe case study,* Webinar, September 26. Retrieved from http://www.bersin.com/Practice/Detail.aspx?id=16806

This case study is about Kelly Services. Garr, S. G. (2012). *Abandoning performance scores.* Bersin & Associates case study. Retrieved from http://www.bersin.com/Practice/Detail.aspx?id=15349

HC Online. (2012). Performance reviews: Scrap them. *Human Capital Magazine.* Retrieved from http://www.hcamag.com/hr-news/performance-reviews-scrap-them-121553.aspx

Luijke, J. (2011, January 16). Atlassian's big experiment with performance reviews. *Management Information Exchange.* Retrieved from http://www.managementexchange.com/story/atlassians-big- experiment-performance-reviews

McCord, P. (2014). How Netflix reinvented HR. *Harvard Business Review, 92,* 71–76.

Pletz, J. (2013). *The end of "valued performers" at Motorola.* Retrieved from http://www.chicagobusiness.com/article/20131102/ISSUE01/311029980/the-end-of-valued- performers-at-motorola

Chapter 9. We Versus Me

1. I want to give full credit to Sheena Iyengar, Mark Lepper, and Lee Ross for finding this quote which opens their paper: *Independence from whom? Interdependence with whom? Cultural perspectives on ingroups versus outgroups.* It is brilliant and captures the essence of meritocracy and individualism. It is from Cummings, E. E. (1958). A poet's advice to students. In G. J. Firmage (Ed.), *E. E. Cummings: A miscellany.* New York, NY: Argophile Press.

2. Morris, M. W., & Peng, K. (1994). Culture and cause: American and Chinese attributions for social and physical events. *Journal of Personality and Social Psychology, 67,* 949–971.

3. Kim, H., & Marcus, H. R. (1999). Deviance or uniqueness, harmony or conformity? A cultural analysis. *Journal of Personality and Social Psychology, 77,* 785–800.

4. For an overview of cultural differences, see Hofstede, G. (2001). *Culture's consequences: Comparing values, behaviors, institutions, and organizations across nations.* Thousand Oaks, CA: Sage.

5. For more information about these different views of the self, see Markus, H. R., & Kitayama, S. (1991). Culture and the self: Implications for cognition, emotion, and motivation. *Psychological Review, 98,* 224–253.

6. See the following for more details on these statistics:

   Gorman, C. A., Ray, J., Nugent, C., Thibodeaux, C. N., List, S., Lonkar, S., Bradley, S., Mason, M., Pittington, L., & Pokhrel-Willet, S. (2012). *A preliminary survey of performance management practices in the United States.* Paper presented at the 2012 annual conference of the Society for Industrial and Organizational Psychologists, San Diego, CA.

   Mercer (2011, May). *Next generation of pay-for-performance.* Survey report.

   Pascarella, P. (1997). Compensating teams. *Across the board, 34,* 16–22.

7. Young, M. (1958). *The rise of meritocracy.* London, England: Thames and Hudson.

8. Smith, A. (1776). *An inquiry into the nature and causes of the wealth of nations.* London, England: W. Strahan and T. Cadel.

9. See for example:

   Capelli, P., & Rogovsky, N. (1994). New work systems and skill requirements. *International Labour Review, 133,* 205–220.

   Cohen, S. G., & Bailey, D. E. (1997). What makes teams work: Group effectiveness research from the shop floor to the executive suite. *Journal of Management, 23,* 239–290.

   Cross, R., Rebele, R., & Grant, A. (2016, January/February). Collaborative overload. *Harvard Business Review.*

   Deloitte. (2016). *The new organization: Different by design.* Global Human Capital Trends Report, Seattle, WA:Deloitte University Press.

   Edmondson, A. C. (2012). *Teaming: How organizations learn, innovate, and compete in the knowledge economy.* San Francisco, CA: Jossey-Bass.

   Hackman, J. R. (2002). *Leading teams: Setting the stage for great performances.* Boston, MA: Harvard Business Press.

   Lawler, E. E., Mohrman, S. A., & Ledford, G. E., Jr. (1995). *Creating high performance organizations: Practices and results of employee involvement and total quality management in Fortune 1000 companies.* San Francisco, CA: Jossey-Bass.

10. See the following:

    Cambers, E., Foulon, M., Handfield-Jones, H., Hankin, S., Michaels, E., III (1998). The war for talent. *The McKinsey Quarterly 3,* 44–57.

    Smart, B. (2005). *Topgrading: How leading companies win by hiring, coaching, and keeping the best people.* New York, NY: Penguin Group.

11. Helft, M. (2011, May 17). For buyers of web start-ups, quest to corral young talent. *The New York Times.* Retrieved from http://www.nytimes.com/2011/05/18/technology/18talent.html?_r=0

12. Taylor, B. (2011, June 20). Great people are overrated. *Harvard Business Review*. Retrieved from https://hbr.org/2011/06/great-people-are -overrated

13. Fact-checking the statements by Zuckerberg and Andreessen requires that we be more explicit. On what attribute are we distributing programmers? Marc Andreessen said that five great programmers can completely outperform 1,000 mediocre programmers. How do we measure programmer performance? What does the distribution of programmer performance look like? The number of outliers and how different they are from everyone else in the distribution depends on the nature of the distribution of the attribute you are measuring. There is some debate in the scientific literature about how job performance is distributed. Most assume performance is distributed normally like a bell curve (symmetrical with smaller tails on either end) while others suggest it is distributed according to a power curve (ski run) with a bunch of people on the low end with a long, "heavy tail" to the high end with more outliers (stars) as Zuckerberg and Andreessen would suggest. If we assume for the moment that performance was distributed normally, we can use some general rules of thumb to see if claims made by Zuckerberg and Andreessen are plausible. A "star" is an outlier on the high side of a distribution of performance. One simple convention in statistics defines an outlier as any observation that is three or more standard deviations away from the mean or average. Standard deviation (SD) measures how much variation there is in a distribution—how spread out the observations are. If performance is distributed normally, 68% of the scores fall within 1 SD above and below the average, 95% fall within 2 SDs above and below the average, and over 99% fall within 3 SDs. One conventional estimate of the SD of the dollar value of job performance is 40% of their salary. If the average programmer earns $200,000, then the SD of the dollar value of job performance for a programmer is estimated to be $80,000. An outlier would be defined as anyone with a value above $420,000 (3 × $80,000 + $200,000), which is a little over 2× the average. This is a far cry from the estimates provided by Zuckerberg or Andreessen. Even if you were much more liberal in your definition of an outlier, defining it as any observation that is 10 SDs away from the average, the value of the outlier ($1,000,000—10 × $80,000 + $200,000) would only be about 5× the average, again, far from the claims of Zuckerberg and Andreessen. Another way of looking at their claims comes from the research done by Industrial psychologists Frank Schmidt and John Hunter who summarized the productivity and output differences reported in 85 years of published studies. They compared superior workers (at the 84th percentile—1 SD above the average) with average workers at the 50th percentile. For high-skill jobs, superior workers were 32% more productive and for professional and managerial jobs, superior workers were 48% more productive. If we assume professional workers that are one SD above the average are 1.48 times more productive than average, then we might assume workers 3 standard deviations are 2.44 times more productive than the average worker (3 × .48 + 1). Again, this esti-

mate is a far cry from the differences Zuckerberg or Andreessen are reporting. Conventional rules of thumb suggest little support for their claims.

See Schmidt, F. L., & Hunter, J. E. (1998). The validity and utility of selection methods in personnel psychology: Practical and theoretical implications of 85 years of research findings. *Psychological Bulletin, 124,* 262–274.

The above analysis says nothing about the accuracy with which we are measuring performance. The research I presented in Chapter 4 suggests we do a poor job of measuring performance and these distributions have lots of error in them. In fact the majority of the variation in these distributions is likely to be due to error. I would question if we can really measure programmer performance reliably in the first place. Even if we could and we determined we had outliers in this distribution, how much better are they than the rest? While top programmers are no doubt better performers than average programmers, they are not likely to be anywhere near 100 or 200 times as good.

14. Pfeffer, J., & Sutton, R. I. (2006). *Hard facts, dangerous half-truths and total nonsense: Profiting from evidence-based management.* Boston, MA: Harvard Business School Press.

15. Gladwell, M. (2002, July 22). The talent myth: Are smart people overrated? *The New Yorker.*

16. Taylor, B. (2011a, June 20). Great people are overrated. *Harvard Business Review.* Retrieved from https://hbr.org/2011/06/great-people-are -overrated

    Taylor, B. (2011b, June 21). Great people are overrated (Part II). *Harvard Business Review.* Retrieved from https://hbr.org/2011/06/great-people -are-overrated-par

17. Groysberg, B., Nanda, A., & Nohria, N. (2004, May). The risky business of hiring stars, *Harvard Business Review.*

    Groysberg, B. (2011). *Chasing stars: They myth of talent and the portability of performance.* Princeton, NJ: Princeton University Press.

18. For an engaging and compelling discussion of this point, see Sutton, R. (2006). *Fight the war for talent right: Bring aboard intact teams and networks.* Retrieved from http://bobsutton.typepad.com/my_weblog/2006/10/fight_ the_war_f.html

19. See the following for more examples and more details:

    Kugler, T., Kausel, E. F., & Kocher, M. (2012). Are groups more rational than individuals? A review of interactive decision making in groups. *Cognitive Science, 3,* 471–482.

    Laughlin, P. R., Bonner, B. L., & Miner, A. G. (2002). Groups perform better than the best individuals on letters-to-numbers problems. *Organizational Behavior and Human Decision Processes, 88,* 605–620.

    Laughlin, P. R., Hatch, E. C., Silver, J. S., & Boh, L. (2006). Groups perform better than the best individuals on letters-to-numbers problems: The effect of group size. *Journal of Personality and Social Psychology, 90,* 644–651.

    Pavitt, C. (1994). *Small group communication: A theoretical approach.* Scottsdale, AZ: Gorsuch Scarisbrick Publishers

Schultze, T., Mojzisch, A., & Schulz-Hardt, S. (2012). Why groups perform better than individuals at quantitative judgment tasks: Group-to-individual transfer as an alternative to differential weighting. *Organizational Behavior and Human Decision Processes, 118,* 24–36.

20. Duhigg, C. (2016, February 25). What Google learned from its quest to build the perfect team. *The New York Times.* Retrieved from https://www.nytimes.com/2016/02/28/magazine/what-google-learned-from-its-quest-to-build-the-perfect-team.html?_r=0

21. Donovan, M. (2015). *Google case study.* Presentation at Society of Industrial and Organizational Psychologists, Leading Edge Consortium: Building a high-performance organization: A fresh look at performance management.

22. For and engaging discussion of Scott Atran's views of this topic, listen to the following podcast: *The psychology of radicalization: How terrorist groups attract young followers.* December 15,, 2015. Retrieved from http://www.npr.org/templates/transcript/transcript.php?storyId=459697926

    For additional details, see Atran, S. (2016). The devoted actor: Unconditional commitment and intractable conflict across cultures. *Current Anthropology, 57,* 192–203.

23. Bower, B. (2016, June 23). New studies explore why ordinary people turn terrorist. *Science News.*

24. For example, see:

    Baumeister, R. F., & Leary, M. R. (1995). The need to belong: Desire for interpersonal attachments as a fundamental human motivation. *Psychological Bulletin, 117,* 497–529.

    Maslow, A. H. (1968). *Toward a psychology of being.* New York, NY: Van Nostrand.

25. Ryan, R. M., & Deci, E. L. (2000). Self-determination theory and the facilitation of intrinsic motivation, social development, and well-being. *American Psychologist, 55,* 68–78.

26. Cacioppo, J. T., & Patrick, W. (2008). *Loneliness: Human nature and the need for social connection.* New York, NY: W. W. Norton.

27. Baumeister, R. F., Twenge, J. M., & Nuss, C. K. (2002). Effects of social exclusion on cognitive processes: Anticipated aloneness reduces intelligent thought. *Journal of Personality and Social Psychology, 83,* 817–827.

28. For example, see:

    Buckley, K., Winkel, R., & Leary, M. (2004). Reactions to acceptance and rejection: Effects of level and sequence of relational evaluation. *Journal of Experimental Social Psychology, 40,* 14 –28.

    Williams, K. D. (2001). *Ostracism: The power of silence.* New York, NY: Guilford Press.

29. For additional details, see:

    Balliet, D., & Ferris, D. L. (2012). Ostracism and prosocial behavior: A social dilemma perspective. *Organizational Behavior and Human Decision Processes, 120,* 298–308.

Baumeister, R. F., DeWall, C. N., Ciarocco, N. J., & Twenge, J. M. (2005). Social exclusion impairs self- regulation. *Journal of Personality and Social Psychology, 88,* 589–604.

Ferris, D. L., Brown, D. J., Berry, J. W., & Lian, H. (2008). The development and validation of the workplace ostracism scale. *Journal of Applied Psychology, 93,* 1348–1366.

Hitlan, R. T., Kelly, K. M., Schepman, S., Schneider, K. T., & Zarate, M. A. (2006). Language exclusion and the consequences of perceived ostracism in the workplace. *Group Dynamics, 10,* 56–70.

Wu, L. Z., Wei, L. Q., & Hui, C. (2011). Dispositional antecedents and consequences of workplace ostracism: An empirical investigation. *Frontiers of Business Research in China, 5,* 23–44.

Wu, L. Z., Yim, F. H. K., Kwan, H. K., & Zhang, X. (2012). Coping with workplace ostracism: The roles of ingratiation and political skill in employee psychological distress. *Journal of Management Studies, 49,* 178–199.

30. Walton, G. M., Cohen, G. L., Cwir, D., & Spencer, S. J. (2012). Mere belonging: The power of social connections. *Journal of Personality and Social Psychology, 102,* 513–532.

31. Gehlbach, H., Brinkworth, M. E., King, A. M., Hsu, L. M., McIntyre, J., & Rogers, T. (2016). Creating birds of similar feathers: Leveraging similarity to improve teacher–student relationships and academic achievement. *Journal of Educational Psychology, 108,* 342–352.

32. There have been two major reviews of this research:

Kleingeld, A., van Mierlo, H., & Arends, L. (2011). The effect of goal setting on group performance: A meta-analysis. *Journal of Applied Psychology, 96,* 1289–1304.

O'Leary-Kelley, A. M., Martocchio, J. J., & Frink, D. D. (1994). A review of the influence of group goals on group performance. *Academy of Management Journal, 37,* 1285–1301

33. For example, see:

Hu, J., & Liden, R. C. (2011). Antecedents of team potency and team effectiveness: An examination of goal and process clarity and servant leadership. *Journal of Applied Psychology, 96,* 851–862.

Sawyer, J. E. (1992). Goal and process clarity: Specification of multiple constructs of role ambiguity and a structural equation model of their antecedents and consequences. *Journal of Applied Psychology, 77,* 130–142.

Weldon, E., Jehn, K. A., & Pradhan, P. (1991). Processes that mediate the relationship between a group goal and improved group performance. *Journal of Personality and Social Psychology, 61,* 555–569.

Weldon, E., & Weingart, L. R. (1993). Group goals and group performance. *British Journal of Social Psychology, 32,* 307–334.

34. Johnson, D. W. (2003). Social interdependence: Interrelationships among theory, research, and practice. *American Psychologist, 58,* 931–945.

35. See for example:

Balliet & Ferris, 2012, *op. cit.*

Ferris, D. L., Brown, D. J., Berry, J. W., & Lian, H. (2008). The development and validation of the workplace ostracism scale. *Journal of Applied Psychology, 93,* 1348–1366.

36. Deloitte documented the shift needed in two recent reports:

Deloitte (2016). *Human capital trends 2016: The new organization: Different by design.*

McDowell, T., Agarwal, D., Miller, D., Okamoto T., & Page, T. (2016). *Organizational design: The rise of team.* Seattle, WA: Deloitte University Press.

37. Kruse, D. L., Freeman, R. B., & Blasi, J. R. (2010). *Shared capitalism at work: Employee ownership, profit and gain sharing, and broad-based stock options.* National Bureau of Economic Research conference report. Chicago, IL: University of Chicago Press.

38. The most popular program was profit sharing, but this was only used by about a third of companies in their study. About a quarter used gain-sharing programs, about 20% used employee ownership programs and about 10% used stock options. Less than half of the firms used any one of these programs. Contrast these numbers with the percentage of firms using individual P4P programs, which is well-above 80% or more.

39. Productivity gains for profit sharing programs were as high as 7.4% (the average was 4.4%). For a review of the effectiveness of profit sharing, see the following:

Kruse, D. L. (1993). *Profit sharing: Does it make a difference?* Kalamazoo, MI: Upjohn Institute for Employment Research.

Weitzman, M. L., & Kruse, D. L. (1990). Profit sharing and productivity. In A. S. Blinder (Ed.), *Paying for productivity* (pp. 95–140). Washington, DC: Brookings Institution.

The following studies looked at the effectiveness of all types of incentive programs, including group and organizational plans:

Condly, S. J., Clark, R. E., & Stolovitch, H. D. (2003). The effects of incentives on workplace performance: A meta-analytic review of research studies. *Performance Improvement Quarterly, 16,* 46–63.

Judiesch, M. K. (1994). *The effects of incentive compensation systems on productivity, individual differences in output variability and selection utility.* Doctoral dissertation, University of Iowa, Iowa City.

Locke, E. A., Feren, D. B., McCaleb, V. M., Shaw, K. N., & Denny, A. T. (1980). The relative effectiveness of four ways of motivating employee performance. In K. D. Duncan, M. M. Gruenberg, & D. Wallis, *Changes in working life* (pp. 363–88). New York, NY: Wiley.

The following studies looked at the effectiveness of employee ownership:

Doucouliagos, C. (1995). Worker participation and productivity in labor-managed and participatory capitalist firms: A meta- analysis. *Industrial and Labor Relations Review 49,* 58– 77.

Freeman, S. F. (2007). *Effects of ESOP adoption and employee ownership: Thirty years of research and experience.* Working paper no. 07- 01. Organizational Dynamics Programs, University of Pennsylvania, Philadelphia.

Kaarsemaker, E. C. A. (2006a). *Employee ownership and human resource management: A theoretical and empirical treatise with a digression on the Dutch context.* Doctoral dissertation. Radboud University Nijmegen, the Netherlands.

Kaarsemaker, E. C. A. (2006b). *Employee ownership and its consequences: Synthesis- generated evidence for the effects of employee ownership and gaps in the research literature.* York, England: University of York.

Kim, E. H., & Ouimet, P. (2008, October). *Employee capitalism or corporate socialism? Broad- based employee stock ownership.* Working paper. Ross School of Business, University of Michigan, Ann Arbor.

Kramer, B. (2008). *Employee ownership and participation effects on firm outcomes.* Doctoral dissertation. Department of Economics, City University of New York.

Kruse, D., & Blasi, J. (1997). Employee ownership, employee attitudes, and firm performance: A review of the evidence. In D. Lewin, D. J. B. Mitchell, & M. A. Zaidi (Eds.), *Human resources management handbook: Part 1* (pp. 131– 151). Greenwich, CT: JAI Press.

Kruse, D. (2002, February 13). *Research evidence on prevalence and effects of employee ownership.* Testimony before the Subcommittee on Employer-Employee Relations, Committee on Education and the Workforce, U.S. House of Representatives.

For more information on ESOP programs, see:

Logue, J., & Greider, W. (2002). *The real world of employee ownership.* Ithaca, NY: ILR Press.

Logue, J., & Yates, J. S. (1999). Worker ownership American style: Pluralism, participation and performance. *Economic and Industrial Democracy 20,* 225–252.

For more information on stock-options programs, see:

Blasi, J., Kruse, D., & Bernstein, A. (2003). *In the company of owners.* New York, NY: Basic Books.

For more information on gain-sharing research, see:

Doucouliagos, *op. cit.*

Welbourne, T. M., & Gomez-Mejia L. (1995). Gain-sharing: A critical review and a future research agenda. *Journal of Management, 21,* 559–609.

40. Adams, C. P. (2002). *Does size really matter? Empirical evidence on group incentives.* Working paper. Bureau of Economics, Federal Trade Commission.

41. See the following for reviews of this research:

Albanese, R., & Van Fleet, D. D. (1985). Rational behavior in groups: The free-riding tendency. *Academy of Management Review, 10,* 244–255.

Anderson, L. R., & Holt, C. A. (2004). Experimental economics and public choice. *The Encyclopedia of Public Choice,* 564–567.

Falk, A., Fischbacher, U., & Gachter, S. (2004). Living in two neighborhoods: Social interactions in the lab. *Institute for the Study of Labor Discussion Paper Series, No. 1381.*

Fehr, E., & Gächter, S. (2000). Cooperation and punishment in public goods experiments. *American Economic Review, 90,* 980–94.

Mas, A., & Moretti, E. (2009). Peers at work. *American Economic Review, 99,* 112–145.

Van Lange, P. A. M., Balliet, D., Parks, C. D., & Van Vugt, M. (2014). *Social dilemmas: The psychology of human cooperation.* New York, NY: Oxford University Press.

42. Several researchers have studied the most effective ways to minimize free riding tendencies and productivity loss in groups:

Communication. The more group members have open channels to communicate with each other, the more social tendencies and normative pressures can operate, the lower the tendency for free riding. Trust will be higher and the group identity will be stronger.

Team-based work systems. The more the work is structured using team-based work systems with high levels of monitoring, communication, planning, peer evaluation, etc., the less free riding will occur.

Ability to exclude, punish noncontributors. When group members can sanction and punish other group members, free riding is minimized.

Peer evaluation. When peers have the ability to provide feedback and input on one another, free riding is less likely to occur.

Public work environment. People are less likely to free ride when they are less anonymous, when they and their contributions are more public.

Positive framing. Free riding is less likely to occur when there is less of an appearance of a conflict between the interests of the individual and the group and when they see cooperation as a more effective strategy.

Clear norms for behavior. When clear norms exist for appropriate behavior, free riding is less likely.

Group cohesiveness and identify. The more the group has a sense of purpose and identity and when individual contributions are seen as expected and indispensable, free riding is less likely.

Altruistic appeals. Free riding will be lower if the group appeals to members to display altruistic concerns and communicates a sense of duty among members.

The following articles discuss ways to counteract the effects of free riding:

Balliet, D. (2010). Communication and cooperation in social dilemmas: A meta-analytic review. *Journal of Conflict Resolution, 54,* 39–57.

Balliet, D., & Van Lange, P. A. M. (2013). Trust, punishment, and cooperation across 18 societies: A meta-analysis. *Perspectives on Psychological Science, 8,* 363–379.

Chaudhuri, A. (2011). Sustaining cooperation in laboratory public goods experiments: A selective survey of the literature. *Experimental Economics, 14*, 47–83.

Fehr & Gächter, 2000, *op. cit.*

Fehr, E., & Gächter, S. (2002). Altruistic punishment in humans. *Nature, 415,* 137–140.

Shepperd, J. A. (1993). Productivity loss in performance groups: A motivation analysis. *Psychological Bulletin, 113,* 1, 67–81.

Zelmer, J. (2003). Linear public goods experiments: A meta-analysis. *Experimental Economics, 6,* 299–310.

43. For a review of the research on spill-over effects see:

    Falk et al., 2004, *op. cit.*

    Mas & Moretti, 2009, *op. cit.*

44. Kandel, E., & Lazear, E. P. (1992). Peer pressure and partnerships. *Journal of Political Economy, 100,* 801–817.

45. For an overview of Google's work, see: Duhigg, C. (2016, February 28). What Google learned from its quest to build the perfect team. *The New York Times.*

46. For a good overview of their approach, see the video of Rick Klau's workshop: How Google sets goals: OKRs conducted in 2012: Retrieved from https://www. youtube.com/watch?v=mJB83EZtAjc

47. Rick is a partner with Google ventures and discusses the origins of this process dating back to when John Doerr proposed it to founders Sergey Brin and Larry Page as the foundational model for planning at Google.

48. For more information on Cisco's reinvention of PM, see:

    Goodall, A. (2015, April 20). *Little Platoons: Reinvention of PM at Cisco.* Presentation at Talent Management Alliance conference: Assessing and developing high potentials. Atlanta, GA.

    Goodall, A., & Herpolsheimer, S. (2016, September 22). *How Cisco is activating team excellence with data.* Bersin by Deloitte Innovating Performance Management Webinar Series Part 1. Retrieved from http://www.bersin .com/News/EventDetails.aspx?id=20095

    Human Resources Online. (2016 January 4). *How Cisco accelerates the performance of its teams.* Retrieved from http://www.humanresourcesonline. net/case-study-cisco-accelerates-performance-teams/

49. Much of this is documented in Buckingham, M., & Goodall, A. (2016, April). Reinventing performance management. *Harvard Business Review.*

50. They adopted the "Standout" platform from Marcus Buckingham and tailored it for their purposes at Cisco.

51. Luckerson, V. (2015, May 29). Netflix accounts for more than a third of all internet traffic. *Time Magazine.* Retrieved from http://time.com/3901378/ netflix-internet-traffic/

52. For an overview of Netflix's approach, see McCord, P. (2014 January/February). How Netflix reinvented HR. *Harvard Business Review,* 71–76.

53. Luijke, J. (2011, January 16). Atlassian's big experiment with performance reviews. *Management Information Exchange.* Retrieved from http://www. managementexchange.com/story/atlassians-big-experiment- performance-reviews

54. Ostlund, D. (2012, January 4). *Why do we pay sales commissions?* Retrieved from http://blog.fogcreek.com/why-do-we-pay-sales-commissions/

55. For examples of other companies that have abandoned sales commissions, see the following:

Perman, S. (2013, November 20). For some, paying commissions no longer makes sense. *The New York Times.* Retrieved from http://www.nytimes. com/2013/11/21/business/smallbusiness/for-some-paying-sales-commissions-no-longer-makes-sense.html?_r=0

Pink, D. (2012, July/August). A radical prescription for sales. *Harvard Business Review,* 76–77.

56. SAS Institute and Southwest Airlines were prominently featured in Pfeffer, J., & Sutton, R. I. (2006). *Hard facts, dangerous half-truths and total nonsense: Profiting from evidence-based management.* Boston, MA: Harvard Business School Press.

Chapter 10. Next Generation Performance Management: PM 2.0

1. Covey, S. R. (1989). *The 7 habits of highly effective people.* New York, NY: Simon & Schuster.

2. Others call this behavior "contextual performance," acknowledging that the job description covers areas that directly support getting to the output of one's job but there are other important things that need to be done to maximize the overall success of the group and organization. See the following references for more details:

Borman, W. C., & Motowidlo, S. J. (1993). Expanding the criterion domain to include elements of contextual performance. In N. Schmitt, W. C. Borman, & Associates (Eds.), *Personnel selection in organizations* (pp. 71–98). San-Francisco, CA: Jossey-Bass.

Organ, D. W. (1988). *Organizational citizenship behavior: The good soldier syndrome.* Lexington, MA: Lexington Books.

3. The U.S. Army has a well-developed process for conducting these reviews. See Darling, M., Parry, C., & Moore, J. (2005). Learning in the thick of it. *Harvard Business Review, 83,* 84–92.

4. Rock, D. (2006). *Quiet leadership.* New York, NY: HarperCollins.

5. There are lots of these tools hitting the market and there is no guarantee these will be around at the time you are reading this. One example of a tool for gathering electronic feedback simply is called 15Five. This tool allows a supervisor or employee to solicit feedback from a standard panel of people

and it automatically pushes the questions to them and aggregates their responses. Here are the links to 15Five and some other tools and software applications (iDoneThis, 7Geese) http://www.15five.com/; https://idonethis.com/; https://www.7geese.com/product/

6. For more information on strength-based performance appraisal and goal setting, see:

Bouskila-Yam, O., & Kluger, A. N. (2011). Strength-based performance appraisal and goal setting. *Human Resource Management Review, 21,* 137–147.

Kluger, A. N., & Nir, D. (2010). The feedforward interview. *Human Resources Management Review, 20,* 235–246.

7. For a brief overview of their research on resonant and dissonant leaders, see:

Boyatzis, R. (2012, January/February). Neuroscience and the link between inspirational leadership and resonant relationships. *Ivey Business Journal.*

8. Rubin, I. M., Plovnick, M. S., & Fry, R. E. (1977). Task oriented team development. New York, NY: McGraw-Hill.

9. Experts call this psychological safety. For an overview of how this concept applies to work teams in particular, see Edmonds, A. C. (2003). Managing the risk of learning: Psychological safety in work teams. In M. A. West, D. Tjosvold, and K. G. Smith (Eds). West Sussex, *International handbook of organizational teamwork and cooperative working.* London, England: Wiley and Sons.

10. Cohesion is a key part of what makes a team effective. For additional details on the role of cohesion and other factors in making teams effective, see:

Kozlowski, S. W. J., & Ilgen, D. R. (2006). Enhancing the effectiveness of work groups and teams. *Psychological Science in the Public Interest, 7,* 77–124.

For details on the antecedents of cohesion, see: Grossman, R. (2014). *How do teams become cohesive? A meta-analysis of cohesion's antecedents.* Doctoral dissertation. University of Central Florida, Orlando.

11. Heslin, P. A., & Klehe, U. C. (2006). Self-efficacy. In S. G. Rogelberg (Ed.), *Encyclopedia of industrial/organizational psychology* (Vol. 2; pp. 705–708). Thousand Oaks, CA: Sage. Nikols, F. (2011). *The goals grid: A versatile, multi-purpose tool.* Mount Vernon, OH: Distance Consulting, LLC.

12. Mercer (2013). 2013 *Global performance management survey report.*

13. Institute for Corporate Productivity. (2012). *HR Technology: The state of software as a service (SaaS). HR Technology: Directions for 2012.* Survey report. Retrieved from http://go.i4cp.com/webinar-2012-state-of-hr-technology

14. Firms like the Institute for Corporate Productivity (i4cp) and the Gartner Group provide thorough reviews of these technologies and the key players. The interested reader can also consult a number of other useful sources on this topic:

Cardy, R. L., & Miller, J. S. (2005). eHR and performance management: A consideration of positive potential and the dark side. In H. G. Gueutal & D. L. Stone (Eds.) *The brave new world eHR: Human resources management in the digital age* (pp. 138–165). San Francisco, CA: Jossey-Bass.

Farr, J. L., Fairchild, J., & Cassidy, S. E. (2014). Technology and performance appraisal. In M. D. Coovert & L. Foster (Eds.) *The psychology of workplace technology*. New York, NY: Routledge.

Gueutal, H. G., & Falbe, C. M. (2005). Trends in edelivery methods. In H. G. Gueutal & D. L. Stone (Eds.) *The brave new world of eHR: Human resources management in the digital age* (pp. 190– 225). San Francisco, CA: Jossey-Bass.

Johnson, R. D., & Gueutal, H. G. (2011). *Transforming HR through technology: The use of e-HR and HRIS in organizations*. Alexandria, VA: Society for Human Resource Management Effective Practice Guidelines Series.

15. De Bono, E. (1992). *Serious creativity: Using the power of lateral thinking to create new ideas*. New York, NY: HarperBusiness.

About the Author

ALAN COLQUITT is a talent management, organizational change and analytics leader with experience and expertise in all aspects of talent management, human capital analytics, and organization change. He has worked as an internal consultant in the pharmaceutical and consumer products industries, building organizational capability and consulting with and advising executives, HR professionals, and other HR staff groups. He is frequently sought out as an expert advisor to other private and public companies, consulting organizations, professional organizations, and academic institutions.

Alan received his bachelor's degree in Psychology from Indiana University and his masters and PhD in Industrial and Organization Psychology from Wayne State University. He is a licensed psychologist in the state of Indiana and a member of the Society for Industrial and Organizational Psychology (SIOP), the American Psychological Association, the Human Resources Planning Society, and the Academy of Management. He currently holds adjunct professor appointments at Indiana University-Purdue University at Indianapolis (IUPUI) and Butler University.

Alan is a frequent speaker and presenter at meetings, professional conferences, and other forums on a wide variety of talent management and human capital analytics topics. His work has been published in several media outlets from books and academic and practitioner journals to magazines

Next Generation Performance Management, pages 213–214
Copyright © 2017 by Information Age Publishing
All rights of reproduction in any form reserved.

and online blog sites. He has represented Eli Lilly and Company in many external groups and forums including the Conference Board, the Mayflower Group, the Attrition and Retention Consortium, and the Institute for Corporate Productivity.

His expertise spans talent management, analytics, and team and organization diagnosis, design and change. Areas of particular interest include: Performance management; pay-for-performance; workforce analytics; talent acquisition; leadership assessment and development; organization change; and workforce strategy.

He has been around performance management his entire career and he is an expert in every sense of the word. It has been done to him for 30 years and he has done it to others for 25 years. He has designed it, changed it, and owned it. He has spent the last 7 years studying the science behind it, summarizing what he has learned and sharing it with others in the hopes of changing the way organizations think about this process.

CPSIA information can be obtained
at www.ICGtesting.com
Printed in the USA
BVHW04s1333280718
522769BV00003B/55/P